MW01005667

"This is a brilliant, insig
nuggets from digging d
book of Job. Many of th
and Scripture from one of the top old-earth creation scientists
writing today." —**Norman Geisler,** Distinguished Professor of
Apologetics, Veritas Evangelical Seminary (www.VeritasSeminary.
com), Murrieta, CA

"Yet another sparkling gem from the treasure house that is the
mind of Hugh Ross! A fabulous and typically thoughtful treatment
of many vitally important subjects." —**Eric Metaxas,** *New York
Times* bestselling author of *Bonhoeffer: Pastor, Martyr, Prophet,
Spy* and *Amazing Grace: William Wilberforce and the Heroic Campaign
to End Slavery*

"*Hidden Treasures in the Book of Job* offers surprising and accurate
scientific insights few consider. Hugh Ross brilliantly analyzes
these details with great scrutiny to highlight the fact that Scripture
presents compelling information regarding our greatest scientific
complexities. I highly recommend this work for those considering
the evidence of the Bible's scientific claims." —**John Ankerberg,**
founder and president of *The John Ankerberg Show*

"This book has the potential to bring many to Christ. It's an elegant
explanation of how Scripture, the scientific facts of nature, and the
tragedy of human suffering all point people to God. Hugh Ross will
even help you love your dog and explain to you why your dog can love
you back! This is such a neat book. It's sophisticated and simple and
arguably groundbreaking. I can't wait to use it in the classroom."
—**Sarah Sumner,** dean of A. W. Tozer Theological Seminary

"*Hidden Treasures in the Book of Job* is a treasure in and of itself.
It is enormously engaging in both its content and its style. It is one
of the most up-to-date scientific, as well as biblical, responses in the
evolution, creation, young earth debate, yet all offered with clear
facts, gentleness of tone, and convincing logic." —**Walter C. Kaiser
Jr.,** president emeritus, Gordon-Conwell Theological Seminary

"Hugh Ross's academic grasp, scientific background, and Scriptural and biblical insight join to qualify him for providing us this helpful contribution for study in Job—one of the 'wisdom books' of the Holy Scriptures. Once again I am delighted to see the appearance of another one of Hugh's works." —**Jack Hayford,** founding pastor of The Church On The Way; chancellor of The King's University

"Thanks to Hugh, nearly every time I gaze up at the stars on a moonlit night or even report on the latest scientific story on my radio show, I can't help but hear that famous Rich Mullins chorus wafting through my mind: 'Our God is an awesome God.' Perhaps more than anyone else, Hugh has helped me to see that awesomeness all around me, from the immense grandeur of the cosmos to the infinite precision of the human genome. Thanks, Hugh, for giving me eyes to see." —**Frank Pastore,** host of *The Frank Pastore Show*

"Once again, Hugh Ross has provided readers with a resource that is well researched and thoroughly engaging. In *Hidden Treasures in the Book of Job,* he addresses vitally important topics such as the problem of evil, the relationship between science and faith, the nature of the soul, and key issues related to creation vs. evolution. All of this—plus insightful commentary on Job, one of the most intriguing parts of the Bible—makes *Hidden Treasures* itself a treasure from one of the church's most gifted apologists." —**Alex McFarland,** nationally syndicated radio and TV host

"Reading *Hidden Treasures in the Book of Job* was jaw dropping. I constantly marvel at the vantage point from which the brilliant mind of Hugh Ross views things, most of which go unnoticed by those of us whose narrow perspective is far more tied to the terrestrial. The sparkling and sometimes mind-warping ideas and thoughts Hugh puts on display made me feel like a little kid whose concept of time, space, creation, and eternity is about as advanced as the Chewbacca action figure I am bringing to show-and-tell." —**Rick Bundschuh,** pastor, Kauai Christian Fellowship; author of *Deep Like Me* and coauthor of *Soul Surfer*

HIDDEN TREASURES
in the
BOOK *of* JOB

*How the Oldest Book in the Bible
Answers Today's Scientific Questions*

HUGH ROSS

BakerBooks
a division of Baker Publishing Group
Grand Rapids, Michigan

© 2011 by Reasons To Believe

Published by Baker Books
a division of Baker Publishing Group
P.O. Box 6287, Grand Rapids, MI 49516-6287
www.bakerbooks.com

Paperback edition published 2013
ISBN 978-0-8010-1606-6

Printed in the United States of America

The Library of Congress has cataloged the hardcover edition as follows:
Ross, Hugh (Hugh Norman), 1945–
    Hidden treasures in the book of Job : how the oldest book in the Bible answers today's scientific questions / Hugh Ross.
        p.   cm.
    Includes bibliographical references and index.
    ISBN 978-0-8010-7210-9 (pbk.)
    1. Bible. O.T. Job—Criticism, interpretation, etc. 2. Science—Biblical teaching. I. Title.
BS1415.52.R67 2011
223'.106—dc22   2011012341

13   14   15   16   17   18   19   7   6   5   4   3   2   1

In keeping with biblical principles of creation stewardship, Baker Publishing Group advocates the responsible use of our natural resources. As a member of the Green Press Initiative, our company uses recycled paper when possible. The text paper of this book is composed in part of post-consumer waste.

Contents

Prologue

My friends cautioned me not to write this book. They warned me, "No one who attempts to write *any* kind of commentary on Job can escape without some new experience in suffering." They had a point. How can anyone interpret Job accurately and compassionately apart from the benefit of direct insight into how God works through suffering?

No need to worry, I told my friends. It was not my intention to address the theme of suffering. My purpose was to focus on the science-related content of the book of Job, especially on passages describing God's involvement in creation. As I dived into my research, however, I began to see some tight connections between the biblical account of natural history and the historic Christian doctrines of sin, evil, and suffering. I came to appreciate God's plan for our ultimate redemption more than ever. So I hoped I would be able to include at least some of these observations in the book.

Almost immediately my friends' cautions proved prophetic. On one of my typical morning trail runs, a crippling pain gripped my chest. It grabbed me harder each time I tried to keep going—even downhill. Once I made my way home, my wife, Kathy, drove me to the ER. By the time a doctor came to check on me, the pain had mostly subsided. And the next day, when I passed the treadmill test with flying colors, the medical team declared me healthy and sent me home.

Kathy felt certain something was seriously wrong. She called my cardiologist and insisted on an angiogram. Reluctantly, he agreed to the procedure. Imagine his surprise to discover that a major artery, nicknamed the "widow maker," was all but completely blocked. A few hours later I had bypass surgery. And I'm glad to report it went well.

Back home again less than a week later, I called my dad (in Canada) to reassure him I was doing fine, already back to walking around the neighborhood. During the call I noticed that my dad's breathing seemed labored. He could hardly finish a sentence without becoming short of breath. With a sense of urgency sparked by my own close call, I insisted he seek medical attention right away. The next day he called me from the hospital, feeling better but definitely not great. Within days the jarring diagnosis came back: mesothelioma. He was gone in just six weeks. With his passing I lost one of my biggest fans and greatest sources of encouragement.

As my recovery progressed, so did the writing. Life returned to a semblance of normal, with only a slight interruption when I experienced asthma for the first time in my life. But after a few months my doctor hit upon the right combination of inhalers, and I felt fine. The manuscript was coming along nicely, nearing the halfway point in fact, when Kathy and I received the kind of phone call every parent dreads. Shortly after 11:30 one night, a nurse informed us we should make our way quickly to the hospital—one we'd never heard of some distance from our home. Before we could ask any questions she said, "Your son Joel has been stabbed, and he's being wheeled into surgery at this moment."

Upon entering the intensive care waiting room, we discovered to our horror that one of the friends Joel had spent the evening with, the son of a well-known and well-loved pastor, had also been stabbed—and had not survived. All this violence erupted from a brief encounter with strangers in a so-called safe neighborhood!

How close we came to losing Joel became evident the next morning. A nurse who'd assisted in the operating room couldn't hide her surprise and relief to learn that Joel was still alive. It took several months, including a return trip to the hospital, for Joel to recover physically. The other wounds will take longer to heal, and we anticipate they'll be painfully reopened when the trial of his attackers gets underway.

A few months and three fender benders later, while writing the last three chapters of this book, my physician called with results from my annual physical. He noted that my PSA number had risen just slightly from the previous year. Though still on the low side, it indicated I should perhaps see a urologist. After all the recent surprises, he decided to take the cautious route. Once again, stunning news hit me. Despite a complete lack of symptoms, I found my body invaded by an aggressive cancer. In fact, the specialist refused to discuss any specific treatment plan until first conducting bone and organ scans.

The tests showed all clear, but after nearly a month of waiting for these additional results, I wanted the cancer out immediately! Thank the Lord for doctors who did everything possible to speed up my surgery date, and it's good they did. My surgeon observed that even another week's delay might have allowed the malignancy to spread to other parts of my body.

During my recovery period, which included my ministry's first cruise conference to Alaska, I gladly returned to writing, grateful for the chance to finish the final chapter of my draft. My plan was to hand it off to Kathy for a round of edits, but that's when yet another dark cloud rolled over us. Kathy's usually sprightly father went to the hospital complaining of stomach pains. The ER doctors could find nothing wrong with his GI tract, assumed it was just a bout of indigestion, and despite his obvious weakness and shortness of breath (not to mention his daughter's protests) released him to go home. While tying his shoelaces, he sat up to catch his breath, but he never did. He went "home" that night, indeed, with Kathy standing right beside him. Again we were devastated by the loss of someone near and precious to us.

My two fathers had always helped me withstand public attacks. Ever since the launch of Reasons To Believe more than two dozen years ago, I've had to bear the public distortions of my beliefs and the assassination of my character by those who disagree with my creation perspective. During the past few years those kinds of assaults had worsened and spread.

Compared to Job, however, my sufferings seemed slight. Unlike Job, I had the privilege of seeing some immediate benefits. My relationship with my wife and two sons deepened in ways they might not have otherwise. Some wonderful opportunities to share reasons for my hope in Christ and scientific evidence supporting it occurred during my hospitalization and recovery process.

As I researched and wrote about Job's trials, what impressed me most profoundly was that Job did not waste his suffering. He used the trauma he experienced to draw closer to God and to learn deep truths that would enlighten his friends and ultimately benefit all humanity, as well as observers in the angelic realm.

Thanks to my "light and momentary troubles" (2 Cor. 4:17), this book (and I) did some growing. Not only did I gain fresh insight to the interconnectedness of creation theology with the reality of evil and suffering, I also began to see in the creation texts of Job certain aspects of science-and-creation theology I had previously overlooked.

While this book has changed somewhat since I set out to write it, it still focuses predominantly on creation and science. Though many books address the message God gives us through Job about the meaning of suffering (and also what suffering does *not* mean), what I've written in these pages may represent the first attempt to examine Job as a key resource in understanding creation and how to care for creation. It also shows how this ancient book anticipates discoveries that have recently emerged from the frontiers of scientific research—as well as some yet to come.

Today the topic of science and faith, especially with reference to creation, stirs up as much hostility and conflict as virtually any subject a person could name. The fact that creation is a hot button for those who don't yet follow Christ or accept the truth of the Bible probably comes as no great surprise. After all, if creation is true, then there must be a Creator, a supernatural Being to whom we might well have to answer for our use of the gift of life. If science and Scripture agree, then we would have to take biblical truth claims seriously.

Over the past two hundred years, despite exponential growth in the body of data from which to develop a more thorough understanding of both natural history and relevant Bible passages, hostility and controversy seem to have intensified. What began as a skirmish over which explanation—natural process or divine miracle—provides the best account of Earth's and life's existence and development has exploded into a multi-pronged battle. On the topic of creation alone, combatants include nontheistic evolutionists, young-earth creationists, day-age creationists, framework and analogical-day creationists, deistic and theistic evolutionists, advocates of "fully-gifted creation," Genesis-as-myth creationists, Genesis-as-polemic creationists, evolutionary creationists, and the list continues to expand.

While some take a more militant stance than others, each group tends to promote its position as *the* superior one, or the only viable one. Too often the scholarly critique of alternative positions turns into vicious, unscholarly, emotion-laced attack. I've seen unvarnished condescension and financial intimidation. Few disagreements have led to more bitter acrimony or have damaged the reputation of Christians more severely. Christians and non-Christians alike have been appalled, and rightly so.

Sadly, instead of rebuking and correcting ungodly behavior, many Christian leaders and congregations choose simply to avoid any discussion of creation issues and controversies. Fearing church splits and loss of funding, they prefer to eliminate *any* teaching on creation and science. They effectively apply Wite-Out to the first eleven chapters of Genesis and all other creation passages, including those texts in Job that offer stunning revelations of God's involvement in shaping our world.

The decision to ignore teaching on creation harms the fellowship of Christ's followers in at least five ways:

1. It thwarts our mission. Jesus called us to make disciples of all peoples. In a world abounding with skeptics, one of the best ways to persuade people that the God of the Bible exists is to demonstrate the necessity of a transcendent Creator.
2. It establishes a dangerous precedent. It communicates that controversies are to be avoided rather than resolved.
3. It obscures foundational Christian doctrines. According to the Bible, the world of nature reveals not only God's existence but also his righteousness and other aspects of his divine nature and attributes.
4. It discourages systematic theology. The integration of truth as revealed in the sixty-six books of Scripture with what is revealed in nature's "book" (i.e., the data available across all

scientific disciplines) is invaluable to developing a consistent and comprehensive theology of the Christian faith.

5. It rewards immature behavior. It sends the message that if a person makes a big enough fuss he or she can control what is and is not worthy of significant discussion.

The strategy of withdrawal has crippled both the church and the scientific community. The church has lost out on much-needed scientific input and especially scientific support for some of its core theological positions. The scientific community has suffered from a lack of spiritual and ethical balance and direction. Worse, the withdrawal communicates to society at large that science and faith are irreconcilably at odds and that anyone attempting to keep a foot in both camps must live with contradictions.

The alternative strategy of attack adopted by some has simply escalated the hostility and negativity. Evolutionists complain that Christians focus all their energies on "evolution bashing." Christians protest that evolutionists won't allow them any voice in discussions of science education and research. Meanwhile, different groups within the church wage battle for exclusive control over instruction about science in general and creation in particular.

What is needed is a strategy of engagement. Christians who take the Bible as a trustworthy revelation from God need to study science and engage with scientists at the highest academic and research levels. We need to present a compelling scientific case for the veracity of biblical commentary on the history of the universe, Earth, life, and humanity; show how the Bible serves as an accurate predictor of scientific discoveries; and demonstrate how a creation model provides a more productive stimulus for ongoing research than does naturalism. At the same time, Christians trained in science and experienced in research need to interact with fellow believers, including those with little or no background in science, making every effort to communicate clearly, humbly, and patiently. They need to bring enthusiasm for how all this revelation from God can be integrated in a consistent manner and enrich our worship of the Savior.

Instead of launching debates to win battles for our pet causes, we can initiate dialogue in search of truth. With truth as the goal—and the humility to approach it as learners—everyone wins and unnecessary division ceases.

My message is that believers need never be fearful of "irreconcilable differences" between the book of nature and the book of Scripture. Nor is there any warrant for nonbelievers to discount the Bible and the Christian faith for "contradicting science." The book of Job, likely the Bible's oldest book (see chapter 2), lays a solid foundation for the "two books" doctrine set forth in the Belgic Confession. According to that Reformation creed, both the book of Scripture and the book of nature are reliable and trustworthy in every respect, and therefore consistent both internally and externally (see chapter 5).

Job helps us resolve nearly all the Genesis creation controversies. It challenges skeptics to test the Bible at a much deeper level through its provision of an extra and more detailed layer of scientific description of natural history. For the Christian who wants to give better reasons for steadfast hope in Christ, Job is loaded with powerful apologetics tools. Several of these tools, including the most potent ones, have yet to enter the awareness of most pastors and lay outreach leaders.

Job, the man, had no peer in terms of his grace, humility, and wisdom. Little clouded his capacity to see the great spiritual truths God had revealed to all people through nature's record. With a heart attuned to God's Spirit, Job discerned from the record of nature the broad outline of God's plan for his eternal salvation.

To a large degree Job is a forgotten resource for science-based apologetics. My hope in writing is that readers will find this book's focus on the science and creation content of Job a liberating experience in answering their questions and concerns about the Christian faith, in healing divisions within the church, and in challenging nonbelievers with evidence they've never yet considered.

1

Answers for Today's Issues

During my four days in the hospital following coronary bypass surgery, I received visits from five different chaplains. These dear people brought kind, caring words. Though I was grateful for their compassion, their visits, for the most part, became outreach opportunities for me.

In my conversations with four of them I was amazed to discover that none viewed the Bible as the inspired and totally trustworthy Word of God. Each considered the content of the Bible's first few chapters as hopelessly at odds with established scientific fact. Yet they were fascinated when I told them about the book I was working on (this one), especially when I commented that certain passages in Job provide interpretative keys to understanding the Genesis creation accounts.

As I shared what I see as some of those keys, each of the four acknowledged that the Bible and nature's record might possibly be concordant after all. They were particularly impressed to see that the book of Job apparently anticipated several stunning scientific discoveries of the past few decades. I encouraged them all to read the entire book with new eyes for scientific content and spiritual truth.

The new millennium's dawn has blessed humanity with a knowledge explosion every bit as dramatic as the "bang" that brought the universe into existence—or the Avalon and Cambrian events that brought vast numbers of new and different animals into existence.

At no other time in history have such spectacular and widespread increases in affluence, technology, education, and communication occurred. These advances have yielded a wealth of new knowledge.

All this knowledge, however, has done little to satisfy people's deepest longings and to answer their most pressing questions. If anything, the knowledge explosion has raised more questions, doubts, and fears. People everywhere express confusion and bewilderment as they attempt to assimilate this burst of new information. Many, especially younger people, look with suspicion and skepticism on our so-called advances as they see global problems growing rather than shrinking.

The book of Job, probably the most ancient book in the Bible (see chapter 2), is a book for *today*, perhaps more so than for any day since it was recorded. Its prophetic accuracy in foreshadowing some of the most astonishing scientific discoveries of recent decades, even of the past few years, demonstrates its relevance to twenty-first-century issues. Is it possible, then, that this centuries-old book can point us in the direction of helpful answers to current challenges and threats to humanity's existence and well-being? Can it suggest areas of research and avenues of inquiry that will lead to beneficial breakthroughs?

I'm convinced it can. For example, as I discuss in chapter 4, Job offers significant insights for addressing the perplexing and controversial global warming concerns. Job also contains passages that give clues to mysteries currently under investigation by cognitive neuroscientists, such as the origin and development of what I refer to in chapters 7–11 as "soulish" attributes (intellect, volition, and emotion) of advanced animals.

God's wisdom embedded in Job seems to have anticipated not only knowledge advances but also the anxiety and insecurity future generations would face as their knowledge and technology progressed. In many respects, the debate between Job and his friends targeted future generations rather than their own. As the apostle Peter declared, "They were not serving themselves but you" (1 Pet. 1:12).

Resolving Bible Difficulties

One way the book of Job serves future generations, including our own, is that it helps readers test and refine their interpretation of other Bible passages about natural history. In the book of Acts, the Berean Jews were considered "of more noble character than those in Thessalonica" because they "examined the Scriptures every day to see if what Paul said was true" (Acts 17:11). This same Paul exhorted the Thessalonians to "test and prove all things" (1 Thess. 5:21 AMP).

In chapters 3 through 6, I show how certain statements in Job help elucidate some of the more difficult to interpret verses on creation found elsewhere in the Bible. Such illumination from Job can help believers respond to skeptics' charges that the Bible is filled with scientific errors and contradictions. The clarity that Job brings can also help resolve some needless controversies threatening to divide Christians and split congregations.

Essential Cues for Interpretation

According to the historical Christian perspective, the Bible authors intended that their words be taken literally unless contextual cues indicate otherwise. The challenge for readers lies in determining when and how a passage shifts from literal to metaphorical or employs some other figure of speech.

Perhaps more than any other book of the Bible, Job makes use of similes, metaphors, and other forms of figurative expression. For example, I count well over a dozen figures just in the passage describing the behemoth and leviathan (more on this in chapter 12). Careful reading reveals numerous contextual markers, including the words "like" and "as" (in English translations) within those passages.

Given that Job likely predates other books of Scripture, it lays a foundation for understanding certain imagery used by later Bible authors. Many word pictures that have puzzled readers for centuries or have provided skeptics with excuses *not* to believe are rooted, defined, and explained in Job. In chapters 5 and 6, I offer multiple examples of how Job's descriptive language settles questions that have troubled Bible students for years as well as questions that have emerged only recently. Job helps settle debates over the meaning of references to the "expanse" in Genesis 1, the uniqueness of humans as compared with other animals, and the nature of death.

Creation Clarification

As the dramatic opening passage of the Bible, Genesis 1 receives and deserves recognition as a paramount declaration of God's identity and role in creation. Yet it is not truly the earliest creation account, as you will see in chapter 2. Job's epic dialogue was available to the ancient Hebrews before Moses's book was written.

Job provides many answers to the creation and evolution controversies that today occupy so much of both secular and Christian thought. While Genesis may be the most familiar and obvious creation narrative, it is neither the sole nor the supreme source of biblical revelation regarding the origin and history of the cosmos and life. In reality, Job contains far more content on creation events and nature's record. Because it is more than a narrative highlight of major events, Job's commentary is more specific and detailed than the Genesis account.

What's more, the book of Job is just one biblical source of amplification and clarification on creation. Psalms, Proverbs, Ecclesiastes, Isaiah, Romans, 1 Corinthians, 2 Peter, and Revelation all provide chapter-length or longer accounts of God's involvement in the realm of nature, specifically in creation (see Appendix on page 223). Throughout the Bible, one finds such commentary in both extended passages and brief references.

This wealth of creation content makes the Bible unique among the "holy books" of the world's major religions. This treasure enables readers, through thoughtful integration, to discern from the Bible a reasonably clear, detailed, and unambiguous story of the origin and history of the universe, Earth, and life.

Healing Genesis Phobia

In my many years of ministry, speaking in hundreds of schools and churches throughout America and other parts of the world, I've been stunned and grieved to discover how many pastors and teachers avoid diving deeply into the first eleven chapters of Genesis and into the apologetics questions and challenges those chapters raise. Many peace-loving pastors or enthusiastic teachers realize the tension and potential divisiveness stirred by discussion of these chapters. Their own training in colleges and seminaries has presented them with a wide array of positions, all zealously defended, including the position that no position is actually defensible.

The problem I see is that ignoring a controversy never makes it go away. Conflict over how to interpret the Bible's first several chapters will continue whether or not Christian leaders choose to offer any instruction on them. Skeptics tend to interpret Christian leaders' avoidance of Genesis 1–11 as an obvious concession that the Bible is scientifically flawed and indefensible. As a result, truth seekers may be discouraged from examining the rest of the Bible.

What motivates both the scientist and evangelist within me is the conviction that this insecurity and anxiety need not continue to interfere with our efforts to spread the Good News—the message that our Creator invites us to know him and live with him forever. In chapter 2, as I make a case for the antiquity of Job's story, I argue that Job serves in one sense as a foreword and introduction to Genesis. On the topic of God's involvement in the natural realm, Job is a *primary* text. Job colorfully sets the stage for the orderly and succinct Genesis narrative.

Chapters 4–6 show how Job can transform Genesis 1–11 from a scientific embarrassment, a source of mockery among skeptics, into Christians' most potent tool for demonstrating that the Bible is a supernaturally inspired, trustworthy, and relevant revelation to mankind. If we use Job to show doubters that the Bible is accurate and wholly reliable both historically and scientifically, we may find them much more willing to trust it as a guide for how we should live and relate to God. If we study Job among fellow Christians, we may find that it restores and matures our faith in all that the Bible teaches. Let's take a look at some of the particulars.

Identifying Darwin's Mistake

In his books *On the Origin of Species* and *The Descent of Man*, Charles Darwin concluded that the difference between humans and the higher animals, as between higher animals and lower animals, is one of *degree* only and not of *kind*. Genesis 1 tells us the difference is of both degree *and* kind. It describes three distinct origins of Earth's life: purely physical life, such as plants and insects; life that is both physical and soulish, including birds, mammals, and a few species of reptiles; and life that is physical, soulish, and spiritual, namely—and only—human life.

Job offers abundant and significant information about the three different kinds of life. In chapters 7 and 8, I examine Job's awareness of the distinctive characteristics of each. Job also reveals how the three different sets of life-forms were designed by God to relate to one another.

Creation and Roles of "Soulish" Animals

Genesis 1 refers to the second category of life by the Hebrew term *nepesh*. This word is used for "soulish" creatures, animals with the capacity for a limited range of thought, choice, and feeling, but without the spiritual qualities possessed by humans. The book of Job offers some remarkable insights into the ways these higher animals relate to humans and shows that God endowed soulish animals with unique capacities to serve and please humanity, each creature in its own special way.

Job even provides a top ten list of animals that have played essential roles both in the launch of civilization and in sustaining human well-being today. The ancient observer describes how the different kinds of soulish animals offer valuable instruction and assistance to humanity. In chapters 8–11, I describe some of the amazing attributes soulish creatures manifested long before humans even existed, which readied them to meet humanity's needs from the very first moment people appeared on Earth.

Creation Care Manual

The first instructions God gave to humanity, specifically to Adam and Eve, concerned their responsibility to manage Earth's resources for the benefit of all life (see Gen. 1:28–31). In many respects, the book of Job serves as an instruction manual teaching humans exactly how to manage the planet's resources for the advantage of all. Job provides this instruction by asking specific questions.

As a scientist reading Job, I see how God structured questions to guide humans in the kind of research we need to conduct in order to wisely manage Earth's abundant but limited resources. Chapters 4–10 explore these questions and note that in spite of humanity's remarkable scientific achievements, most of the questions remain unanswered to this day. The National Science Foundation here in the United States, as well as scientific organizations in other leading nations of the world, would do well to take advantage of Job in developing their plans and funding for ongoing research.

Good Science, Good Faith

Another lesson I've learned from my years in ministry is that when skeptics and seekers receive thoughtful, reasonable answers to their questions about science, creation, evolution, and human behavior, they gain a desire to learn more about God and the possibility of developing a relationship with him. In the early days, I expected that after giving a lecture on science and God before an audience of skeptics, the question-and-answer time would be dominated by science questions. But that was not and still is not the case. Typically, the audience peppers me with questions about the Bible and Christian theology, often asking for clarification of difficult doctrinal issues.

The first time I spoke in a public high school about scientific evidences for God, the president of the student society of atheists practically leaped in the air to ask the first question: "What can I do to avoid judgment?" Although for a moment some classmates wondered if he was joking, they quickly realized he was serious.

The book of Job reflects what I've observed time and again: questions about science and nature's record lead naturally into questions about faith, especially about humanity's standing before a righteous God. A study of nature, and especially of God's creatures, emphasizes the gulf between humanity and the One who made everything for his own purposes. It sparks questions about if or how that gulf can be bridged. Chapters 11–15 address the faith issues that arise from the conversation among Job and his four friends, issues of equal importance and concern to us today as we continue to gain a better understanding of God's work in creating the universe and the earth to sustain life in general and humans in particular.

Age-Old Problem of Evil and Suffering

It goes without saying that Job, the man, and Job, the book, primarily address the questions raised by encounters with evil and suffering. This issue of evil and suffering is the focal point of virtually every commentary on Job that I've been able to find. The book you now read offers a different commentary. My motivation in writing is to show how Job imparts answers to some of the biggest science-faith issues of the twenty-first century. I leave comprehensive commentary on evil and suffering to others[1] and to some of my previous writings.[2]

This book does, however, touch on the problem of evil and suffering where this problem remains a significant factor in creation-versus-evolution and science-versus-faith debates (see chapter 13). Some things don't seem to change through the centuries.

Of course, Job himself needed time to comprehend and appreciate why he had to endure so much evil and suffering. However, Job never wavered in his conviction that God, if he so desired, could offer some good reasons for subjecting one of his worshipers to torment and devastation. Nor did Job ever waver in his confidence that nature's record was a trustworthy revelation from God not only about the nature of the physical realm but also about life's most important spiritual issues. Job's steadfast persistence and faith in God—and in God's revelation—offers an example of how to conduct our scientific and theological research today in those areas where the observed results may not make immediate sense.

Book for Today

Who can help but wonder how the most ancient of Scripture's sixty-six books yields such a rich abundance of penetrating answers to some of the thorniest and most divisive issues of our day? Thanks to the words recorded in Job, a real and lasting reconciliation of God's two revelations—general revelation through nature and special revelation through the Bible—appears within reach.

The epic dialogue between Job and his friends is remarkable on many fronts. In addition to being remarkable for its content, Job is also remarkable in terms of its participants, its timing, and its location. These features of the dialogue and how it came about represent a fascinating story in itself.

2

Gathering of the Greatest Minds

Sometimes the best way to answer a question is by asking another question—or even two, in some cases. Recently, a scowling student approached the microphone during my talk at his university campus. He wanted to know how any reputable astronomer could possibly give credence to the biblical claim that the sun was created *after* plant life appeared. At least that's what he had heard the Genesis story said.

My response began with a question about specifically who or what would have benefited from the appearance of the sun, moon, and stars in the sky. As he wrestled for a while with that question, I raised another: "Do you know what the book of Job tells us about the surface conditions of the primordial Earth?"

The aim of these questions was to help this skeptical student discover for himself why it's possible for intelligent, scientifically literate people to accept the truthfulness—not in part but in whole—of God's Word. I figured if he discovered rather than simply heard some answers, it would have a deeper impact on his thinking and his willingness to consider the core message of Scripture about God's love for him and God's purpose for his life.

As any researcher knows, a crucial first step in finding answers to difficult problems and challenges is to ask the right questions. Most have also discovered the importance of asking the right questions of the right people in the right way.

To fully appreciate the creation and science content in the book of Job, we need to consider some contextual questions: Who was Job? Who were the others mentioned? When and where did the story take place? What event(s) gave rise to the dialogue between Job and these other individuals?

In today's society, as in the past, bringing great minds together to discuss complex issues can yield great results. That's why we hold conferences, forums, symposia—gatherings where leading experts on a particular topic can share their latest discoveries and insights and propose solutions to unsolved problems. Such interaction is especially productive when a variety of disciplines are represented. These gatherings include vigorous debate over the relative merits of the various solutions proposed.

Such debates, however, are not at all like the political, legal, and religious debates that dominate modern news media or the competitions that typify high school and college debate clubs. The goal is not to win or demolish the credibility of one's opponent. Rather, it is to work together toward a rigorous and thorough evaluation of the strongest evidences and arguments that will lead to the best resolution of a particular problem. The ultimate goal is to study and address the problem in a way that leads to solving more problems and answering more questions within the discipline and perhaps beyond. Such is the spirit of the "debate" documented in the book of Job.

Greatest Debates

The key to understanding the message of Job is to see the book as a transcript of one of humanity's all-time most important debates—full of presumptions, questions, rebuttals—and ultimately as a quest for truth. Why did the Creator and sovereign Master of all things and events allow Job, a devout worshiper, to experience such unimaginable suffering? This great debate was instigated by an even bigger debate, a confrontation between the two most powerful beings in existence: God and Lucifer, or Satan, the most powerful being God ever created.

The question God deemed worthy to address was this: Would a man live righteously, honoring God, if he experienced loss and suffering unrelated to his own decisions and actions?

Satan mocked God's plan for redeeming humanity. He insisted that, however righteous a human might appear, submission to God's authority and responding to God's offer of redemption from sin is essentially motivated by self-interest based on the desire for guaranteed physical and material blessings or protection. Take away the blessings, Satan argued, and watch the righteousness, trust, and worship evaporate.

For the sake of the entire heavenly and earthly hosts, God accepted Satan's challenge. He allowed Satan to remove all the material blessings and even loved ones from the premier example of human righteousness, a man named Job. When that initial test failed to produce the results Satan had anticipated, the Arch Rebel challenged God to put Job through another level of testing: remove Job's health and vitality, exposing him to infection, pain, and suffering. So, with no knowledge of the debate taking place in the heavenly realm, Job was subjected to material devastation, the emotional agonies of losing his beloved children, unrelenting bodily misery, and even gross disfigurement.

The appalling state to which Job was reduced understandably gave rise to the earthly, human debate we can now observe as if we were present. This dialogue likely involved the greatest minds then alive. The debate centered on the relationship between evil and suffering.

To call this interaction the greatest of all human debates seems no exaggeration. Consider that the existence of evil and suffering remains to this day the only "positive" rationale nontheists ever seem to marshal against God's existence. The modern formulation of this argument, which we've all heard in one form or another, goes like this: if an all-powerful, all-loving God were to exist, such a God would immediately take action to remove all evil and suffering from human experience, or never let it happen in the first place. Since evil and suffering obviously do exist, God must not.

(I am not implying that atheists present no other arguments for their no-God stance. Rather, I'm suggesting their other arguments all tend to be "negative." They consist primarily of jabs against theists' weak, subjective arguments in favor of God's existence or against whatever they dislike about God's plan for redeeming humanity.)

The debate between Job and his philosophical friends deserves consideration as the greatest debate of all time for another reason. Unlike many of today's leading scholars, Job and his friends apparently grasped the intimate connection between the problem of evil and suffering and the question of purposeful creation versus undirected evolution (for further discussion see chapter 13). Furthermore, they seemed to comprehend that their debate transcended their personal relationships and perhaps even their own time. I can't help but wonder if they had some inkling they were debating for the benefit of all humanity.

Great Debaters

The debate between Job and his friends may be the greatest of all debates for a third reason: the caliber of the debaters. Job, Eliphaz, Zophar, and Bildad were likely the intellectual powerhouses of their day and the leading spiritual lights of their culture. Scholars refer to them as "princes of the people and sages of renown."[1] One advantage of their ancient (though not primitive) "education" shows in the breadth of their knowledge. Unlike many intellectuals today, they were less specialized in their studies and thus more adept at seeing the bigger picture, not to mention the connections between material and nonmaterial reality.

There is no doubt about Job's stature. Apparently God and Satan had no dispute over who could be called the most righteous man alive. Twice the prophet Ezekiel recognized Job along with Noah and Daniel as the three most righteous men of the Old Testament era (Ezek. 14:14, 20).

Eliphaz, who took the lead in the debate against Job, is identified in the text as a Temanite. Teman is a city in Edom. Edom encompasses the southern portion of what is now the nation of Jordan. Teman was famous in the ancient world for its exceptionally wise scholars.[2] Ancient literature indicates this fame persisted for centuries.

The prophet Jeremiah comments on Teman in a series of rhetorical questions: "Is there no longer wisdom in Teman? Has counsel perished from the prudent? Has their wisdom decayed?" (Jer. 49:7). Given the eight-hundred-mile distance between Teman and Job's home in the land of Uz (see fig. 2.1) and the investment required to undertake such a journey, it seems likely that Teman's leaders sent their most gifted scholar, Job's friend and peer, to offer comfort. It makes sense that Eliphaz, the most revered, was probably the Temanite best known to Job, and the text indicates (see Job 2:11 and 42:10) that, despite the distance, Eliphaz was among Job's dearest friends.

The text suggests that Zophar and Bildad were of virtually equal abilities to Eliphaz and also close friends to Job. Apparently, when word of Job's devastating losses and sufferings spread, the world of that time sent their three most eminent wise men to offer comfort and counsel. Who else could even try?

Debate Recorder

Another indication of the debate's momentous nature was the careful, detailed manner in which the debate was recorded. Given the early date when this debate must have occurred (see p. 30), recording this conversation would have been no easy matter. It probably required a dedicated team, and someone of especially high position and skill to lead that team.

Several details support the conclusion that the record-keeping supervisor was Elihu. First, Elihu was much younger than Job, Eliphaz, Zophar, and Bildad, perhaps as much as a generation (or more) younger. In spite of his youth, however, he outmatched the combined wisdom of Eliphaz, Zophar, and Bildad (see Job 32–37). It appears from Elihu's own words (see Job 32:6–22) and from the fact he was present at the debate that Elihu was the intellectual and spiritual prodigy of his time. As such, he would have recognized the importance of recording the conversation for posterity. Other leaders, as well as Job and his associates, would have confirmed Elihu's qualification for the role.

This scene from Job brings to mind a personal experience, on a much smaller scale, to be sure. During my graduate school days at the University of Toronto, each June the faculty would bring four of the world's leading astronomers to give lectures and to engage our department in dialogue. A few of us took notes as usual, but our note-taking was especially detailed whenever the four astronomers interacted with one another. We realized we were witnessing a historic event that might never be repeated. I imagine the young man Elihu felt no differently.

In the book of Job, God has the last word. The Almighty delivers both a commendation and a mild rebuke to Job, and a strong rebuke to Eliphaz, Zophar, and Bildad. However, the text includes no comment concerning Elihu or his extensive participation in the debate. Such an omission would be consistent with Elihu's role as recorder-in-chief. In that capacity he would be sensitive to keep the focus on the debate's main participants. Elihu's service as recorder would also explain why his presence is not mentioned until he actually addresses the others, as documented in Job 32.

Location and Date

Job resided in the land of Uz (1:1), located immediately south of Chaldea in the region near the northwest shore of the Persian Gulf (see fig. 2.1). Job 2, the chapter introducing the debate, indicates Job's friends each came from their homelands—in the case of Eliphaz, a far distant city—to meet with him. With Job so terribly incapacitated, it seems highly unlikely he traveled to them.

Although the book of Job follows seventeen other books in the arrangement of the Old Testament canon, its position does not reflect the timing of the story it tells. The Bible's books are not placed in order according to a single chronological sequence. Rather, the Old Testament is divided into three sections, and within each section the books are arranged chronologically. The first section includes all the books designated as history; the second, poetry; and the third, prophecy.[3] Job is the first book in the poetry section. Its placement there tells us it's the oldest of the poetic books, but a reader must look to its content to determine whether Job predates or postdates the earliest of the historical books (Genesis) or of the prophetic books (Isaiah).

Several clues suggest the story of Job predates the writing of Genesis and the rest of the Pentateuch (the Bible's first five books). Scholars

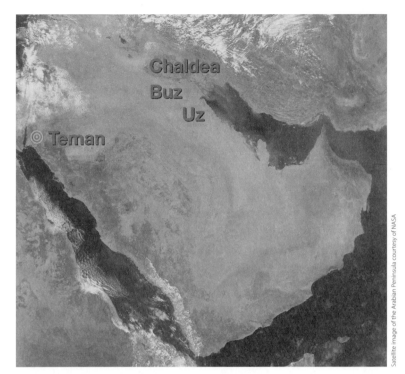

Figure 2.1: Geography of the Debate Recorded in Job
The text identifies Job's homeland, Uz. Elihu is said to have lived in the adjoining land of Buz. A raiding party from Chaldea carried off all of Job's camels. Job's friend Eliphaz traveled from the distant city of Teman.

tend to agree that it more closely coincides with the era of Abraham (initially Abram), the patriarch, who left Ur in Chaldea (Gen. 11:31) an estimated 660 years before Moses and the establishment of the Ten Commandments and the Hebrews' civil and ceremonial laws.

Right away the reader sees that Job, as the family head, makes the sacrificial offerings. From Moses's era onward, priests carried out that task in a particular way. Old Testament scholars often comment that the book of Job contains no references to Hebrew culture.[4] It seems evident, then, that neither the Mosaic sacrifice system nor other elements recognized as Hebraic social customs had yet come into existence.

Because Job references neither political nor economic events, it would appear that he lived in an era before what we know of as nations had emerged as socioeconomic, sociopolitical entities. It seems that city-states were the primary sociopolitical entities of Job's time. Furthermore, historians find references to both Job the book and Job the man in extrabiblical writings dated as early as 2000 BC.[5]

Job's long life span also suggests an early date consistent with the time of the patriarchs. Genesis tells of God's decree, at Noah's time, that the maximum human life span would be shortened from about 970 years down to 120 years. Through genealogical records we see the decline in longevity occurred along an exponential curve (Gen. 11:10–26). By Moses's time and thereafter, that limit was fully in effect. Yet Job lived at least twenty years beyond it (see Job 42:16; Gen. 6:3; 11:10–26).

The fact that the Hebrew language did not yet exist in written form at the time of Abraham and the patriarchs may explain the poetic form in which the book of Job was recorded.[6] Such a style character-izes many ancient stories because it facilitated memorization, a way to preserve the account's accuracy until Hebrew writing developed. No record exists to identify who put the account of Job into writ-ten Hebrew. Scholarly speculation ranges from Moses to Joshua to Solomon to Isaiah.[7]

Creation Preview

A patriarchal date for the book of Job would make Job far and away the earliest piece of inspired Scripture. The probability that Job was available either in written or oral form before Genesis was written profoundly impacts our interpretive perspective and approach to the Genesis creation accounts.

In many respects, Job serves as an introduction or preface to Gen-esis. The gaps in the Genesis creation accounts that skeptics love to ridicule are not really gaps at all if the content of Job was familiar to the original recipients of Genesis. Why would Moses need or want to repeat what was already widely understood from Job's epic poem?

For later readers and students of Genesis, the key to understanding the creation and flood accounts lies in recognizing them as reviews or overviews of the broader, more expansive (though nonchronological) creation content in Job. In one sense, Job provides the introductory context that informs not only the Genesis creation passage but all the Bible's creation accounts (see Appendix, p. 223). Job, rather than Genesis, is the biblical text where discussion of creation and evolution should rightly begin.

Deuteronomy Foreshadowed

Not only does the book of Job provide an introduction to the first words of Scripture (Gen. 1–9), it also foreshadows Moses's final words in Deuteronomy. Just as Genesis is not the earliest revelation from God on the subject of creation, neither is Deuteronomy the earliest word on the problem of evil or on God's plan to redeem humanity from the fatal illusion of spiritual autonomy. Many skeptics have criticized Deuteronomy for its apparent obscurity, specifically on these two topics. However, the charge evaporates in the light of Job's familiar story.

Moses and his contemporaries already possessed a preview of God's redemptive plan in the words of Job. Deuteronomy simply echoes and reinforces what they had already heard and likely memorized. They also understood something about the value and purpose of suffering and the necessity of humanity's exposure to evil.

By understanding the historical position and context of Job—the events, people, place, and timing—we gain insight into other Bible books. These insights can help deepen and amplify our understanding of those books.

Asking Big Questions

The dialogue that took place between Job, his friends, Elihu, and God occurred as much as four thousand years ago. Yet the questions these men wrestled with—and those that God posed—still hold a central place in our minds and hearts to this day. The Bible's most ancient book merits recognition and study as one of the most relevant for twenty-first-century readers.

No other book of Scripture contains as many questions as Job does. By my count, the number exceeds two hundred. And God poses over eighty questions in response to those two hundred. In all these questions, I see God guiding and motivating us to discover a wealth of answers we desperately need for addressing the problems and challenges of our time—of all time, for that matter.

As the Bible's premier question-and-answer book, Job addresses the timeless questions raised by people throughout all ages. But amazingly, it also anticipates questions raised by explosive advances in technology and education. The next three chapters examine some of the insights Job provides for addressing such questions.

3

Answers to Timeless Questions

For more than thirty years I've been teaching a Sunday morning class called Paradoxes. The class seems to attract people of all ages, both Christians and non-Christians. What binds us together is the desire to discuss the paradoxical issues of science and Scripture and life. For the past year or so, a skeptic named Al has kept us on our toes with his vigorous defenses of naturalism and critiques of Christian apologetics.

One Sunday Al complained about how hard it is to believe in a God whom we can't see, hear, or touch. "If God really wanted us to know him and follow him," Al asked, "why wouldn't he have made his existence more obvious?"

Good question. My initial response was to point out that it represents a crucial, sometimes first, step in a person's journey toward faith. Who doesn't ask this question in one form or another at some point in life? Job and his friends certainly did.

Next I asked Al and the class to engage in a thought experiment. If we could access God through our five senses, what would we discover about God's identity and attributes? After some lively class discussion, Al himself offered an answer: "A god we could know that way would not be the all-powerful, all-knowing, and everywhere-present God of the Bible." Without realizing it, Al echoed the words of the apostle Paul. A God who truly *is* God would be one "whom no one has seen or can see" because this God "lives in unapproachable light" (1 Tim. 6:16).

Almost immediately an outcry arose from other class members: "Wait a minute! Jesus was God, and yet he was visible and touchable by human beings." This response led to a lengthy discussion of a great paradox, one that Job and his friends grappled with long before the divine Redeemer came to Earth in human form.

Jesus of Nazareth was fully God—but he willingly chose to accept, for a time, the confines of a human body to accomplish a purpose only God himself could fulfill:

> Who, being in very nature God, did not consider equality with God something to be used to his own advantage; rather, he made himself nothing by taking the very nature of a servant, being made in human likeness. And being found in appearance as a man, he humbled himself by becoming obedient to death—even death on a cross! Therefore God exalted him to the highest place. (Phil. 2:6–9)

For a time and a reason, God took visible, touchable form on Earth, and yet all the while God was and is more. God has access to a reality beyond the dimensions of the universe.

Many faith questions are like Al's. They're universal, asked by people all over the world from all walks of life and through all of human history:

1. Who, what, or where is God?
2. Does God see or care about my life?
3. Why doesn't God answer my questions?
4. How can God be near and yet beyond my reach?
5. Why does God allow suffering and death?
6. Why is human life so short?
7. Why do good things happen to bad people?
8. Why do bad things happen to good people?
9. How does God communicate to us?
10. Do angels really exist?

These are some of the core questions Job and his friends grapple with, for their own sake and for ours.

Finding God

Have you ever met a true atheist? I've encountered many individuals who adopt that label, but so far they've all been people with complaints against God—or against those who purportedly know him. In all his torment, Job never denied God's existence or cursed God, as his wife suggested he do (2:9). But when Job cried out in anguish, raising many of the questions listed above, Eliphaz, Bildad, and Zophar responded in the same unhelpful way some well-intentioned believers do in the face of challenges and complaints. They rebuked Job and magnified his suffering with their "righteous" defense of God and his ways.

Each of us, if we're honest, indulges in moments of grumbling against God. Because a faithful man named Job voiced his pain, confusion, and anger, all of humanity can benefit from his integrity and, ultimately, from the insights and awareness he received.

Within and Beyond

Without the benefit of biblical instruction, Job and his friends somehow discerned and articulated for later generations one of Christianity's unique, core beliefs—that God is both immanent (existing and operating everywhere within his creation) and transcendent (existing and operating beyond his creation without limitation). In today's terms, we would say that God exists beyond the cosmic space-time dimensions to which humans are restricted, making physical contact with God impossible, and yet God remains simultaneously and continuously in proximity to every person and thing within cosmic space-time dimensions. (The scientific evidence to support this view has emerged in the last few decades.)[1] These ancient sages expressed and embraced the paradox long ago.

Job has much to say of God's nearness and awareness:

You [God] examine them [every person] every morning and test them every moment. (7:18)

You [God] gave me life and showed me kindness, and in your providence watched over my spirit. (10:12)

If I sinned, you [God] would be watching me. (10:14)

His [God's] eyes are on their [every person's] ways. (24:23)

He [God] views the ends of the earth and sees everything under the heavens. (28:24)

His friends echo these thoughts. Bildad questioned rhetorically, "On whom does his [God's] light not rise?" (25:3). Elihu added, "His [God's] eyes are on the ways of mortals; he sees their every step" (34:21).

Job also described God's transcendence: "When he passes me, I cannot see him; when he goes by, I cannot perceive him" (9:11). Later he declares, "If I go to the east, he [God] is not there; if I go to the west, I do not find him. When he is at work in the north, I do not see him; when he turns to the south, I catch no glimpse of him. But he knows the way that I take" (23:8–10).

Zophar offered this perspective: "Can you probe the limits of the Almighty? They are higher than the heavens above—what can you do? They are deeper than the depths below—what can you know?" (11:7–8). In Elihu's words, "The Almighty is beyond our reach" (37:23).

Centuries later, the prophet Jeremiah restates the paradox in succinct terms. Speaking for God he writes, "Am I only a God nearby . . . and not a God far away? Who can hide in secret places so that I cannot see them? Do not I fill heaven and earth?" (Jer. 23:23–24).

Mathematicians have developed ways to illustrate how God can be near and beyond us at the same time. One way is to picture a two-dimensional realm inhabited by two-dimensional beings. These "flatlanders," having access to length and width only, would be incapable of making contact with a three-dimensional (3D) being hovering even a tiny fraction of an inch above their plane. But that 3D being would be capable of gaining and maintaining a perspective on them beyond what they could possibly have on each other—either with or without their awareness of its presence. And, of course, a 3D being could certainly choose to make contact with the flatlanders and impact their existence in a variety of ways.

A Reason for Death

One of the most difficult struggles of life comes in grappling with the horrible reality of death. Skeptics sometimes use death as an argument to support their rejection of faith. Their line of reasoning goes something like this:

1. The God of the Bible claims to be all-loving and all-powerful.
2. An all-loving, all-powerful God would not subject his creatures to an experience as profoundly dreadful and irreversible as death.
3. Therefore, the biblical God must not be God, if there is a God.

Many believers also wrestle with questions about death: Why did God allow it in the first place? Why does God take some people through death's door so early, or so late, or right in the middle of some activity that is beneficial to humanity?

Death is a subject most of us avoid talking about until some painful circumstance brings it to the forefront. No wonder it became a central issue in Job's discussion with his friends. Death had just taken not one but *all* of Job's sons and daughters. Death had robbed him of a father's great hopes and dreams.

At the height of his suffering, Job (understandably) wondered whether he might have been better off dying in his mother's womb and thus spared the trouble and torment of his current state (3:10–13, 16–19). This expression reveals a normal emotional response to extreme distress. Jesus himself longed for "escape" from the anticipated horrors of his torture and execution (Matt. 26:36–46; Luke 22:42–44).

Although they lived long before any written Scriptures were available, Job and his friends held firmly to their conviction that death is something other than the cessation of all consciousness. They believed death is a doorway into a realm beyond life as we know it. Job sees it as the doorway to ongoing "peace" and "rest" (3:13). Zophar describes it as the doorway to "terrors," "total darkness," and "fire" for those who exalt themselves above God (20:25–26).

One insight that emerges from this conversation is that a person's view of death reflects his or her view of life and what life is about. As Job and Eliphaz saw it, life is a time not only of joy and pleasure but also of "trouble," "sufferings," and "hard service" (5:7; 7:1; 9:28; 14:1, 14) during which God continually examines and tests human hearts (7:17–19).

In contrast to Eliphaz, Bildad, and Zophar, Job acknowledged his inability to pass life's tests without God's direct intervention. He spoke of his need for a divine Advocate (9:33–34; 16:19–21), a Redeemer (19:25–27), to stand before God in his behalf. With wisdom that could have come only from the Holy Spirit, Job declared that God in his mercy would provide "the pledge" divine justice demands (17:3).

Job and his friends represent all of humanity in their thoughts and concerns about life beyond death. They demonstrate one of the characteristics that distinguish humans from all of Earth's other life-forms. Humans alone have a capacity—and a compulsion—to consider the meaning, value, and purpose of life and to ponder existence beyond the grave (Job 33:16–30; 19:25–27; Ezek. 18:4–32). This unique dimension of human life is what Job refers to as the human spirit (Job 6:4; 7:11; 10:12; 27:3; 32:8; 32:18).

Necessity of Short Lives

Although he lived decades longer than anyone could possibly live today (Job 42:16), Job saw his life as fleetingly brief (7:6–9, 21; 9:25–26; 10:20; 14:1–2; 16:22; 17:1). So did Bildad (8:9). Like nearly all at one time or another, Job and his friends pondered life's brevity, considering why a loving God would limit our earthly existence to so few trips around the sun.

Job offered some remarkable observations. He seemed to recognize that a relatively short human life span effectively protects humanity by limiting the expression of evil. He describes how the death of the wicked delivers the righteous from evil assaults (24:19–24; 27:18–23). The principle here is that when a person becomes irreversibly committed to doing evil, a longer life span would result in an escalation of harm.

This principle found dramatic demonstration in the days before Noah's flood. Though early humans were capable of living past nine hundred years, the lack of population growth indicates that few died of natural causes. It seems the vast majority had their lives cut short by murder. Mathematical calculations suggest that the average life span in pre-flood times was likely less than the average life span in the world's developed nations today.[2]

Those who complain about the brevity of life fail to realize that potentially longer life spans can actually shorten human longevity. When God decreed in Genesis 6:3 that the maximum human life span would be abbreviated to about 120 years, he acted to protect humanity and extend the average human lifetime. He shielded humans committed to righteous living from becoming completely overwhelmed by those humans bent on rapacious greed and violence.

Daily headlines tell the story. Whom do wicked people prey upon? Most often they inflict their evil on the ordinary, unsuspecting, law-abiding citizens, not on others like themselves. Longer life spans would only allow malignancy to spread. In Noah's generation the entire human population, other than Noah and his family, became reprobate.

Through the millennia since Noah, God has allowed humanity to see that seven decades (or thereabouts) is adequate time for a person to choose his or her eternal destiny, pursue a life of worship and blessing, and pass along a legacy of virtue. Yet through life's ups and downs, good times and hard times, we waver, as Job did, between viewing life as too short or too long (Job 26–31). How much more do those of us who lack Job's humility and wisdom question God's timing?

A useful analogy for our earthly lives would be the final exam for a tough college course. As a student, I always felt the time I had to complete my final examinations was far too short. The three to six hours my professors allotted was never enough time to adequately answer all their questions. On one occasion, however, my professor snatched my exam paper away from me after I had been sitting in the exam room for only about an hour. He told me it was pointless for me to suffer through another two hours given that my performance so far had already established I deserved the class's highest grade. Similarly, it often takes less time than we think to complete our God-assigned tasks on Earth.

Mystery of Death

In the debate between Job and his friends, Job did almost all the talking about death. This is not surprising given Job's physical suffering and misery. He naturally presumed his death was imminent.

Job understood, however, that regardless of external circumstances or the state of his physical health, God had predetermined the exact length of his life. "A person's days are determined; you have decreed the number of his months and have set limits he cannot exceed" (14:5). As King David later concurred, God predetermines from before the time of our birth the precise number of days each one of us will live (Ps. 139:16).

Job also recognized that even a single second of life on Earth is a miracle of God. He said, "In his hand is the life of every creature and the breath of all mankind" (12:10). Elihu acknowledged that death, not life, is the outcome of nature and natural processes when he said, "If it were his intention and he withdrew his spirit and breath, all humanity would perish together and mankind would return to the dust" (34:14–15). In other words, only by God's grace do any of us get to breathe our next breath.

As noted earlier (pp. 39–40), fulfilling God's purposes in our earthly lives is hard work. Death is an opportunity to rest from one's labor. Job pointed out to his friends that in death, "I would be lying down in peace; I would be asleep and at rest" (3:13). Only a few verses later, Job adds, "There the weary are at rest" (3:17).

Christ, the Creator of the universe and all life, also uses the analogy of sleep for death (see Matt. 9:18–26; Mark 5:21–43; Luke 8:49–56; John 11:11–15). So does the apostle Paul (see 1 Cor. 11:30; 15:6, 18–20, 51; 1 Thess. 4:13–17). Sleep is an excellent analogy. The dead in Christ are aware of events taking place among the living (Heb. 11:4–12:1; Rev. 6:9–11), but they are unable to do anything to influence either those events or the living. They are passive observers.

The passivity of the dead, however, is not eternal. A time will come when they will awake from their slumber and rise to full vitality. Job, having comprehended and received God's offer of eternal salvation as revealed through God's book of nature (more on this in chapter 13), declared with unshakeable confidence, "After my skin has been destroyed, yet in my flesh I will see God; I myself will see him with my own eyes—I, and not another. How my heart yearns within me!" (19:26–27).

Another mystery for the living is the doorway to death. God brought up this point to Job and his friends when he asked, "Have the gates of death been shown to you? Have you seen the gates of the deepest darkness?" (38:17). The mystery of crossing over the threshold from life to death can bring considerable anxiety to someone facing imminent death. However, for those who have made their peace with God in submitting to his authority and have received his offer of eternal salvation, the comforting knowledge exists that the Savior himself will come and personally escort the believer across death's threshold. As King David stated, "Even though I walk through the valley of the shadow of death, I fear no evil, for You are with me; Your rod and Your staff, they comfort me" (Ps. 23:4 NASB). As recorded in Acts, just before the young deacon Stephen crossed over death's threshold, Jesus visibly appeared to him (7:54–60). The believer, therefore, need not fear the death event.

Blessing the Wicked

Job and his friends disagreed most sharply on the manner in which God deals with ungodly people. Eliphaz, Bildad, and Zophar all insisted that God ensures bad things happen to bad people and good things happen to good people in this life. They were convinced the calamities and suffering that had befallen Job were consequences meted out by God for some hidden sin in Job's life. Based on this certainty, Job's friends repeatedly admonished him to repent.

Job strongly rejected his friends' premise that his sufferings revealed some unconfessed wickedness. Admitting that he had indeed sinned in his life, he claimed to be blameless of anything that might have warranted this sudden and overwhelming flood of what looked to them like divine punishment. As far as Job was aware, each time he had done wrong to his fellow man, he had followed up with whatever restitution was necessary to make it right. Knowing that his offenses against God could never be recompensed by his own good deeds, Job acknowledged his need of an Intercessor, a Redeemer (for more on this see chapter 13). And because Job placed his full trust in the Redeemer, rather than in his best efforts to satisfy God, Job was assured that he stood blamelessly before his Creator. *No,* he reasoned, *there must be some explanation—other than divine disciplinary action—for the devastating catastrophes visited upon me.*

Job made a second argument against his friends' conclusion by observing how the wicked do not always receive justice in this life. Job pointed out how frequently the ungodly are blessed with long life, good health, great prosperity, and even the respect and admiration of friends and family (21:7–34). He recognized God's sovereignty in all this. He saw God as responsible for all the tragedies that had overtaken him as well as for the seeming rewards heaped upon faithless, prideful, self-serving people.

What Job wanted most of all was a reasonable explanation of what had happened to him, some understanding of why God allowed him to be so tormented. Job's friends reacted as if he had accused God of wrongdoing. Job's certainty that God was visiting these troubles upon him for some reason *other* than to chastise him seemed to bother them far more than anything else.

Job eventually came to understand that God allowed his sufferings and also chose to heap up blessings on wicked people to accomplish a greater good. In Job's case, that good included rescuing three friends from their folly and its potential consequences (see pp. 40, 43), not to mention countless "friends" over the centuries since then. The good also included, and still includes, God's willingness to give people every possible chance to recognize him as the source of all blessings. God's justice certainly prevails in the end.

A biblical example of a sinful man who finally acknowledged that his great wealth came from God and belonged to God is Zacchaeus (Luke 19:1–10). Israel's King Solomon gave additional insight to what Job discerned when he wrote:

> Though the righteous fall seven times, they rise again, but the wicked stumble when calamity strikes. Do not gloat when your enemy falls; when they stumble, do not let your heart rejoice, or the LORD will see and disapprove and turn his wrath away from them. Do not fret because of evildoers or be envious of the wicked, for the evildoer has no future hope, and the lamp of the wicked will be snuffed out. (Prov. 24:16–20)

In other words, God blesses those who resist him for the same reason he blesses anyone. God gives us all abundant opportunity to recognize the good things in our lives as too wonderful to be explained by "luck" or by our own efforts. God wants us to acknowledge the good things as more than we deserve, clear expressions of his gracious generosity. God blesses even those who oppose him so that they might come to realize the source of all the good things in their lives. In awakening to the source of their blessings, they might repent of their rebellion against him, as Zacchaeus did, and begin to give God the glory for the great things he has done.

Many recipients of God's blessings, however, refuse to acknowledge, thank, and worship him. Instead, they take the credit he deserves. A famous example is Babylon's King Nebuchadnezzar. One day as he was "walking on the roof of the royal palace of Babylon," Nebuchadnezzar said, "Is not this the great Babylon I have built as the royal residence, by my mighty power and for the glory of my majesty?" (Dan. 4:29–30). Once Nebuchadnezzar uttered these words, his so-called power was taken away from him. His mind was gone and he was forced to live out in the open fields among the cattle (4:31–33).

As with Nebuchadnezzar, God may snatch away blessings from prideful people so that in the midst of their loss they might turn from ignoring his presence and authority. God often uses reversals as wakeup calls to bring people to their senses, to turn them away from counterfeit gods. Though it took seven years, Nebuchadnezzar did finally bow before God, giving him the honor and glory he deserves (4:34–35). Afterward, God restored Nebuchadnezzar to the throne, and the splendor of Nebuchadnezzar's holdings "became even greater than before" (4:36). At the pinnacle of his success, Nebuchadnezzar publicly declared, "Everything he [God] does is right and all his ways are just. And those who walk in pride he is able to humble" (4:37).

Another outcome of God snatching away his blessings from ungodly people is to test the hearts of those who see themselves as godly. Those who repent and turn to God need the counsel and instructive example of his followers—those whose hearts are fully devoted to him. Any gloating over others' losses reveals a heart that is *not* fully devoted to God and overflowing with his love. Gloating is evidence of envy and pride—not what a humbled, hurting person needs. In fact, gloating is so damaging that when it happens, God quickly restores the blessings he has just removed (Prov. 24:17–18). God then seeks out someone else to minister to the nonbeliever.

God wants his people to understand that the removal of blessings is his way of setting up opportunities for them to minister his grace to those who don't yet comprehend or grasp it. As Elihu says, God makes sinners "listen to correction and commands them to repent of their evil" (Job 36:10). God does everything to encourage people to turn from their sinful ways. But listening to correction won't happen if God's followers gloat over others' losses. So if gloating occurs, it exposes the need for believers to repent and grow in grace.

God's Hidden Goodness

In the midst of his anguish Job struggled to hold onto the belief articulated by Paul in the New Testament "that in all things God works for the good of those who love him, who have been called according to his purpose" (Rom. 8:28). Like anyone else, Job had trouble imagining what good could possibly come from his situation. He wondered how long God might make him endure this pain, suffering, and shame before the good would materialize. He began to wonder if he would ever see it. Many of us experience similar impatience in the midst of trials. We want to know, and know now!

The book of Job provides some profound insights as to why, with rare exceptions, we do not and cannot fully know the answers to such wonderings. It illustrates why in most situations we must wait for what seems—or may actually be—an eternity before we find out what good our suffering yields.

What we learn from the book's opening chapters is that events in Job's life were initiated by events that occurred in a realm outside cosmic space and time. They emerged from an exchange between God and Satan in the presence of the angels. If Job had known the backstory, he would have responded quite differently to the circumstances that befell him, and the dialogue between him and his friends and between him and God would have taken another direction altogether. This knowledge would have altered both the debate in heaven and the one on Earth. As a result, everyone would have lost out on the immeasurable benefit that accrued for Job, his friends, the rest of humanity, *and* the angelic hosts as well.

I would not say Job and his friends were totally unaware of angels (see Job 4:13–16; 15:15). However, it appears that like most of us, they grossly underestimated the degree to which these transdimensional beings impact events in the earthly realm. As the apostle Paul explains, "Our struggle is not against flesh and blood, but against the rulers, against the authorities, against the powers of this dark world and against the spiritual forces of evil in the heavenly realms" (Eph. 6:12). Unseen combatants influence the affairs of humanity. Forces of darkness are at work among all peoples. Yet in our battle against the forces of evil we are not alone. God sends his obedient angels to assist us, usually in ways that are hidden from our view and awareness. As the author of Hebrews assures, "Are not all angels ministering spirits sent to serve those who will inherit salvation?" (1:14). He adds an exhortation, "Do not forget to show hospitality to strangers, for by so doing some people have shown hospitality to angels without knowing it" (13:2).

In other words, much more is going on behind the scenes—both in this world and the realm beyond—than we realize. If our knowing would serve God's good purposes and plans, he would let us know. But even in my limited reasoning ability, I can picture that such knowledge would be less than best. It could potentially diminish our credibility, integrity, and compassion, causing us to miss out on important lessons and interfering with our training for future ministry.

Job is by no means the only biblical example of the paradoxical hardship and advantage of *not* knowing God's plan and of waiting a long time for answers to our cries. A dramatic example may be seen in the life of Joseph. Others include David, Daniel, Jacob, Moses, and Stephen. Their lack of knowing demanded and built trust, which is the foundation to growing in faith, hope, and love. The author of Hebrews elaborates on this point as he takes readers on a tour through faith's hall of fame (11:4–12:28).

More about Angels

Several Bible passages either state or imply that angels are created beings (Col. 1:15–17; Heb. 1:6–7). Only the book of Job, however, gives any clues as to when God created them. Job 38:4–7 tells us the angels were witnesses as God "laid the earth's foundation." Exactly what this Hebrew phrase means cannot be precisely determined. It may refer to the formation of Earth when it first became recognizable as a planet. It may refer to that moment when the buildup of Earth's mass was complete. It may refer to that era in Earth's history when liquid water covered the planetary surface or perhaps to the time when landmasses first appeared. It could even refer to the time when God set in motion the space, time, matter, and energy from which he created the earth. At the very least, the expression indicates that angels have existed for the past 3.8 billion years or more.

Whether the creation of angels predates the creation of the universe we do not know. Nor can anyone say how long a time span separates the angels' rebellion and Satan's entry to the Garden of Eden. Revelation 12 indicates that a third of the angels followed Lucifer (Satan), the most powerful and magnificent angel, in a rebellion against God's authority. This event may or may not have preceded the creation of the universe or the formation of Earth. One thing we know for certain, however: angels are part of God's created order, and their lives and roles cross into the human realm in significant ways, both seen and unseen, as illustrated in Job.

Seemingly "Bad" Acts of God

Insurance companies refer to natural disasters as "acts of God." This label serves to distinguish between catastrophes blamed on human error or malevolence and those caused by the indiscriminate forces of nature.

Job recognized that natural calamities arise from the pervasive law of decay (entropy) God has imposed on the entire physical realm—"a mountain erodes and crumbles," "a rock is moved from its place," "water wears away stones," and "torrents wash away the soil" (14:18–19). God wields sovereign control over all nature's functions, including the operation of entropy (8:13–16; 12:8–10; 22:12–18; 23:13–16). On that point Job and his friends agreed. But they clashed mightily over the divine purposes behind such events.

Job's friends embraced the ancient and enduring notion that God purposely "aims" natural disasters to inflict punishment on evildoers

(4:8–9; 15:20–35; 18:8–16; 20:5–29) while protecting the innocent from harm (4:7; 5:19–22; 11:13–19). Job argued that natural catastrophes befall both the righteous and the unrighteous alike (9:22–23). In rejecting the direct cause-and-effect relationship between destructive natural events and the people affected by them, Job concurred with nature's Creator. Jesus addressed the same issue with his followers many centuries later. They asked whether suffering a natural disaster or violent act implies that the sufferer is more sinful and deserving of punishment than those who are untouched by it (Luke 13:1–5). Jesus's answer was no.

Everyone who has ever lived has exerted his or her will against God and his rightful authority as Creator. For that reason we all deserve death and even eternal separation from God. However, as Job so eloquently declares (see for example 16:19–21; 17:3; 19:25–29), God has established a way to redeem us from our sin and its consequences, and that way involves the law of decay and death.

The New Testament fills in the details of that plan. As the apostle Paul explains, "[T]he creation was subjected to frustration . . . by the will of the one who subjected it" so that "the creation itself will be liberated from its bondage to decay" (Rom. 8:20–21). Paul goes on to say that the entire creation has been groaning right up to the present time as a consequence of this bondage (8:22). He adds that the law of decay will cease to operate once the full number of people who choose to accept God's redemption has been reached (8:18–24). According to John's Revelation, that's the moment when evil—and even the possibility of evil—will be permanently removed from God's creation (20:11–21:8).

Recent studies reveal that the law of decay, or the second law of thermodynamics, has been optimally fine-tuned by God to restrain humanity's expression of evil and to motivate pursuit of virtue.[3] Once evil is finally conquered and permanently removed, God will have no further need for the law of decay. For now, however, the crucial role of this law in our physical existence as well as in restraining evil and motivating virtue explains why God allows people, both good and bad, to suffer its effects. The Bible shows that on some occasions God shields people from natural disasters to accomplish a redemptive purpose (Acts 27:1–28:10). Even less frequently, God intervenes in the natural order to bring a disaster upon certain individuals, but only when and if the intervention results in an essential restraint of evil.

Often people are tempted to blame Satan for all the hurricanes, tornadoes, volcanoes, earthquakes, fires, floods, and droughts that bring pain and loss to themselves or others. Many even cite the first two chapters of Job as proof of Satan's culpability. However, while Job 1–2 suggests that Satan has the power to bring about such catastrophes, he can only do so by permission from God. God has the final word.

This thought may provide no comfort to someone who has experienced devastation. Nature's disasters are among the things that drive us to question God's goodness. However, God's sovereignty over nature provides no excuse to malign his character or his motives toward us. Along with Job, we must sometimes suffer without knowing a reason why, trusting in God's eventual goodness. As Paul declares, "In all things God works for the good of those who love him, who have been called according to his purpose" (Rom. 8:28).

Looking at natural disasters from a scientific perspective, we can see that any diminishing of such events would demand less efficient operation of the law of decay, and the consequence would be a less effective restraint of evil. It's important for people to understand how the seemingly destructive natural phenomena that befall humanity and the rest of life on Earth actually serve beneficial purposes, even apart from the restraint of evil. Every act of God plays a beneficial role in sustaining Earth's life, and humanity in particular. For example, tectonic activity, which is responsible for earthquakes and volcanoes, ensures that continental landmasses and islands permanently remain upon Earth's surface. It also guarantees adequate recycling of nutrients essential for the long-term sustenance of abundant life both in the oceans and on the continents. Yet the current level of plate tectonic activity is not so high as to make the building and maintenance of cities and transportation arteries infeasible.

Given the Creator's multiple purposes for the universe and the earth, he established physical laws—including laws that govern wildfires, floods, droughts, lightning strikes, hurricanes, tornadoes, and ice ages—and fine-tuned them for the maximum benefit of life in general and of humans in particular.[4]

Why Must We Endure Hurricanes?

In the aftermath of Hurricane Katrina and other massive storms, one wonders why God would subject the planet to such forces. Given the laws of physics the Creator used in shaping the universe,[5] the absence of such storms would mean either less rainfall, less evenly distributed rainfall, lower quality living space on the continents, or more extreme day-to-night temperature differences. The present number and intensity of hurricanes yields the optimal balance between advanced life's well-being and collateral damage.

Hurricanes serve a number of beneficial purposes. They substantially increase chlorophyll concentrations along continental shelves,[6] bringing nourishment to many species located there. Hurricanes' powerful winds lift huge quantities of sea-salt aerosols from the oceans, and these play a critical role in raindrop formation.[7] They also ensure that enough rain falls to support a large, diverse land life population. In addition, these aerosols and the clouds they form efficiently scatter solar radiation, allowing hurricanes to act as a global thermostat.[8] When tropical oceans get too hot, they generate hurricanes. The aerosols and clouds produced by hurricanes serve to cool down the tropical oceans.

Every form of severe weather, not just hurricanes, brings beneficial effects. The book of Job makes frequent references to God's control of lightning (36:30–33; 37:3–5, 11, 15; 38:24–27, 35). Lightning is a major contributor to nitrogen fixation, a crucial nutrient supply for plants. Lightning also generates wildfires, which remove growth inhibitors, infuse soils with water-retaining and mineral-rich charcoal, and facilitate the growth of arbuscular mycorrhizal fungi, a vital nitrogen fixater for vascular plants.[9] The lightning strike rate on Earth is optimal for maintaining a high quality of life. Scientists observe the same level of optimization in every other form of "bad" weather.[10]

An Inquisitive Generation

The ability to read and understand God's other book, the book of nature, has been growing exponentially in recent decades. The knowledge base in some scientific disciplines doubles every decade or less. This knowledge explosion has generated more science-faith and science-Bible questions than ever.

Both believers and nonbelievers are raising questions, as they should. God does not discourage honest questions or the quest for answers. Just like the ancient man named Job and my skeptical friend Al, we can bring our questions to God and seek out answers by studying all of his books. Amazingly, the oldest among all the Bible's sixty-six books provides some of the most up-to-date answers to current, complex questions emerging from nature's book. The next chapter delves into those questions and answers.

4

Answers to New Questions

It seems like everywhere I've spoken since the release of Al Gore's *An Inconvenient Truth* I've been asked to comment on global warming. The debate over whether or to what extent it's really happening has escalated sharply since "Climategate," an information leak revealing a serious breach of scientific integrity. One thing is certain: the debate itself is heating up on a global scale.

Some people ask, "Do you believe global warming is real?" This question indicates confusion over what data or whom to trust. Others ask, "What's causing global warming, and what must we do about it?" This question indicates the rampant confusion over which of the drastic steps proposed by experts (if any) might help stave off their anticipated ecological collapse. Each questioner expects me to take a side, defending one set of data over another, and then to recommend action accordingly.

In this emotionally charged atmosphere, my approach is to take the discussion in an unexpected direction. I point out that the Bible's oldest book offers the best prescription for maintaining global climatic stability. I further surprise people by stating that the recommendations offered in Job require no sacrifice of either ethics or economics. Before going into some of the specific insights Job offers, I like to remind everyone

that Job is a book for all time, including our time. This ancient revelation speaks to the science-faith issues of today and tomorrow as well.
Not that this scientific relevance should come as a total surprise.
Given how pointedly Job addresses the big questions faced by all
generations and cultures, perhaps we could have anticipated it would
also address specific problems and uncertainties challenging humanity's most populous generation—questions about origins, evolution,
physics, and cosmology, as well as global warming. All these topics
receive attention in the final chapters of the book, where God speaks
directly to Job and his friends, including us.

Evolution Question

The book of Job leaves little room for doubt that God frequently,
profoundly, and miraculously intervenes in shaping the universe, the
world, and life for humanity's existence—and in ways we humans
can discern. Its message is echoed repeatedly in the Psalms (see pp.
18, 32). "The heavens proclaim his righteousness, and all peoples see
his glory" (Ps. 97:6). "How many are your works, LORD! In wisdom
you made them all; the earth is full of your creatures" (Ps. 104:24).

God challenges Job and his friends with a long list of rhetorical
questions that opens with the words "Where were you when . . . ?"
(38:4). It goes without saying that long before Job and his friends were
born, God was at work. He "laid the earth's foundation," "made the
clouds its [the primordial ocean's] garment and wrapped it in thick
darkness," and established "doors and bars" (that is, physical boundaries) for Earth's seas (38:4, 9, 10). In a similar vein, God humbles Job
and his friends with withering irony: "Surely you know, for you were
already born! You have lived so many years!" (38:21). In these and many
other declarations recorded in Job, God contradicts the basic tenets
of naturalism and deism, evolutionism and young-earth creationism.

"Bad" Designs in Nature

As life scientists have made discoveries that advance our understanding
of cells and living systems, some have come across what they consider

faulty or useless designs. The inverted retina in the eyes of all birds and mammals is one example. Another is the human appendix. Skeptics frequently point to these examples of so-called bad designs in nature as proof against God's existence.[1] They argue that an all-powerful, all-wise, all-loving Creator would create only perfectly designed, fully functional systems and parts.

Job and his friends certainly embraced the belief that God is omnipotent, omniscient, and constantly loving (5:9–10; 9:4, 10, 19; 10:10–12; 11:7–9; 12:7–10, 13; 21:22; 23:13; 26:14; 28:12–28; 33:12–13; 34:10, 13–15; 36:5, 10, 22–26, 31; 37:4–5, 23). Thus, they concluded that no actual faults would or could be found in anything God has done or made (8:3; 9:19; 10:8; 12:7–10; 21:22; 28:12–28; 33:12–13; 34:10, 12, 19; 36:23–24; 37:23). What God created he matched perfectly to its purpose and context.

Herein lies the difference. Today's skeptics label designs "bad" or "useless" in nature when they may in fact serve a particular but as yet misunderstood or misidentified purpose in the context of God's created order. These people seem hesitant to admit that they may be overlooking or cannot yet recognize the benefit or the functionality of the design they observe.

Job and his friends understood that because of human limitations, no one knows everything there is to know about any creature or phenomenon in the natural realm. This limitation applies as much to the twenty-first century's most brilliant and best-funded research scientists as it did to any of Job's contemporaries. From a biblical perspective, we can expect that even today, many of God's designs in nature remain hidden from our understanding. But they are not permanently hidden. Therefore, the bad—or useless—design argument can be evaluated.

If flawed designs were a pervasive reality, ongoing research into Earth's creatures and the ways they relate to one another would reveal increasing evidence of defectiveness. The number of known imperfections would grow and the degree of faultiness would become increasingly measurable. If, on the other hand, these apparent flaws are merely artifacts of human ignorance and misunderstanding, research should deliver the opposite result. It should reveal the precision and elegance of design.

The record to date favors the latter result. Research advances seem to confirm the belief expressed by Job and his friends. For example, scientists have recently determined that while the inverted retina indeed is far less sensitive to light than its counterpart found in octopi species, this lower light sensitivity is crucial for birds' and mammals' sight retention in an environment with high incident light.[2] Bright sunlight would quickly bring about catastrophic photochemical injury to a retina like that of the octopus. The inverted retina also permits the photoreceptor cells to be densely packed so as to provide high-resolution capability in both low- and high-light environments.[3]

The human appendix represents another example of premature judgment. While research shows it serves no significant purpose in the digestion of food, as originally thought, it turns out the appendix does fulfill an important role in the body's immune system.[4]

These two reversals of opinion belong to a much longer list, one that continues to grow. On that basis, skeptics who insist nature is rife with bad or useless designs would do well to heed Job's words: "Surely I spoke of things I did not understand, things too wonderful for me to know" (42:3).

Big Bang Universe

Job is the earliest Old Testament writer to describe the continuous, ongoing expansion of the universe (9:8). Other Old Testament authors also made statements about cosmic expansion (Ps. 104:2; Isa. 40:22; 42:5; 44:24; 45:12; 48:13; 51:13; Jer. 10:12; 51:15; Zech. 12:1). Amazingly, not until the twentieth century did any scientist even hint at the possibility of an expanding universe.

Job's description of continuous cosmic expansion ranks as one of the most far-reaching and dramatic biblical forecasts of later scientific discovery. Job accurately—and uniquely—predicted a monumental scientific breakthrough some four thousand years in advance!

To quote Job's words, "He [God] alone stretches out the heavens" (9:8). The Hebrew verb *natah*, translated as "stretches out," implies an ongoing, continual expansion. In stating that God alone expands the universe, Job implies there is something supernatural about this cosmic stretching.

Recently, astronomers found what may be considered "supernatural" in the expansion's finely tuned rate. First, they determined that if the universe had expanded only slightly more rapidly throughout cosmic history, the stars and planets necessary for possible formation and support of life would never have formed. In such a scenario, gravity would not be strong enough to concentrate gas and dust sufficiently to make these astronomical objects. On the other hand, if the universe had expanded slightly more slowly, the only bodies that would ever have formed would be black holes and neutron stars. In either case, physical life would be impossible at any time and at any location in the universe. For life to be possible, the universe must continuously expand at the precise rates throughout its entire history. In fact, the physical factors that play the most crucial roles in governing cosmic expansion manifest levels of fine-tuning that rank as the most spectacular evidence for supernatural design measured to date (see pp. 60–63).

Job's friend Bildad described another cosmic feature. In his words, "Dominion and awe belong to God; he establishes order in the heights of heaven" (25:2). Here Bildad broke away from ancient Near-Eastern religious mythology, which deified the sun, moon, and stars because of their power over earthly life. Instead, he spoke of the one God who rules over the heavens and is responsible for the order observable there. Bildad's view of the awesomeness and orderliness of the universe has been abundantly affirmed by scientific advances.

Job and his friends had no way to know or even estimate how large or distant the stars must be. Their eyes could detect only about seven thousand stars. Thanks to the Hubble Space Telescope, astronomers recognize that about fifty billion trillion stars exist within the total extent of the theoretically observable universe.[5] These fifty billion trillion stars make up only 1 percent of the universe's total mass, which in turn comprises just one-quarter of all the universe's stuff. The universe indeed appears awesome in its vastness.

The universe's orderly, reliable nature is a theme from Job repeated by other Bible authors. Jeremiah, for example, declares that the laws governing the heavens and Earth are fixed (33:25). That is, we can count on the laws of physics to be constant. Thus, two of the most prominent features of what the world now calls the big bang, or what I refer to as a biblical creation model, were first described in Job. Other Bible books identify additional major components of big bang cosmology (Gen. 1:1; 2:3–4; Ps. 148:5; Isa. 40:26; 45:18; Jer. 33:25; John 1:3; Rom. 8:18–22; Col. 1:15–17; Heb. 11:3).

Who, then, deserves credit for coming up with the big bang model for the universe? Albert Einstein? Georges Henri Lemaître? Edwin Hubble? In the scientific age, each of these individuals played an important part. However, Job, Moses, the psalmists, Isaiah, Jeremiah, Paul, and the author of Hebrews described it first, *many* centuries earlier.[6]

Quest for the "Theory of Everything"

Einstein spent his last decades pursuing what's called a "unified field theory" of physics. He was convinced, as were nearly all physicists of his time, that the elegance and beauty they saw throughout the world of physics meant that a single overarching theory would someday explain the operation of all four fundamental forces (gravity, electromagnetism, and the strong and weak nuclear forces). Just as Scottish physicist James Clerk Maxwell showed that magnetism and electrostatics emerged from a single force, Einstein hoped to develop a theory explaining how all the fundamental forces of physics were once unified.

Einstein and his peers lacked the instruments to test and refine an array of hypotheses. With the advent of powerful particle accelerators in the 1970s, physicists began to establish in exhaustive detail exactly how the electromagnetic force unified with the weak nuclear force and to identify several pathways toward the unification of the electroweak force with the strong nuclear force. These achievements persuaded physicists all the more that a unified field theory must exist to explain the operation of everything in physics. Their ongoing successes gave birth to a new term—the "theory of everything," or TOE.

Many physicists have become so enamored with TOE as to assert that it will explain not just all physics but literally everything. They say it will reveal all knowledge. In his all-time bestselling science book, Stephen Hawking wrote,

A complete, consistent, unified theory is only the first step: our goal is a complete *understanding* of the events around us, and of our own existence. . . . It would be the ultimate triumph of human reason—for then we would know the mind of God.[7]

Job and his friends recognized that humans are endowed with unique intellectual capacity (38:36). They observed that in powers of the mind humans rank far above all other earthly creatures (35:11). Unlike many scholars today, however, they acknowledged the existence of fundamental limitations on human intellectual capabilities.

Zophar pointed out that there are certain mysteries of God that humans can never fully fathom. Likewise, he observed there are hard limits to what humans can do and know. God, on the other hand, is unconstrained by such limits (11:7–8). Job acknowledged God's power as beyond anything a human can possibly muster, far beyond what a human can even measure or comprehend (9:1–14). Elihu also described God as "exalted in power" (37:23).

As for wisdom, Job said, "God understands the way to it and he alone knows where it dwells, for he views the ends of the earth and sees everything under the heavens" (28:23–24). Elihu exclaimed, "How great is God—beyond our understanding! . . . he does great things beyond our understanding" (36:26; 37:5).

Finally, the Lord himself spoke to Job and his friends (38:1). He began with this question: "Do you know the laws of the heavens?" (38:33). This question remains a challenge for our time. After millenia of advances in knowledge and technology, the world's most brilliant scientists have acquired only partial knowledge of the laws of the heavens. The presumption that we humans can attain *all* knowledge, a TOE, or an understanding of God's mind, seems absurdly arrogant (more on this topic to follow).

God asks, "Who has put wisdom in the innermost being or given understanding to the mind?" (38:36 NASB). With this question he reminds Job and his associates that their wisdom and understanding did not originate within themselves. It was a gift granted to them. A gift is always less than the gift giver.

Throughout Scripture, God claims sovereignty—complete knowledge and influence—over every thought, word, and action of every human life.[8] Such knowledge and power God shares with no one else. What's more, God exercises this control without diminishing free will.

We humans find it difficult enough to know our own minds and to exercise a modicum of control over our own thoughts, much less to know or control those of others. The briefest foray into neuroscience research is enough to reveal the complexity of the brain, its physics and chemistry among other features. How much more complex the operation of the human mind!

Ironically, the very theorems developed and tested by physicists and mathematicians, including Hawking himself, establish hard limits on the extent of human knowledge. The space-time theorems and incompleteness theorems, which are common knowledge among physicists who claim that a TOE and the "mind of God" are within reach, rule out the possibility that either can ever be attained.[9]

Only a few decades after astronomers and physicists discovered that matter and energy originated in the finite past, Hawking and Roger Penrose proved that space and time had a beginning.[10] These findings imply that humanity's capacity for making detections and measurements must always be limited to what exists within the cosmic space-time dimensions. When applied to the universe, the incompleteness theorem demands this conclusion: no one can know, based only on information accessible within the universe, that the universe can only be what it is. In other words, only a Being who can exist and make measurements both within *and beyond* the universe's space-time dimensions possesses the potential to arrive at a TOE. Job and his friends apparently recognized the absurdity of the notion that any creature could ever be equal to or greater than the transcendent Creator.

Mystery of Cosmic Darkness

Another question God put to Job and his friends points to a mystery that researchers have only begun to unravel. It's a question about darkness:

> What is the way to the abode of light? And where does darkness reside? Can you take them to their places? Do you know the paths to their dwellings? (38:19–20)

What a strange question! God treats darkness as if it is something that resides somewhere in the universe. This treatment, whether or not it represents poetic license, clearly contradicts the common, centuries-old definition of darkness.

As recently as the late twentieth century, dictionaries and science textbooks defined *darkness* as "the absence of light," not as an actual substance with a specific physical location. Within the last few years, however, researchers discovered that God's question in Job 38 reveals an astonishing truth about the nature of darkness. Astronomers now recognize what they see through their telescopes as comprising only 0.27 percent of all the contents of the universe. Darkness comprises the other 99.73 percent. It seems likely, then, that God's question about darkness springs from the fact that dark stuff represents the dominant physical component of the cosmos.

The latest research tells us that the dark stuff gives impressive testimony to God's handiwork in designing the universe for the benefit of all life. The quantities and locations of the different kinds of dark stuff provide spectacular evidence for supernatural design. To ensure the universe expands at precisely the right rates throughout its history so that the right kinds of stars and planets form at the right time and location so that advanced life can exist, the densities of all three types of cosmic darkness must be exquisitely fine-tuned (see sidebar on p. 62). One of these three types, dark energy, must be fine-tuned to within one part in 10^{122}. That ratio is so extreme it's difficult even for astronomers to visualize—vastly greater than the difference between the mass of a single electron and the mass of the entire universe.[11]

Such an intricate level of fine-tuning logically justifies the conclusion that a supernatural Creator skillfully and intentionally fixed the cosmic dark energy density. Human experience attests that intellect, knowledge, creativity, and power are required to achieve a high level of fine-tuning in any design project. These are the characteristics of a personal being. So it makes sense to think of the Creator as a personal being.

Once they confirmed the existence and abundance of these kinds of dark stuff, astronomers went on to discover how carefully these kinds are positioned in space for the benefit of life in general and humans in particular. Advanced life is possible only in a specifically sized,

Different Kinds of Dark Stuff

The Swiss-American astronomer Fritz Zwicky was the first scientist to recognize that dark (nonradiant) "something" must comprise a substantial portion of the universe's makeup. As far back as the 1930s, his study of the dynamics of nearby galaxies and galaxy clusters indicated their stability depends heavily on the abundance of some kind of matter characterized by mass but not by noticeable radiance.

In the 1990s, detailed maps of the radiation left over from the big bang (the cosmic microwave background radiation) together with a fairly accurate measurement of the cosmic expansion rate revealed that only about a sixth of the universe's dark matter is what would be called "ordinary" matter—matter comprised of such ordinary particles as protons, neutrons, and electrons. These ordinary particles can and do interact with light (photons). When highly concentrated in stars and nebulae, this ordinary matter begins to radiate and is no longer dark, but most (90 percent) either stays dark or returns to being dark. Ordinary matter makes up 17.5 percent of the universe's total matter.

Exotic dark matter accounts for the remaining 82.5 percent of the universe's matter and 23.3 percent of the universe's total "content," most of which is *not* matter at all. This exotic matter interacts only weakly, at best, with photons. It is made up of particles such as neutrinos and what physicists tentatively refer to as axions and neutralinos. Regardless of the form it takes, exotic matter is always dark.

The universe's main component is something called dark energy, or space energy density. Some 72.1 percent of the physical universe is this "something," which is even harder to describe than it is to name. It can best be portrayed as the self-stretching property (like an anti-elastic band) of the space surface of the universe, and its abundance controls the rate at which the universe expands.

sufficiently stable spiral galaxy. The spiral arms must be neither too large nor too small, and they must be separated by a certain distance. Further, the spiral arms must retain a high degree of symmetry for many billions of years. All of these particulars depend on the precise location of both ordinary dark matter and exotic dark matter in relation to the galaxy.

Life can exist in our Milky Way only because our galaxy resides within a giant halo of ordinary dark matter, the diameter of which is nearly ten times larger than the visible galaxy. Beyond this ordinary dark matter halo sits an even larger halo of exotic dark matter. Again, this halo must have a specific mass and diameter.

Scientific confirmation that darkness is a physical entity with specific physical locations represents not only a dramatic research breakthrough but also one of the most powerful evidences in favor of biblical accuracy. Job's book foreshadowed a set of profound scientific discoveries thousands of years in advance. This predictive success gives a hint of the significance of God's questions as recorded in Job 38–39. Can it be that these questions provide guidance for researchers today? That's a possibility I hope to affirm in the pages of this book.

Global Warming Guidelines

Despite highly publicized exaggerations and distortions,[12] an increase in the average global temperature has been confirmed by multiple measurements around the world.[13] The data exist in the public record for all to see. Photographs show measurable shrinkage of the polar ice cap. The northwest passage through the Canadian arctic archipelago, for centuries a barrier to shipping, now stands open.

The fact that human activity contributes to the observed global warming cannot be denied.[14] The rise in fossil fuel consumption and various agricultural practices have increased carbon dioxide abundance in the atmosphere at least to some degree. While detailed atmospheric models demonstrate that the greenhouse effect of this extra carbon dioxide accounts for much of the observed rise in global temperatures,[15] researchers cannot say exactly how much can be attributed to human activity. Natural temperature cycles may equal or even exceed the human factor.

While pundits point to global warming as the greatest evil mankind has ever inflicted on the natural environment, some atmospheric physicists say global warming may not be such a bad thing. Over the past few million years, Earth has endured multiple 100,000-year temperature cycles correlated with characteristic variations in Earth's orbit about the sun. In each cycle, a 90,000-year-long ice age follows a 10,000-year-long warm interglacial period.[16] The most recent of these interglacial periods began 15,000 years ago. Our warming activities seem to have extended its duration.

Agricultural practices inaugurated about 8,000 years ago have contributed most significantly to the temperature increase.[17] The primary credit goes to the domestication of cows and the flooding of rice fields, which together have nearly doubled the methane (a much more potent greenhouse gas than carbon dioxide) quantity in Earth's atmosphere. Most scientists concur, however, that human contributions to the greenhouse effect have more than compensated for the natural progression toward an ice age. As a result, humanity faces a number of climate crises. Researchers and others agree something must be done—and soon. If they would look to the book of Job, they would find guidance toward solutions far superior to the Nobel Prize–winning proposals by former US vice president Al Gore.

Much of Job 38 focuses on precipitation—mist, rain, hail, and snow. In these passages we read that God exquisitely designed precipitation levels to provide an optimal environment for Earth's life. The implication seems clear: we should address climate crises by first correcting whatever damage we have caused to Earth's precipitation patterns. The most alarming examples of human disturbance of regional and global rainfall patterns is the expansion of the Sahara and Gobi deserts. Over the past two thousand years the Sahara has grown ten times larger.[18] The Gobi is three times larger.[19] These deserts, among others, have been enlarged as people have grazed their herds at the desert boundaries and then stripped remaining vegetation for cooking fuel.

One helpful response to global warming would be to assist people living on the fringes of the Sahara, Gobi, and other expanding deserts in replanting these areas. Even if it means providing them with free fossil fuels, the trade-off would be worthwhile. The Israelis have demonstrated that this approach works. Independent scientific studies confirm that if the replanting is done in a prescribed manner, vegetation will flourish again where it long ago thrived.[20] The presence of this new vegetation, in turn, significantly augments the quantity of precipitation and cooling.

Ten percent of all the water in Earth's atmosphere comes as a result of flowering plants' transpiration (drawing up water from the soil through their roots and releasing much of that water via evaporation into the atmosphere).[21] Nonflowering plants also contribute water to the atmosphere. In many parts of the world, such as the eastern portion of North America, the presence of flowering plants approximately doubles the amount of precipitation.[22] If the Sahara and Gobi deserts were replanted, these regions could become, as they were two thousand years ago, the breadbaskets for Europe and China. At the same time, the abundance of vegetation would soak up significant quantities of greenhouse gases, thereby helping to moderate the planet's atmospheric temperature.

Job 39 brings to mind another way to manage the human contribution to global warming. This passage includes a list of bird and mammal species that seems random at first glance and yet, on closer examination, clearly proves otherwise. Each of the creatures listed once played a unique and significant role in the launch of civilization (see chapter 10). The ostrich, for one, can help us again. Meat from ostriches is a healthy red meat, potentially cheaper to produce than the meat from cattle. Ostrich meat is low in saturated fat and cholesterol and is the recommended meat for people suffering from diabetes. With a sufficiently large population of domesticated ostriches, ostrich meat could well be the cheapest and best of all meats to produce because ostriches need much less land than cattle. Per pound of meat produced, ostriches emit only a small fraction of the methane and carbon dioxide generated by cows.

Few people seem to know that domesticated cows deliver more greenhouse gases to the atmosphere than do all the world's vehicles—autos, trucks, trains, aircraft, ships—combined. Deforestation to create pasturelands for cows and other prodigious greenhouse-gas producers, including sheep and goats, also contributes more to global warming than do all the world's vehicles.[23] Domestication of ostriches could deliver a triple benefit. By replacing large numbers of greenhouse-gas emitters and allowing much of the world's pastureland to be reforested, ostriches would offer a crucial health benefit, a much-needed economic boost, and a large part of the cure for global warming.

Another creature with large potential to help with global warming is the whale. In his discourses Job mentions whales twice (7:12; 12:8–10). In both instances Job suggests that no matter how big or how small the creature, God created each life-form with specific characteristics for specific reasons. The most extensive of the creation psalms, Psalm 104, echoes this message:

> How many are your works, Lord! In wisdom you made them all; the earth is full of your creatures. There is the sea, vast and spacious, teeming with creatures beyond number—living things both large and small. There the ships go to and fro, and the Leviathan, which you formed to frolic there. All creatures look to you to give them their food at the proper time. (vv. 24–27).

Of all animals existing from ancient times till now, whales are the largest. Blue whales can attain 110 feet (34 m) in length and weigh as much as 400,000 pounds (182 tonnes). By comparison, the largest dinosaur to roam the earth weighed an estimated 200,000 pounds (91 tonnes). Whales are not only enormous but also warm-blooded. Consequently, they expel huge quantities of carbon dioxide and water vapor into the atmosphere in their normal respiration. For this reason many global warming activists once touted the near extinction of whales during the great hunts of the eighteenth, nineteenth, and early twentieth centuries as a good thing. New research shows us how much more we need to learn about nature's wonders.

A team of eight biologists and oceanographers—seven from Australia and one from Germany—led by Flinders University biologist Trish Lavery, discovered that sperm whales actually remove greater quantities of greenhouse gas from the atmosphere than they add.[24] The whale accomplishes this feat by its eating and elimination habits.

Sperm whales are Earth's largest predators at 67 feet (20.5 m) and 126,000 pounds (57 tonnes), and sporting an enormous jawbone holding fifty-plus teeth, each tooth weighing 2.2 pounds (1 kg). They prey upon giant squid and colossal squid, creatures that attain fifty feet in length and inhabit the dark depths of the world's oceans. Sperm whales, these monstrous squids' only predators, have been known to dive as deep as 9,800 feet (3 km) in search of a meal.

Uniquely designed for deep dives, the sperm whale's flexible ribcage permits lung collapse, which reduces nitrogen intake, minimizing the effects of the bends. Their blood can store a huge quantity of oxygen owing to an extremely high red blood cell count, and their metabolism can drastically decrease to conserve oxygen. Scientists believe the spermaceti organ, located in the forehead, serves to regulate buoyancy during dives.

While sperm whales do eat some fish, the iron-rich giant squid and colossal squid make up the bulk of their diet. When feeding, whales undertake dives of thirty to ninety minutes interspersed with rest periods of about eight minutes near the surface, during which they defecate. According to Lavery's team, as much as 85 to 90 percent of the iron a sperm whale ingests is expelled in the form of ferrous salts. Since most of this eliminated matter is liquid, nearly all of the iron is delivered with great efficiency to the ocean's photic zone, where phytoplankton live.

Phytoplankton forms the base of the food chain for all oceanic life. So the more phytoplankton, the greater the total biomass the oceans can support. Phytoplankton account for more of the oxygen pumped into the atmosphere and more of the carbon dioxide removed from the atmosphere than all other life-forms combined. The major limit on the growth of phytoplankton, particularly in the southern oceans, is the availability (or unavailability) of soluble iron.

The 12,000 sperm whales that populate the Southern Ocean surrounding Antarctica deliver 55 tons (50 tonnes) of iron per year to the phytoplankton dwelling there. The phytoplankton exploit that iron, ultimately removing 440,000 tons (400,000 tonnes) of carbon from the atmosphere. Given that these 12,000 whales add only 176,000 tons (160,000 tonnes) of carbon to the atmosphere through their breathing, the sperm whale population in the Southern Ocean removes a net 264,000 tons (240,000 tonnes) of carbon from the atmosphere every year. In other words, even the drastically reduced population of sperm whales remaining in the world's oceans today is playing a huge role in helping to manage global warming.

Paradoxically, sperm whales also stimulate the growth of giant and colossal squid populations. Nature's cycle works this way: as the whale-nourished phytoplankton die, they sink to the ocean depths where their carcasses become food for the deep ocean animals that are the food source for squids. So, while sperm whales prey upon giant and colossal squids, they contribute—via phytoplankton—to an increase in the squid population as well as the population of all the fish species phytoplankton support in the deep oceans. (The same kind of positive-feedback relationship occurs between baleen whales and krill and all the sea life krill support.)

As we turn back the clock, we see the reverse side of this picture. The depletion of the sperm whale population brought about by industrial whaling drastically reduced the phytoplankton biomass, surface and deep sea fish populations, and giant and colossal squid populations. Furthermore, according to the Lavery team's calculations, the decrease in sperm whale population led to the retention of an extra 2.2 million tons (2 million tonnes) of carbon in the atmosphere annually.[25]

The study closes with an appeal to all nations to work together to restore the global whale populations to their pre–Industrial Revolution robustness. Not only would this restoration help alleviate global warming, it would allow all manner of marine life to regain healthy population levels, which in turn would support a sustainable fishing industry far beyond what is possible today. In dramatic fashion, these scientists have shown the world that sperm whales are not to be taken for granted. They are a unique species, designed to serve and preserve the planet's life, including human life.

The book of Job highlights the theme that God has marvelously designed the universe, the earth, and all its life in such a way as to harmonize ethics and economics. When we humans face a crisis or dilemma that appears to force a choice between ethics and economics, we can be sure God has provided a solution that compromises neither. Through the book of Job, God calls humanity to resist the temptation of quick fixes, particularly those that demand either a breach of ethics or a loss of economic stability. This exhortation applies at all levels—global, national, regional, municipal, and familial.

Predictive Success

One basis for concluding that the book of Job must be supernaturally inspired is the relevance of its content to the questions, challenges, and controversies of later generations, including our own. Another mark of divine inspiration is the book's successful anticipation, or prediction, of some of humanity's most important scientific discoveries, including those of my own lifetime. The ancient words address some of the twenty-first century's biggest questions about the nature of the universe and the survival of civilization.

Job's demonstrated predictive success also applies to controversies concerning the Bible's first eleven chapters. It provides help in responding to atheists' and agnostics' attacks on the Bible, especially to their ridicule of its opening pages. It provides help in responding to fellow believers' attacks on one another regarding their interpretation of Genesis 1–11. In anticipation of these controversies, the book of Job provides an extensive and essential resource. The next two chapters show the way.

5

Answers to Creation-Day Controversies

Nearly three thousand people crowded into Gregory Gymnasium at the University of Texas–Austin for a Skeptics Forum on Creation and Evolution. Specifically, they came to hear my colleague, biochemist Fuz Rana, and me defend our (still-developing) biblical creation model. According to the plan, Fuz and I would take twenty-five minutes each to review our model's highlights and show the various ways our model has been, and can be, scientifically tested. Then a featured guest, Michael Shermer, would offer thirty minutes of critique, and after a brief response from each of us, a panel of UT faculty would ask us questions. At Fuz's and my request, the plan also included time for questions from the audience.

As so often happens with good plans, this one unraveled, and Fuz and I feel as if the audience received less than they came for. The scientific critique that was to come from the guest and the panelists never materialized. Shermer, executive director of the Skeptics Society and a columnist for *Scientific American*, totally ignored our presentation. Rather than respond to any of our points, which he had been given in advance, he devoted over thirty minutes to a combination of promoting his society's journal, describing his theory of how religion evolved, and mocking the "obvious errors" in Genesis 1—that is, in his particular interpretation of the passage. Ironically, and disingenuously, he claimed the only reason intelligent, well-educated persons would say the Bible is true would be to defend the religion of their childhood. Alas, Fuz and I were left with no time to respond to Shermer's *mis*interpretation of Genesis 1 or to point out what he already knew—that neither of us grew up in a Christian home. After we briefly interacted with panel members and fielded a few questions (more were comments) from the floor, the forum ended.

Many people pressed forward to talk with Fuz and me. What surprised us most about our interactions with them was how few had actually read Genesis 1 for themselves. Without that background, they had no basis for evaluating either Shermer's or our interpretation of the text. It seemed none had even considered that other parts of the Bible could shed light on the meaning of the Bible's first page.

More to the Creation Story

The Bible includes more than two dozen in-depth accounts of creation (see Appendix). Only one, Genesis 1, offers a numerically sequenced chronology of creation miracle highlights. The other biblical creation accounts describe certain aspects of God's creative activity but without direct reference to order or chronology.

Job 38–39 tells the creation story in its own dramatic way, describing what occurred during the various stages of God's creative work but without numbering events or arranging them in chronological order. Job provides another perspective, most likely the first perspective given Job's ancient date. It conveys details not included in Genesis 1, and although it leaves out other details, it helps fill most of the gaps in the Genesis story that frequently draw ridicule from skeptics, such as the timing of Earth's formation and that of other bodies. Where Genesis 1 is implicit in explaining a particular creation event, such as the origin of the sun, moon, and stars, Job 38 is especially explicit. Thus Job provides an interpretive guide. It answers many of the challenges raised by today's skeptics.

Universe and Earth at the Same Time?

To quote Michael Shermer, the Bible "gets it wrong from the very first verse." He continued, "The heavens and the earth were *not* created at the same time, as the Bible says." Then he read the verse, "In the beginning God created the heavens and the earth," confident he had established his point. Aware of the several-billion-year gap between the universe's origin and the origin of the earth, many skeptics in the audience began to elbow each other and nod.

I read Genesis 1 for the first time when I was seventeen, in the midst of a personal study of the holy books undergirding the world's major religions. While I began with some degree of certainty that God exists—because of the way the universe began and was structured—I assumed all the holy books would prove to be humanly crafted frauds. My aim was to confirm this belief by identifying provable errors and contradictions within those books. The task seemed relatively easy—until I came up against the Bible.

I noted many places in the sixty-six books where a *possible* error or contradiction could be inferred, but after a two-year study I could find no *provably* false statement, except in the mouths of God's enemies. As I read the Bible's opening verse, nothing indicated to me that the cosmos and Earth originated simultaneously. I saw only that God made them at some time in the past called "the beginning." I was impressed that the author acknowledged a beginning, since for centuries philosophers and others described the universe as infinitely old.

Continuing to read through the Bible, I saw the phrase "the heavens and the earth" repeated eight more times in the Old Testament. The phrase "heaven and earth" appeared nineteen times. Neither of these phrases shows up in Job's creation narrative, which includes many separate references to Earth, heaven, and the heavens. In those passages where "the heavens and the earth" expression appeared, I observed a contextual similarity. Each seemed to indicate the entirety of physical creation. In passages referring to "heaven [singular] and earth," the author seemed to imply the totality of both the physical (or earthly), and spiritual (or heavenly) realms.

After a while it dawned on me to inquire about differences between the language of the original manuscripts and the English language

Bible I was reading. I began to wonder if "the heavens and the earth" might be the only expression in ancient Hebrew for the entire physical universe, the whole realm we refer to as nature. What I discovered helped significantly. The number of words in the ancient Hebrew lexicon amounts to a small fraction (less than a hundredth) of the number of English words. Nouns are particularly in short supply; verbs a bit less so.

Twenty-seven years later, during a week at Trinity Evangelical Divinity School, I had the privilege of interacting with some of the world's most distinguished Hebrew and Old Testament scholars. During that week, Bruce Waltke delivered four lectures on the meaning of the Bible's first three sentences. As a fellow guest lecturer, I had the privilege of spending time each day with Waltke and two of his colleagues, Kenneth Kantzer and famed linguist Gleason Archer. Over lunch we engaged in some intense discussions of the words of Genesis 1.

What I had pieced together years ago from textbooks, they confirmed for me face-to-face. Indeed, biblical Hebrew has no one noun for "cosmos" or "universe." The Hebrew word for the earth, *'erets*, has four different literal definitions, and the Hebrew word for heaven or heavens, *shamayim*, has three different literal definitions. Waltke explained that biblical Hebrew compensates for its sparseness of nouns by the use of compound nouns and noun phrases. The Hebrew phrase *hashamayim veha'arets* (used in Genesis 1), Waltke pointed out, takes on a definition distinct from either *shamayim* or *'erets* used individually.

Waltke made a case for assigning an even broader definition to *hashamayim veha'arets*. More than simply a reference to the universe, which the ancient Hebrews had no way to conceive of, the phrase refers to the totality of all things physical. It refers not only to all the universe's matter and energy but also to its space-time dimensionality. The universe's creation entails the beginning of everything, even space and time.

Waltke's insight provides a potent response to Shermer's mockery. Rather than implying that galaxies, stars, and the earth were all made simultaneously, Genesis 1:1 explicitly declares the universe as a whole has a starting point. Matter, energy, space, and time, according to Genesis 1:1, are not eternal. They were brought into existence by a Being who exists and operates beyond the limits of matter, energy, space, and time.

Why the Big Time Gap?

In my encounters with atheists, agnostics, and deists I've often heard Genesis 1 derided for its failure to address what God was doing between his creation of the universe and his formation of Earth. After all, two-thirds of the universe's history takes place between the universe's beginning and the earth's formation. If the Bible is God's Word, why would it ignore such a huge chunk of creation chronology? One skeptic asked me, "Was God so bored with his creation that he decided to take a really long nap?"

I like to point out that Moses made no mention of God's activity during that era because Job had already done so. The most explicit passage in Job describing God's activity between creating the universe and forming the earth says, "He alone stretches out the heavens" (9:8). This passage, along with others, indicates that the universe has undergone continual expansion, from the past through the present and continuing on into the future. The emphasis on God's singular role in the expansion implies that the universe cannot expand itself in the manner required to fulfill God's purposes for it. God must guide and control the cosmic expansion so that it gains the capacity to support life, human life, and civilization.

Astronomers today acknowledge the extreme degree of design and fine-tuning necessary for these ends to be accomplished (see pp. 61–63). Instead of napping, God was carefully, exquisitely, and patiently "engineering" the universe. Through this manufacturing he could form the solar system and Earth at just the right time with all the resources to sustain and benefit human existence and civilization for an appropriate epoch he has determined. Meanwhile, the angelic host looks on and learns (Job 38:4–7).

Why Take So Long?

An answer to what God was doing between creating the universe and forming Earth usually leads to a follow-up question: Why did God take so long to bring Earth upon the cosmic scene? Job and his friends acknowledged that God had other options. They regarded his power as limitless. Job said of God, "I know that you can do all things; no purpose of yours can be thwarted" (42:2). Eliphaz, and later Job, declared, "He [God] performs wonders that cannot be fathomed, miracles that cannot be counted" (5:9; 9:10). With alternate physics and dimensionality, God easily could have sped up the process of forming the earth.

God's goals in creating the universe, however, included much more than simply fashioning Earth as a fit habitat for humans. The debate between Job and his friends focused primarily on a deeper, more significant divine purpose—one that involves the experience of evil and suffering. Though these men disagreed sharply on how God is working to conquer evil, removing sin and its effects from his creation while preserving human life, they all acknowledged that God will certainly accomplish this victory.

Despite life's difficulties and Job's horrific sufferings, Job and his friends remained firm in their persuasion that God is good and loving. Thanks to twenty-first-century physics, it has become possible to comprehend that God optimally designed the laws of physics and space-time dimensions in such a way as to quickly and efficiently remove evil, once it appears, from his creation without negating the free will of his creatures.[1] Those laws and dimensions help explain why God took so much time between creating the cosmos and laying down Earth's foundations.

Brass Dome Connection

Shermer's talk that night in Texas included the familiar assertion that creation day two in the Genesis story simply parrots the brass canopy cosmology of the ancient Near East. According to this cosmological perspective, the earth is a flat disk supported on pillars above a primeval ocean (see fig. 5.1). Just below the disk and in between the pillars is the underworld, the realm of the dead. Above the disk is a hemispheric brass vault, which the ancients considered the firmament. The sun, moon, planets, and stars reside on the vault's interior surface, and a vast body of water covers its exterior surface. Small holes in the vault permit rain to fall on the earth.

Taking a page from higher criticism theology, Shermer cited Job 37:18 to "prove" his point. The verse says, "Can you join him [God] in

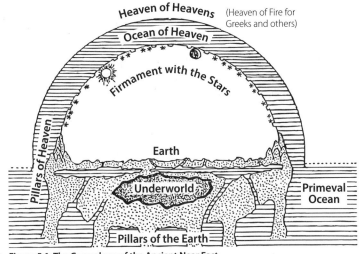

Figure 5.1: The Cosmology of the Ancient Near East
This drawing illustrates the cosmological perspective shared by many ancient civilizations surrounding the emerging Hebrew nation. It depicts the heavens, or firmament, as a hemispheric brass vault to which the sun, moon, stars, and planets are attached.

spreading out the skies, hard as a mirror of cast bronze?" A superficial reading does at least raise the question of a connection with primitive cosmology. However, the word "as" indicates the use of figurative language here. So the careful interpreter must ask, In what way would the skies seem to fit the description "hard as a mirror of cast bronze" *if* this passage does *not* simply echo the vault myth?

An answer emerges from within the passage, just a few sentences later: "Now no one can look at the sun, bright as it is in the skies after the wind has swept them clean" (37:21). In ancient times, glass mirrors did not exist. The best reflective surface humans could produce was a mirror of polished cast bronze. The simile compares the brightness of the sky on a wind-swept day to the painfully bright reflection of light from a cast bronze mirror.

Job 38 provides even more amplification of events associated with the second creation day. In fact, this chapter of Job provides more information about events of that one day than about any other. It elaborates on the various kinds of precipitation—rain, dew, frost, hail, and snow—God established as part of Earth's climatic cycles. The Genesis 1 depiction of God's establishment of an abundant, stable water cycle receives ample attention and clarification in Job 38. This delicately balanced cycle would be essential for supporting life on the emerging continental landmasses when it took hold there later.

Plants Came When?

God's plan for Earth's water cycle included its capacity to support a profusion of land plants that would provide food for land-dwelling animals. Together with land plants these animals would nourish nations of humans and support their civilizations around the world.

Elihu alludes to this plan when he says of God, "He draws up the drops of water, which distill as rain to the streams; the clouds pour down their moisture. . . . This is the way he governs the nations and provides food in abundance" (36:27–28, 31). Following Elihu's discourse, God offers further insight, again in the form of a rhetorical question: "Who cuts a channel for the torrents of rain, and a path for the thunderstorm, to water a land where no one lives, an uninhabited desert, to satisfy a desolate wasteland and make it sprout with grass?" (38:25–27). These words imply that continents were once a desolate wasteland unable to support life. Precipitation falling on the land allowed "grass" to spring up. This plant life made possible land animals, which in turn made possible humans and their civilizations.

As with all physical life, the pattern of its creation on the continental landmasses, as evident throughout Genesis 1, was a progression from simple to more complex. Thus, the first land plants would not have been the deciduous fruit trees that many skeptics read into the events of creation day three, particularly as described in the King James translation.

The words "grass," "seed," "trees," and "fruit," often found in English versions of Genesis 1:11–12 (and Job 38:27) denote specific meaning in English that cannot be attributed to biblical Hebrew. Genesis 1:11 opens with a summary statement of God's creative proclamation, "Let the land produce vegetation." The Hebrew word translated "vegetation" is the same word (deshe') translated "grass" in Job 38:27. It means vegetation or green plant life.[2] It is a word that would apply to any photosynthetic land life.

Three Hebrew nouns are used in Genesis 1:11 as examples of various kinds of vegetation: *zera'*, "seed, that which is scattered, whether of plants, trees, or grain"[3]; *'ets*, plant material that is "hard, firm, . . . for fuel, . . . used of materials for building"[4]; and *peri*, "fruit, whether of the earth and field . . . or of a tree . . . offspring."[5] *Zera'* and *peri* could refer to any plant species that has ever existed, while *'ets* would include all large plants containing cellulose and perhaps all larger-than-microscopic plants whose fibers provide a measure of stiffness. These terms would be appropriate to signify virtually any of Earth's primitive plants.

Only recently has science uncovered any direct evidence of widespread terrestrial vegetation previous to the Cambrian explosion (543 million years ago), when the swarms of small sea animals mentioned at the beginning of creation day five first appeared (Gen. 1:20). Geologists Paul Knauth and Martin Kennedy published that evidence in a report in *Nature*. The report describes their discovery of extensive photosynthetic life on the continents well before the Cambrian event.[6] From their data Knauth and Kennedy concluded that Earth must have seen an explosive appearance of abundant photosynthetic communities on the continents approximately 850 million years ago. They also determined that terrestrial plant life remained as abundant during the 200 million years prior to the Cambrian explosion as it did afterwards. Their work confirms the biblical record and answers another skeptical challenge.

Why Both Rain and Snow?

The poetic elegance of Job 38 in its depiction of precipitation in both its forms—liquid (dew, mist, and rain) and solid (frost, snow, and hail)—has been observed and appreciated for centuries. However, current research reveals the passage offers more, including more evidence of the book's predictive, or anticipatory, value.

Life scientists today recognize that snow, frost, and hail can provide plants and animals with continuous, reliable water sources in regions that do not receive steady, heavy precipitation, especially if their melting is delayed or slowed. We've also come to recognize that a much greater diversity of plant species is possible when moisture is delivered in a broad range of raindrop sizes.

Planetary scientists have discovered that though water is abundant in the universe, the prospect of finding a planet other than Earth with surface water in the precise amounts in all three states—vapor, liquid, and solid—is either extremely remote or nonexistent. Establishment of a generous, widely distributed water cycle circulating all three states of water—timed to begin working just as continental landmasses begin to form—testifies of meticulous design. It testifies, too, of the Designer's careful preparation for Earth's advancing quantity and diversity of life, and eventually humans.

Sun, Moon, and Stars Created When?

The apex of Shermer's and many other skeptics' ridicule of Genesis 1 hangs on the mistaken notion that the sun, moon, and stars originated on the fourth creation day. "How did day-three plants survive without the sun?" they ask. Some creationists say they survived because the days were short or because God temporarily substituted some type of heat and light. This response elicits even more ridicule.

Inadvertently agreeing with the skeptics, young-earth creationists and many or most theistic evolutionists consider the introduction of the sun, moon, and stars on the fourth day to be so problematic as to force a peculiar interpretation or reinterpretation of the text.[7] In their view Genesis 1 either contradicts the scientific record or relates solely and vaguely to certain aspects of the natural realm.

Alternately, some theologians have developed a "framework view" of Genesis 1.[8] They propose the seven-day scheme represents a figurative framework. According to this view, Moses uses the literary device of creation "days" as tableaus, snapshots of divine creative activity. While they accept the events mentioned in Genesis as actual historical occurrences, framework proponents describe them as nonliteral and nonsequential.

Theistic evolutionists and framework proponents who assert that Genesis 1 is something other than an account of nature's origin and history have fallen out of step with believers of past ages. Prior to the twentieth century the majority of Christian and Jewish commentators on Genesis 1 embraced it as an actual report on the origin and history of the physical realm. How could Moses have made it clearer for either ancient or modern readers that Genesis 1 provides a truthful overview of natural history? In public forums and private conversations, atheists and agnostics tell me they regard theistic evolutionists' and framework proponents' interpretive gymnastics as an attempt to dodge admission that the Bible contradicts scientific facts.

Is the Bible really in as much trouble as atheists and agnostics assert and as even some Christians seem to think? Why have Jews and Christians accepted Genesis 1 as an accurate record of natural history, knowing full well for millennia that plants cannot survive for one moment without the sun's heat and light and gravitational influence? If the Bible really taught the sun, moon, and stars were created after light and after plant life, it seems unlikely the Jewish and Christian Scriptures would have endured until today.

In my first serious reading of the Bible, coming from a skeptical perspective, not once did it occur to me that God waited until the fourth creation day to create the sun, moon, and stars. It never crossed my mind because Genesis 1:2 unambiguously identified Earth's water-covered surface as the frame of reference, or point of view, for the six creation days. Even more striking to me, the author of Genesis 1:2 described the initial conditions from which God's creative work moved forward: "Now the earth was formless and empty, darkness was over the surface of the deep, and the Spirit of God was hovering over the waters."

This darkness resulted from one of two options: the absence of light-emitting astronomical bodies or the opacities of Earth's primordial atmosphere and the solar system's primordial debris disk. The latter made more sense in the context of both the first verse, a reference to the heavens, and the third verse where God declares, "Let there be light." These words seem to imply that light sources already existed and now their radiance could come through to Earth's surface. When I read Genesis 1:14, where "lights in the vault of the sky" are first identified, my idea that the sun, moon, and stars had previously existed but only later become visible as distinct objects to Earth-bound observers seemed to make sense.

All this interpretive speculation would have been put to rest if only I had begun my study of the Bible in Job rather than in Genesis. Job's account of creation tells us that after God "laid the earth's foundation"

Does Genesis 1:16 State God Made the Sun, Moon, and Stars on the Fourth Day?

Many young-earth creationists and theistic evolutionists insist that if one interprets Genesis 1 literally, Genesis 1:16 proves that God did not make the sun, moon, and stars until the fourth day of creation. However, a correct understanding of the Hebrew verb form used in the verse leads to the opposite conclusion.

Genesis 1:16 says, "God made two great lights—the greater light to govern the day and the lesser light to govern the night. He also made the stars." The Hebrew verb 'asah is translated here as "made." The form of the Hebrew verb means that the making of the sun, moon, and stars was finished sometime previous to creation day four.

he "made the clouds its garment and wrapped it in thick darkness" (38:4, 9). The pronouns "its" and "it" here refer to the vast sea that covered the entire surface of Earth at the time. Job leaves no room for ambiguity. Darkness initially pervades the surface of the deep (Gen. 1:2) not because the sun and stars hadn't yet been created, but rather because Earth's primordial atmosphere was like a thick blanket that prevented light from penetrating to the surface of Earth's waters.

The latter part of Genesis 1:14 sheds further light on the interpretation: "Let them [the lights in the expanse of the sky] serve as signs to mark sacred times, and days and years." For what or for whom do they serve? As most of us learned in biology class, life-forms fit into one of two categories with respect to reproductive and other survival cycles: those that do not require any awareness of the sun, moon, and stars' location in the sky and those that require, at least on occasion, an awareness of the sun, moon, and stars' positions. All life-forms associated with the first three creation days fall into the first category, needing a translucent but not necessarily transparent sky. All life-forms created on days five and six fall into the second category, needing a transparent sky at least some of the time. The sun, moon, and stars serve as signs in the sky to mark seasons, days, and years so that the various animals God introduced on creation days five and six could know when to feed, migrate, reproduce, and hibernate.

Genesis 1:1–3 and 1:16 (see sidebar, p. 82) offer clues that the sun, moon, and stars were made prior to creation day four, before the plants of creation day three and, in fact, before all six Genesis creation days. However, Job 38 makes the picture crystal clear, explicitly affirming the cause of primordial darkness on Earth's surface, an atmospheric cloak God progressively transformed for the sake of his living creatures. Job renders exegetical gymnastics completely unnecessary.

Job can reinvigorate our response to Article 2 of the Belgic Confession, one of the foundational doctrinal statements of the Protestant Reformation (see sidebar below). This article reminds us that God gave humanity two books of revelation: the book of Scripture (special revelation, propositional revelation) *and* the book of nature (general revelation, illustrative revelation). The God who neither lies nor deceives (see Num. 23:19; Ps. 12:6; 19:7–8; 119:160; Prov. 30:5;

Belgic Confession

One of the great Reformation creeds, the Belgic Confession (1561), Article 2 states:

> We know him [God] by two means: First, by the creation, preservation, and government of the universe, since the universe is before our eyes like a beautiful book in which all creatures, great and small, are as letters to make us ponder the invisible things of God: his eternal power and his divinity, as the apostle Paul says in Romans 1:20. All these things are enough to convict men and to leave them without excuse. Second, he makes himself known to us more openly by his holy and divine Word, as much as we need in this life, for his glory and for the salvation of his own.[9]

Best known as the "two-books doctrine" primarily drawn from Psalm 19, this creedal article rests more securely on Job than on any other portion of Scripture. No other Bible book makes a stronger argument for God's revelation of himself to all humanity through nature's record.

Theologians call the record of nature "general" revelation because it speaks to everyone. Because nature's message is sufficiently clear, no human can legitimately claim to have heard nothing from God. On this doctrine, Job, his three friends, and Elihu agree (5:9–10; 7:17–18; 9:4–10; 10:8–9, 12; 11:7–9; 12:7–10; 25:2–3; 26:6–14; 28:20–28; 34:14–15; 35:9–11; 36:24–33; 37:3–23; 42:2).

John 10:35; Heb. 6:18; 1 John 1:5) has made both books reliable and trustworthy (Ps. 19:1–8; 50:6; 97:6; Rom. 1:18–20). His words in Job 38 clear up any question about whether the timing indicated in Genesis 1 for the formation of the sun, moon, stars, and earth is consistent with what nature's book shows us about the timing of those bodies' formation.

Creation Miracles Concealed or Revealed?

One of the core apologetics issues debated by twenty-first-century Christians can be summed up in this question: To what degree or extent are God's designs and creative acts in the universe, Earth, and Earth's life discernible? Some argue that God implemented his creation plan through natural processes in such a way that his handiwork is hidden from view by human investigators. Others argue that God brought about his creation plan through miraculous interventions that human researchers *can* detect.

Theologians who hold to various evolutionary or framework hypotheses express concern that science either has found or will find evidence contradictory to (or at least insufficiently supportive of) the biblical creation narratives. Many Christian scientists embrace an evolutionary interpretation of nature's record based on a belief that God seldom, if ever, intervened in the origin and development of our Milky Way Galaxy, solar system, Earth, or Earth's life. Many of these scientists and theologians would not deny that God performs creation miracles. They have agreed God performs multiple spectacular creation miracles, but most were front-loaded at the cosmic creation event some 13.7 billion years ago while the rest remain scientifically undetectable. Another version of this theological position is called "fully-gifted creationism." According to this perspective, *all* the creation miracles were front-loaded at the cosmic creation event.

While this perspective may seem equivalent to deism, most of these individuals acknowledge all the miracles recorded in the New Testament. They would say God performs creation miracles in one of two ways: (1) entirely packaged in the universe at its origin; or (2) mostly packaged in the cosmic origin event and thereafter hidden from the probing investigation of human research.

The book of Job potently challenges the notion of mostly or totally hidden divine intervention in creation. When he speaks to Job and his friends in chapters 38 and 39, God lists for them and for future generations the most spectacular and discoverable creation miracles he performed in preparing Earth and its life for human beings (see

Creation Miracles Described in Job 37–39

1. Setting up Earth's interior and surface features for the needs of advanced life (38:4–16)
2. Establishing an abundant, stable water cycle with water in all three states: vapor, liquid, and ice (37:3–21; 38:22–38)
3. Fine-tuning Earth's (gradually slowing) rotation to the precise rates for various life-forms throughout terrestrial history (38:4–6, 12–14)
4. Balancing the oceans' and continents' depths/heights, sizes, shapes, distributions, and movements for civilization's emergence and survival (38:4–11, 22–30)
5. Providing varied terrestrial habitats that allow diverse and abundant species to thrive (37:5–17; 38:22–30)
6. Engineering different kinds of cosmic dark stuff and placing each kind in the exact locations and abundances for the benefit of all Earth's life (38:19–21)
7. Fixing the precise amounts and kinds of precipitation, cloud cover, and lightning strikes to benefit diverse life-forms (37:3–18, 21; 38:22–30, 34–38)
8. Shaping and timing Earth's starry environment for the benefit of each life-form on Earth throughout terrestrial history (38:7, 12, 19, 31–33)
9. Setting all the laws and constants of physics at specific levels to facilitate fulfillment of divine purposes for the cosmos in relation to humanity (37:5–38:38)
10. Endowing birds and mammals with the capacity to form uniquely meaningful relationships among themselves and with humans (38:39–39:30)
11. Endowing humans with unique capacities to engage in an array of meaningful pursuits and relationships with each other, with other creatures, and with their Creator (37.7, 13–24, 38.1–39.30)
12. Equipping ten species of birds and mammals for humans' benefit in the development and sustenance of a global, technologically advanced civilization (38:39–39:30)

sidebar, p. 85). When I recently assembled an inventory of the latest and most remarkable scientific discoveries giving evidence of God's intervention in nature, the list almost entirely overlapped my list of creation miracles described in the Bible's most ancient book.[10]

How can this overlap be explained? One explanation is that four thousand years ago God anticipated and prepared for three significant developments: (1) movement of most of the world's population to cities, away from meaningful contact with nature; (2) a degree of research specialization that impairs recognition of the full extent of God's handiwork in nature; and (3) spiritual blindness and confusion that requires stunning new revelations and reminders of God's existence and calls to worship him alone.

At the time of the debate between Job and his friends, God's creation miracles seemed obvious. In their own words:

> **Job:** "His wisdom is profound, his power is vast" (9:4); "He performs wonders that cannot be fathomed, miracles that cannot be counted" (9:10); "Your hands shaped me and made me" (10:8); "You gave me life and showed me kindness, and in your providence watched over my spirit" (10:12); "Ask the animals, and they will teach you, or the birds in the sky, and they will tell you; or speak to the earth, and it will teach you, or let the fish in the sea inform you. Which of all these does not know that the hand of the LORD has done this? In his hand is the life of every creature and the breath of all mankind" (12:7–10); "These are but the outer fringe of his works. . . . Who then can understand the thunder of his power?" (26:14); "Where then does wisdom come from? Where does understanding dwell? . . . God understands the way to it and he alone knows where it dwells" (28:20, 23).
>
> **Eliphaz:** "He performs wonders that cannot be fathomed, miracles that cannot be counted" (5:9).
>
> **Zophar:** "Can you fathom the mysteries of God? Can you probe the limits of the Almighty? They are higher than the heavens above—what can you do? They are deeper than the depths below—what can you know? Their measure is longer than the earth and wider than the sea" (11:7–9).
>
> **Bildad:** "Dominion and awe belong to God; he establishes order in the heights of heaven. Can his forces be numbered? On whom does his light not rise?" (25:2–3).
>
> **Elihu:** "God my Maker, . . . who teaches us more than he teaches the beasts of the earth and makes us wiser than the birds in the sky"

(35:10–11); "Remember to extol his work, which people have praised in song. All humanity has seen it; mortals gaze on it from afar. How great is God—beyond our understanding!... This is the way he governs the nations and provides food in abundance" (36:24–26, 31); "God's voice thunders in marvelous ways; he does great things beyond our understanding.... Stop and consider God's wonders.... God comes in awesome majesty. The Almighty is beyond our reach and exalted in power" (37:5, 14, 22–23).

A twenty-first-century reader may be tempted to attribute Job's and his contemporaries' confidence in the Creator's work and wisdom to their lack of knowledge that has been made available since the scientific revolution. That's one possible explanation, but I see another, one that seems equally if not more reasonable. In a particular context, these men were better educated than many of today's leading scientists. They were in a better position to be taught by the animals, the earth, and their conscience. They were free of high-tech gadgets and multitudinous distractions that make up the so-called good life.

Without the benefit of the knowledge explosion predicted by the prophet Daniel (12:4), Job and his friends were scholars of a different sort. They were "Naissance" men, predecessors of Renaissance men. They had a broad grasp of the science, philosophy, and theology of their day, an ability to integrate that often appears more helpful in discovering God's fingerprints than deep knowledge of one subset of one academic discipline.

A New Hope

Job's usefulness for answering skeptics' challenges and resolving controversies over the meaning of the Bible's opening words gives us every reason to hope that Job can help us address questions arising from the subsequent Genesis chapters. We explore this in the following chapter with the hope of shedding light on what Genesis 2–11 says about humanity's origin and early history.

6

Answers to More Genesis Controversies

A fistfight broke out about halfway through my talk in Hollywood one evening. In South Africa, a pair of burly men tried to physically prevent me from entering the auditorium where I was scheduled to speak. Several times on university campuses, skeptics have interrupted so loudly and rudely that I've had to abandon my prepared talk and devote the evening to Q&A. In each of these cases, though, the antagonists eventually calmed down and gave earnest attention to my words.

The hostility I faced in each of these situations seems minor compared with what I've encountered in some (not all!) churches. I can anticipate things may go badly when I see a "Hugh Ross Attack Pack" on every seat. Another clue comes when the pastor introducing me informs his congregation he disagrees with my beliefs about science and the Bible but wants to allow me a hearing. The folks in these places usually let me complete my message. After all, we are in church. But when the Q&A session begins, the sparks start to fly. Instead of asking for clarification on points of disagreement, they scold me. They pin beliefs on me I've never held. They imply my mind is so weak and my ego so fragile that I swallowed everything my atheistic professors taught me. They say I seek the favor of men more than of God. They accuse me of faking graciousness as a means to deceive audiences.

They even question whether I'm really a Christian. A few times I've been called a "false prophet" or "tool of Satan." The words written about me on the internet are about the same, if not worse.

What makes these otherwise kindly Christians so upset? They've been taught to defend a particular interpretation of Genesis as if Christianity and their own personal relationship with God depend on it. Despite the reality that biblical Hebrew includes four literal definitions of *yom* (the Hebrew word translated as "day" in Genesis 1), they close their ears and minds before I can explain why I believe *yom* means "a long but finite time period" rather than "twenty-four hours" with respect to the Genesis 1 creation days. Their anger seems amplified by any comments I may give about creation day seven, plant and animal death, Noah's flood, and the universe's future. On all these issues, the book of Job holds important insights to calm hearts and clarify minds without compromising the authority and accuracy of God's Word.

What About Day Seven?

God's choice to rest after six days of creating has led to endless jokes and derision from skeptics. Why would an all-powerful Creator need rest? Typically, preachers in our work-oriented society teach that God rested to provide humanity with a precedent for rest, an example for our good. Seldom have I heard mention of the other meaning for rest, the one used in musical notation. This meaning refers to cessation rather than recovery from weariness. Our enjoyment of music owes much to these brief pauses.

The Creator certainly knows all his creatures benefit from rest periods. In his intimate knowledge of our nature, he sees that our tendency toward selfishness and greed can lead to abuse of ourselves and others, even of our land and animals. One expression of this abuse is deprivation of rest. Perhaps that's one reason he designed Earth's weather patterns in such a way that we are compelled to rest. The words of Job 37:5–12 suggest this possibility:

> God's voice thunders in marvelous ways; he does great things beyond
> our understanding. He says to the snow, "Fall on the earth," and to

the rain shower, "Be a mighty downpour." So that everyone he has made may know his work, he stops all people from their labor. The animals take cover; they remain in their dens. The tempest comes out from its chamber, the cold from the driving winds. The breath of God produces ice, and the broad waters become frozen. He loads the clouds with moisture; he scatters his lightning through them. At his direction they swirl around over the face of the whole earth to do whatever he commands them.

Genesis 2:3 tells us "God blessed the seventh day and made it holy." It seems more likely that instead of taking a nap, the infinite Designer-Artist-Engineer of the physical universe stepped back from his creative production and delighted in it. Perhaps there's a connection between the importance of such moments and his command to keep the seventh day holy, which is near the top of the ten most important rules of life. We humans need more than just the biological benefit of regular rest periods. Unceasing work distracts us from giving attention to the most important relationship in life, the relationship that impacts all we think and value about everything, including all our earthly relationships. Every person needs time to consider God's handiwork both in the external and internal worlds. Regular interludes of cessation from work allow for personal worship and reflection, as well as preparation for life here on Earth and beyond it.

Some people argue backwards from the human Sabbath, one day of the week, to show that the creation days must have been the same twenty-four-hour days. However, the Bible commands sabbaths of different duration for different reasons. The land, for example, is to be worked for six years and permitted to lie fallow during the seventh year. To quote Leviticus, "In the seventh year the land is to have a year of sabbath rest, a sabbath to the LORD" (25:4). Biological principles underlie the agricultural land's work period. A year of rest allows for nutrient restoration of the soil and starvation of soil pests such as nematodes.

As for God, he has no biological needs or constraints. His work "week" could have continued for any length of time. In some sense, it continues still. According to Genesis 1, God completed his *physical* creation work with the fashioning of Adam and Eve and endowing of their spirit. Since then, God has ceased from material creation, which may help explain why many scientists claim to see no direct evidence of God's miraculous handiwork. The vast majority of scientists are biologists, whose research endeavors focus primarily on the natural realm of the present era, when God is no longer active in making new kinds of physical life in the universe. That task is done. His work now applies to preparations for humanity's future, for our ultimate transition to life in the new creation.

God's seventh day does not continue indefinitely. The Bible points our attention ahead to a time when God will call an end to all sin and evil and the suffering they cause. He will remove them from his presence and ours. In the fullness of time (Rom. 8:22–25), when the full number he's chosen have answered his call of "Come!" the Son will usher his followers into a new life on a new day in a new realm. That moment marks the beginning of eternal life in the new creation described in Revelation 21–22.

How Extensive a Flood?

If there's one issue as controversial and emotionally charged as the length of creation days, it's the extent of the Genesis flood (Gen. 6–9). This topic represents not only a contentious point among believers but also a serious challenge to our faith's credibility. The most prominent and hotly debated views on the flood's extent and impact are these two:

1. Noah's flood was global, inundating the entire earth's surface. It destroyed all land-dwelling, air-breathing creatures, both plants and animals, not sequestered on Noah's ark. It also accounts for nearly all the earth's current geologic features and past geologic activity (destroying nearly all ocean creatures in the process) and virtually all fossils and fossil fuel deposits.
2. Noah's flood was regional and partial, relatively tepid in terms of its destructive powers. Rather than destroying all humanity outside the ark, it engulfed only one especially wicked nation and left all others unscathed.

More and more Christians are beginning to embrace a third option, for both biblical and scientific reasons:

3. Noah's flood was "worldwide" with respect to humanity, submerging all regions of Earth where humans and birds and mammals associated with humans lived. Because humans were not globally dispersed at that time, the flood need not have been global to destroy the people and their animals outside Noah's ark.

A reading of most English translations of the Genesis story seems to favor the global deluge position. Genesis 7:19 reads, "They [the waters] rose greatly on the earth, and all the high mountains under the entire heavens were covered." Could these words refer to anything other than a planet-wide flood? To answer that question requires thoughtful consideration and integration of all biblical passages relevant to the story.

The book of Job, a story widely disseminated before Genesis was written (see chapter 2, pp. 30–32), offers an important perspective. As the earliest Bible text to elaborate on natural history, Job seems a logical place to start in seeking to understand what occurred in Noah's time.

Job's description of God's creation work indicates the flood could not have been global. In reference to the events of creation day three, long before Noah, God asks, "Who shut up the sea behind doors when it burst forth from the womb, . . . when I fixed limits for it and set its doors and bars in place, when I said, 'This far you may come and no farther; here is where your proud waves halt'?" (38:8, 10–11). This passage suggests that in the process of forming Earth's continents, God established permanent boundaries for the world's oceans, limits they cannot cross.

Psalm 104 echoes God's words recorded in Job. The psalmist provides a picture of Earth prior to the emergence of continents and islands: "You [God] covered it [the earth] with the watery depths as with a garment; the waters stood above the mountains" (Ps. 104:6). The primordial earth was a water world at first, but Psalm 104:7–8 recounts the story of how God transformed Earth's surface on creation day three, raising up continents and separating the landmasses and oceans. According to Psalm 104:9, that's when God "set a boundary they [the waters] cannot cross; never again will they cover the earth." The words "never again" are explicit and unambiguous in this passage. Given that Noah's flood occurs after the third creation day, its extent cannot be rightly interpreted as global. While Job 38 provides a strong implication that Noah's flood was something other than global, Psalm 104 states the case clearly.

Other Old Testament passages, including Psalm 33:6–11 and Proverbs 8:22–31, underscore the point. Then in the New Testament we read that God brought the flood upon "the world of the ungodly" (2 Pet. 2:5 NASB). Because the ungodly of Noah's era had not yet inhabited Antarctica or Greenland (most likely not yet Australia or North and South America, either), the purpose of the Genesis flood would have been accomplished without the waters covering the entire earth's surface. Again Peter comments, "By these waters also the world of that time was deluged and destroyed" (2 Pet. 3:6). The qualifying phrase "of that time" (*tote* in the original Greek) implies a distinction between Noah's world and Peter's world without reference to the globe or planet (a modern understanding of "world").

The Genesis flood account itself (Gen. 6–9) provides clues to the less-than-global extent of the floodwaters. Genesis 8 describes the receding of the waters after the deluge. From his perspective on top of the ark, Noah could see the tops of the distant hills or mountains on the horizon (v. 5). Later, when he released a dove, the bird "could find nowhere to perch because there was water over all the surface of the earth" (v. 9). The words "over all the surface of the earth" are essentially the same as those found in Genesis 7:19, the passage most frequently quoted as proof that the flood must have been global in extent. The use of such phrases as "all the surface of the earth," "under the entire heavens," and "the whole world" may simply be an indication that Moses and his readers conceived of "earth" and "world" in the context of people rather than planet. The expression "under the entire heavens" may mean "from one horizon to the other."

The people being singled out for judgment in the flood story are the ungodly. Genesis 6:7–12 tells us that all of humanity—except Noah and his immediate family—had rejected God and given themselves over to evil. What moved God to take such drastic measures was his observation that the entire human race outside Noah's family had become utterly reprobate. As reprobates, these people were now incapable of doing, saying, or even thinking anything pleasing to God or ever responding to truth with humility and repentance.

Paul described the pathway to reprobation in his letter to the Romans: "Although they know God's righteous decree that those who do such things deserve death, they not only continue to do these very things but also approve of those who practice them" (1:32). Peter wrote, "They seduce the unstable . . . they entice people who are just escaping from those who live in error" (2 Pet. 2:14, 18). In other words, reprobation equates with moral malignancy, spreading like a deadly cancer. Just as a surgeon will remove a malignant tumor from a person's body to save that person's life, likewise God acted to save the rest of humanity from total spiritual death by removing those who had given themselves to evil.

The surgeon analogy may be helpful in more detail. The size and degree of the malignant growth determines how much tissue the surgeon must excise. Similarly, depending on the degree of moral degradation in the reprobate community, God removes more or fewer of the people, animals, and belongings associated with the depravity. Piecing together Old and New Testament passages on sin's defiling effects, we see that reprobation's impact begins and spreads in the following order:

1. to the sinners first (Rom. 7:8–11)
2. to their progeny (Exod. 20:5)
3. to their domesticated animals (Josh. 6:21)
4. to their material goods (Num. 16:23–33)
5. to their inhabited land (Lev. 18:24–28)

When the Creator performs surgery, his surgical procedure focuses with perfect precision on the dangerous tissue, cutting away no more and no less. Unlike a human surgeon, God needs no margin for error. He removes only that part of society that has become irredeemably malignant.

The account of God's "bargaining" with Abram (Abraham) over the destruction of Sodom and Gomorrah provides a basis for understanding how and when God operates. In this story we see God places strict limits on the expression of his judgment, or wrath (Gen.

18:22–33). He promised Abram, whose nephew lived in Sodom, that if as few as ten righteous people could be found there, he would spare the two cities for the sake of those ten. As it turned out, fewer than ten remained. So God removed from Sodom and Gomorrah the one and only nonreprobate ("righteous" by comparison) person, along with his family, before raining destruction on those cities. Meanwhile, God allowed the wicked Amorites to live on because, as he explained, "the sin of the Amorites has not yet reached its full measure" (Gen. 15:16). Their judgment would come later.

The details of Abram and Lot's story shed additional light on the flood extent. The report of what occurred during the angels' brief stay in Lot's home provides a snapshot of the people surrounding Noah, people we have difficulty even imagining, so extreme was their vile behavior. Most of us today have yet to meet even one individual of whom we could say "every inclination of the thoughts of [his] heart was only evil all the time" (Gen. 6:5). But that describes Noah's neighbors, all of them. Genesis adds, "All the people on earth had corrupted their ways" and were "full of violence" (Gen. 6:11–12). In order to rescue humanity from total self-destruction, God determined to rescue Noah, his family, and his family's animals, and to wipe out all the reprobate people, their progeny, their animals, their material goods, and their land.

If we consider the flood account in light of what the whole of Scripture reveals about the timing and extent of God's judgment, we find a way to resolve the controversy over the flood's geographical extent. The core question is the geographical distribution of humans and of the animals associated with them. Anthropological research indicates early humans lacked the technology and economic means to colonize lands far distant from Mesopotamia and Northern Africa, certainly not such places as Antarctica and Greenland. Archeologists find no evidence of human habitation outside the region surrounding the juncture of Africa, Asia, and Europe until long after what would have been Noah's era.[1] Genesis 11:1–9 records that even after the flood, humanity still resolutely disobeyed God's command to "increase in number; fill the earth" (Gen. 1:28). Instead, Noah's descendants committed to "build ourselves a city, with a tower that reaches to the heavens, so that we may make a name for ourselves; otherwise we will be scattered over the face of the whole earth" (Gen. 11:4). God intervened to disrupt their plan, and they finally began to move into all the lands upon the entire surface of Earth (Gen. 10:1–32; 11:8–9). Outside support for such a scenario comes from parasitic and DNA markers indicating a period when humans spread rapidly from that one region into all the world's continents and islands.[2]

While most of the geographical place names recorded in Genesis 2–8 refer to sites within Mesopotamia, some do not. Notable exceptions are the Pishon and Gihon rivers, which flow out from the southern part of the Arabian Peninsula. Genesis 2 indicates that the Tigris, Euphrates, Pishon, and Gihon rivers all met together in the Garden of Eden. The only locale where these four rivers joined together is the southeastern part of what now is the Persian Gulf. Geological research tells us that roughly 50,000 years ago, before the end of the last ice age, much of what is now the Persian Gulf was dry. Given the mention of all four rivers in association with Eden, this area seems the likely location of early populations and civilization. If so, the Genesis flood must have inundated not only Mesopotamia but also the entire Persian Gulf region (at least) and much of southern Arabia. With help from Job 38 and other Bible passages concerning the great flood of Noah's day, a reasoned response to an acrimonious debate unfolds. The flood is both biblically and scientifically defensible as an inundation much larger than Mesopotamia, as some have proposed, and yet significantly more limited than global in extent.

Church history reveals that this one flood controversy, which arose in the early part of the twentieth century, gave rise to several additional disputes that have continued ever since.[3] In these cases, too, the book of Job assists in bringing about productive dialogue and potential resolution.

When Rain Began to Fall

Some people caught up in the flood debate conclude no rain fell on Earth prior to when Noah's family boarded the ark. This reasoning is based on one or more of the following (mistaken) assumptions: (1) the statement "God had not sent rain on the earth" (Gen. 2:5) is interpreted as describing conditions after rather than before the six creation days; (2) the "mist" that watered Eden (Gen. 2:6)—a fog or dew, not falling drops of water—was a global phenomenon; (3) some kind of water vapor canopy explains why pre-flood people could live for several hundred years; and (4) the rainbow Noah spied after the flood was the first rainbow phenomenon to occur on Earth.

In addressing the major events of creation, Job 38–39 devotes a lot of attention to precipitation, as discussed earlier (see pp. 64, 78–80) in relation to God's establishing of the water cycle (38:22–23, 25–30, 34, 37). Specific forms of precipitation mentioned include rain, hail, snow, "frost from the heavens," and "water jars of the heavens." The text gives no basis for doubting that these forms of precipitation played a role in events of the creation days to follow, and because all the creation days predate the Genesis flood, rainfall must have been part of Earth's scene a long while before the time of the flood.

Elihu's oration extolling God's majesty and transcendence suggests humans always have experienced rainfall. Elihu reminds Job and his friends that God commands the rain, calling forth a downpour that "stops all people from their labor" and allows "everyone he has made" to "know his work" (37:6–7). The words "all" and "every" suggest that this passage applies to all people from the time of creation onward, not just from Noah's time forward. The benefit of rain, including the forced stoppage of human labor, would have belonged to all humanity for all time. We humans have always struggled to balance work and rest. For ancient people, even more than for people today, mere survival required long, hard labor nearly every day. Compulsive workaholics probably have been around since the beginning, and so have tyrants who make excessive demands on others' time and energy. Elihu says God occasionally uses rainstorms to bring work to a halt. This forced relief would have been needed just as much before Noah's time as after.

Is the Universe Eternal?

Another theological dispute of our day centers on God's plan for humanity's future, specifically for that time when, as Revelation says, "God's dwelling place is now among the people, and he will dwell with them"

(21:3). Many people who view the flood as a global event also interpret God's covenant with Noah and his sons (in Genesis 9) as a promise that Earth and its creatures will remain forever, in keeping with God's "everlasting covenant." Their perspective on this passage's meaning shapes their belief about the "new creation" promises in other parts of Scripture, including Revelation 21. They live in anticipation of a time when God will restore the universe and Earth to their original splendor, their condition before Adam and Eve's rebellion in the Garden of Eden.[4]

This widely held doctrine of a restored, eternal universe and Earth seems to rest most heavily on four Bible passages in addition to Genesis 9:

> Praise him [the Lord], sun and moon; praise him, all you shining stars. Praise him, you highest heavens and you waters above the skies. Let them praise the name of the LORD, for at his command they were created, and he established them for ever and ever—he issued a decree that will never pass away. (Ps. 148:3–6)

> I know that everything God does will endure forever; nothing can be added to it and nothing taken from it. (Eccles. 3:14)

> Those who are wise will shine like the brightness of the heavens, and those who lead many to righteousness, like the stars for ever and ever. (Dan. 12:3)

> [God's] works were finished from the foundation of the world. (Heb. 4:3 NASB)

In the English language, these verses appear to support the notion that Earth and the universe we now occupy will remain without end. Here again, however, a look at the Hebrew words and other relevant passages of Scripture alters the picture.

The Hebrew word *'olam*, translated "forever" or "for ever and ever" in these verses, has another literal definition in the lexicons: "indefinite continuance into the very distant future."[5] So a possible literal interpretation of these passages could be that the sun, moon, stars, and the rest of the cosmos will continue for a very long time. Given the two potential meanings, a consideration of other clarifying passages becomes essential to determining which interpretation to take. Let's start with Job.

In his intense suffering, Job spoke of longing for death but also of his eventual hope of resurrection. He referred to the day of his rising when "the heavens are no more" (14:12). Job clearly believed death is not the end for redeemed humans (19:25–27). He envisioned his resurrected life in a realm beyond the cosmos, *after* the universe no longer exists. Job's belief is affirmed by the words of the psalmist: "They [the foundations of the earth and the heavens] will perish, but you [God] remain; they will all wear out like a garment. Like clothing you will change them and they will be discarded" (Ps. 102:26). Isaiah prophesies, "All the stars in the sky will be dissolved and the heavens rolled up like a scroll; . . . the heavens will vanish like smoke. . . . [God] will create new heavens and a new earth. The former things will not be remembered, nor will they come to mind" (Isa. 34:4; 51:6; 65:17).

Having heard Jesus, the Creator incarnate, pronounce that "heaven and earth will pass away" (Matt. 24:35), the apostle Peter wrote, "The heavens will disappear with a roar; the elements will be destroyed by fire . . . Everything will be destroyed in this way . . . That day will bring about the destruction of the heavens by fire, and the elements will melt in the heat. But in keeping with his promise we are looking forward to a new heaven and a new earth" (2 Pet. 3:10–13). In his revelation from God while on the Isle of Patmos, John saw ahead to the final judgment, where Christ is seated on a "great white throne." In this scene, "The earth and the heavens fled from his presence, and there was no place for them" (Rev. 20:11).

From its oldest book to its last, the Bible speaks of a reality beyond the space, time, matter, and energy of the universe, a reality to which spiritual beings belong but the heavens and earth do not. The universe endures for a long time in the context of our earthly existence, and yet it cannot contain the fullness of God nor the reward that awaits those who choose eternal life with him.

Death Before Adam?

If I were to name one controversy with greater power to inflame passions than all others associated with creation, evolution, and judgment, it would have to be whether any animals experienced death prior to Adam and Eve's sin. In my experience this issue is far and away the most divisive aspect of the dispute over the age of the earth and length of creation days. Some sincere, devout Christians have told me (and persuaded countless others) that an all-powerful, all-loving, all-good God could not and would not have allowed *any* of his creation to suffer anything as horrific and distressing as death—unless and until sin (Adam's rebellion) brought it on. Some have told me both privately and publicly, "I cannot worship a God who would do that." These strong words and the conviction behind them imply that death is evil or bad in every context imaginable. Such a conclusion on such a significant issue warrants testing. As always, the whole of God's Word must be brought to bear.

Again, we start with the oldest revelation. In Job's book God has much to say on the subject. One claim jumps out: plant and animal death prior to Adam and Eve's sin may actually have served some purposes we'd be compelled to call "good."

As noted already, Job 38 and 39 are among the most comprehensive creation accounts outside Genesis. In one sense these chapters parallel Genesis 1 in depicting the events of the six creation days. The last few verses zoom in on God's creative activity during creation days five and six. On these days God created some life-forms referred to in Hebrew as *nepesh* and which many Bible scholars call "soulish" animals. The unique characteristics of *nepesh* creatures are their intellectual, emotional, and volitional capacities, including the ability to relate. They bond with others of their species, with others not of their own species (under very unusual circumstances), and most notably with humans. Their behavior toward humans includes serving and pleasing. God appears to have designed them to serve and please in unique and specific ways.

God's message to Job and his friends first singles out two *nepesh* kinds, the lioness and the raven: "Do you hunt the prey for the lioness and satisfy the hunger of the lions when they crouch in their dens or lie in wait in a thicket? Who provides food for the raven when its young cry out to God and wander about for lack of food?" (38:39–41). Given the historical context (the fifth creation day), this passage indicates that carnivorous activity occurred even before humans arrived. Whatever the timing, the verses state unambiguously that God himself provides food for the predator.

The passage goes on to mention two more carnivorous *nepesh*: "Does the hawk take flight by your wisdom and spread its wings toward the south? Does the eagle soar at your command and build its nest on high? It dwells on a cliff and stays there at night; a rocky crag is its stronghold. From there it looks for food; its eyes detect it from afar. Its young ones feast on blood, and where the slain are, there it is" (39:26–30). In no way does God appear to recoil from or express revulsion over the carnivorous activity of the lioness, raven, hawk, or eagle. Since the context remains that of the creation days, physical death must have occurred during some part of God's creation period. Yet all six creation days predate the first humans' sin, and God called his creation good, even very good.

Both history and science confirm that the lioness, raven, hawk, and eagle illustrate important benefits of carnivorous activity (more on that topic later), including certain relational benefits. They can meet their nutritional needs quickly. They need not spend all their waking hours consuming and digesting food. So in addition to exhibiting intelligence and emotional expressiveness, which endear them to humans, they also need little time to eat, which allows them time to relate to humans at remarkably deep levels.

In no way does this interpretation of Job or this view of predation mean death is not grievous. Nor does it contradict Paul's statement in Romans about the death imposed as a dreadful consequence of Adam's sin. Paul wrote, "Sin entered the world through one man, and death through sin, and in this way death came to all people, because all sinned" (Rom. 5:12). Here, Paul carefully specified the kind of death Adam's sin introduced to the world. It is "death through sin." Of all life on Earth, only humans are capable of committing sin. Thus, Paul's words identify the death sin caused as human death, which is both physical and spiritual. This attribution becomes clearer in Paul's comment that "in this way death came to all people." By saying death came to all *people* rather than to all *life*, Paul implied that plant and animal death, essential to the survival and benefit of all living things, does not represent the detrimental outcome of human sin. The death of plants and animals in the pre-Adamic creation does not impugn God's character and goodness. Instead, it speaks of a higher purpose.[6]

Controversy Resolution Principles

As with any biblical controversy, the key to resolution is integration. When we bring together every Scripture passage directly addressing or indirectly correlating the subject, progress can be made toward a consistent interpretation and diminished conflict. One rule of thumb in this process is to interpret implicit statements in light of explicit ones. In every respect, Job's debate proves an especially rich source of material for resolving current disagreements.

Another of these disputes surrounds the meaning of the phrase "the image of God." The controversy goes beyond a semantic debate among Jews and Christians. It involves science and scientists as well. In his book *The Descent of Man*, Charles Darwin made the claim that humans differ from apes *only* in degree and not in kind. This assertion, as much as any other, has stoked the fires of creation-evolution debates. As the next chapter reveals, Job provides many tools for dampening those flames.

7

Unique Attributes of Humans

Sometimes the best question at one of our university events comes *after* the clean-up crew has ejected us from the auditorium. Such was the case at the University of Illinois a few years ago. On that occasion more than 1,500 students and faculty packed Foellinger Auditorium to hear how Fuz Rana and I would defend our belief in creation in front of a panel that included three of the university's distinguished science professors, one of them a Nobel Laureate. Fuz and I were allotted time to highlight a few of our creation model's testable components, and each panelist was given fifteen minutes to respond, followed by Q&A with the audience.

That was the plan, but when one of the panelists rambled on for forty-five minutes, uninterrupted by the moderator, the Q&A time evaporated—a disappointment for the audience as well as for Fuz and me. But all was not lost. As we exited the building a cluster of students and one professor gathered around to ask for our comments on results from recent animal experiments indicating the essential sameness of humans and other animals. This is a question we would have enjoyed discussing with the entire audience! Yet we felt glad for a chance to address it with this group.

The studies to which the students referred included the well-publicized case of a gorilla that, over time, mastered a vocabulary of sorts with the equivalent of three hundred words. The same gorilla had adopted a pet cat. Other experiments they mentioned showed chimpanzees were able to learn how to use tools to recover or capture food. "Don't these findings prove," they asked, "that we humans are simply highly developed apes with a common ancestry?"

Our reply began with a compliment to the remarkably gifted animal trainers and to the animals who demonstrated such intelligent and socially skilled achievements. From there we aimed the discussion toward two key points: (1) multiple recent experiments indicate humans possess capacities categorically distinct from those of all other species; (2) at least some of the deductions derived by previous generations of scholars deserve thoughtful consideration. Often those early scholars spent much more time observing and interacting with animals than do most people today—even than most current researchers.

What Fuz and I skimmed over that day barely scratched the surface. If they took away anything from our comments, I hope they heard that many of the more eloquent and insightful elements of past wisdom about humans and animals come from the book of Job.

Image of God

In the Bible's opening pages, Moses records these words spoken by the Creator: "Let us make mankind in our image, in our likeness, so that they may rule over the fish of the sea and the birds in the sky, over the livestock and all the wild animals, and over all the creatures that move along the ground" (Gen. 1:26). Moses's account continues, "So God created mankind in his own image, in the image of God he created them; male and female he created them" (1:27). This expression, "in his own image," has generated discussion and debate among Jews, Christians, and many other theists for centuries. One point on which all seem to agree is that we humans, like God, have the capacity and responsibility to govern. This governing encompasses management of all Earth's resources, both physical and biological. Genesis 1 makes clear that humanity's role in governance is utterly unique among all Earth's creatures, past and present.

Genesis 2 tells the story of God's earliest interactions with Adam. Initially God introduced Adam to the physical creation, the world of plants and trees primarily. Next he introduced Adam to the "soulish" creation, the world of fascinating life-forms with whom the man could relate in entirely new and wonderful ways. After getting acquainted with them and observing their interrelationships, Adam becomes aware of his uniqueness and, thus, his aloneness. At this point, God introduced Adam to the one earthly creature like him (Eve), the world of human relationship, a whole new and satisfying level of oneness including physical, soulish, and spiritual dimensions. Theologians point out that this three-ness reflects God's image in two obvious ways. According to the Christian doctrine of the Trinity, the one God exists as three persons who transcendently manifest body (the glorified Son; Col. 2:9), soul, and spirit. Also, as the three persons of the Triune God relate to one another at three levels—physical, soulish, and spiritual—so do humans.

The book of Job provides additional, intriguing details. When God entered the debate between Job and his friends, he posed a string of rhetorical questions. At one point he asked, "Who has put wisdom in the innermost being or given understanding to the mind?" (38:36 NASB). This question identifies God as the source of all knowledge and capacity to know. Because his existence transcends all creation, no mere creature—angelic or human—can share his omniscience. Humanity's possession of the image of God does not mean we can ever gain "god" status or achieve Stephen Hawking's stated goal of attaining "the mind of God."[1] Only Jesus of Nazareth can be described as the "exact representation" of God's being in human form (Heb. 1:3).

God says, nonetheless, he granted to humans, and only to humans among Earth's life, a unique capacity to think, gain understanding, and discern what's wise. While many animal species manifest intelligence and amazing instinctual knowledge, none can emulate the human ability to accumulate knowledge and build upon understanding from generation to generation. Nor can they share the human aptitude for invention, communication, abstraction, and assessment.

This question from God may well respond to Job's earlier question and observation. Job said, "Where then does wisdom come from? Where does understanding dwell? It is hidden from the eyes of every living thing, concealed even from the birds in the sky" (28:20–21). Job saw among other creatures no equivalent to the human quality we describe as wisdom. Its source is hidden from the keenest physical eyes, including the eyes of birds. That's not to say birds and other animals do not manifest a kind of wisdom, namely the instinct and intelligence to prepare for future needs. They build nests, store food, and migrate in response to seasonal changes. Many can solve simple problems and know what to do to build strong bonds with other members of their species and with humans (see chapters 8 and 9). In these respects they provide lessons for humans.

Humans, however, have the capacity to make judgments. We discern what's true, right, and enduring. We can choose to behave unwisely. In addition to taking lessons from intelligent creatures like the raven, humans can ponder and evaluate their own and others' thoughts, motives, words, and actions. Humans can choose what has value and meaning and what does not. Humans can investigate the past and consider how it relates to the present and future. This capacity we call wisdom does not correlate with intellect. It differs from intelligence in kind, not in quantity. Job apparently recognized the wisdom each human possesses as a unique gift imparted from a source outside ourselves.

Social Cognition

Without intending to, European and American anthropologists stumbled upon tangible evidence for humanity's qualitative uniqueness. The evidence flowed from a study comparing the intellectual capabilities of adult orangutans and chimpanzees with those of human children aged thirty months.[2] In selecting the children, the researchers took care to eliminate the possible benefit of early literacy or education.

To their amazement, the team discovered that in terms of ability to learn from their physical environment, human toddlers showed no significant advantage over adult apes. However, the children's capacity to comprehend and share knowledge and understanding from their social interactions exceeded by orders of magnitude anything observed among the adult chimpanzees and orangutans. In the researchers' words, "Humans are not just social, but 'ultra-social.' "[3] Spiritual activities such as philosophical, theological, and worldview discourses and corporate worship all require an extraordinary capability to communicate and learn in the context of social interactions. Even the most intelligent mature primates lack that capability. Yet it is strikingly noticeable in immature (very young) humans.

A different study revealed another aspect of humanity's unique spiritual nature—the capacity for malevolence. It appears that only humans among Earth's creatures harm each other for harm's sake.[4] The research team housed chimpanzees in cages that allowed them to withhold food from other chimpanzees by pulling on a rope. The researchers found that the chimpanzees would withhold food (in a statistically significant manner) only from chimpanzees that stole their food—not from others. In others words, they showed no tendency toward behavior that in humans would be defined as "spite" or displaced retaliatory anger.

The research team concluded that spiteful behavior appears unique to humans. Only humans engage in malicious behavior toward fellow humans for no reason other than the impulse to hurt or harm someone. The team also commented on humanity's flip side, "pure altruism." Only humans, not primates, engage in self-sacrificial acts performed to assist or benefit other humans or even animals with whom no social context has ever been or likely will be established. In other words, the study confirmed what the Bible says about humanity's spiritual nature and condition: humans are uniquely sinful and uniquely righteous among all living creatures.

Awareness of God

Job contains the earliest biblical reference to a human response called "the fear of the Lord." Because of the way English speakers, and especially those of recent centuries, use the word "fear," this biblical expression has caused some confusion. The Hebrew word translated "fear" in this phrase is *yir'ah*, which means reverence or piety.[5] *Yir'ah* stands in contrast to another Hebrew word, *pachad*, which means dread or terror.[6]

Job's words point to another aspect of humanity's uniqueness as spiritual creatures. Humans alone, among all Earth's creatures, carry a certain reverence for the divine, an awareness of God and the sacred. People of all times and places express what may be called a religious impulse, a yearning to know and relate to the supernatural realm, and specifically to their Creator. As noted in chapter 3 (pp. 37–38), neither Job nor his friends expressed even the slightest doubt about God's existence or his attributes of omnipotence, omniscience, and omnipresence.

Such a confident belief in God may seem less ubiquitous today than in Job's day. Certainly many people have become more hesitant to declare their belief publicly, especially in western European and English-speaking nations. Even in America, however, surveys consistently show about 85 to 95 percent of the population professes belief in God and an afterlife.[7] The other 5 to 15 percent identify themselves as atheists or agnostics. Yet even these self-proclaimed nonbelievers reflect some level of God-awareness, if only in the form of anger toward God or toward religious people.

I had an opportunity to observe this phenomenon at the Skeptics Society Conference held at the California Institute of Technology in the fall of 2008. The conference theme was religion and science. Its title, "ORIGINS: The BIG Questions." Highlighting the gathering were lectures from leading scientists across a wide range of disciplines, each offering to explain how the natural realm can look the way it does without invoking any deity's existence or involvement. The featured event of the second day was advertised as "The Great God Debate: Does Science Support Belief in a Deity?"[8] pitting me against Victor Stenger, author of *God: The Failed Hypothesis*, among many other books.

From observing the conferees and conference proceedings leading up to the debate, I gathered that most of the audience, some seven hundred atheists and agnostics, unquestioningly embraced the assumption that no scientific evidence exists to support God's existence. I urged them to become more skeptical of their skepticism. After the debate the comments I received from attendees encouraged me greatly. Some said, "Until today I had never heard any scientific support for God." One man told me, "Because of what you said, I can no longer be secure in my atheism."

Many people gathered around to ask me what single piece of evidence for God I considered the strongest. I replied that while the scientific evidences presented in my talk stand out for their potency, many more evidences—historical, philosophical, and theological—also support my faith. Their curiosity grew when I said I had come across a new piece of evidence for God that very day. I hoped they would ask about this "new evidence," and they did.

Throughout the entire conference, I told them, both the speakers and audience vigorously expressed their mocking disdain toward belief in a Creator God, but not just any god. Intense emotion had been directed entirely toward the God of the Bible. The gods of the other religions received a free pass from this scathing scorn. Why? If the people here confidently believe the God of the Bible does not exist, I asked myself, why don't their emotions toward him resemble their feelings toward the tooth fairy, the Easter bunny, and Santa Claus? Their degree of passion and nearly constant focus on the issue of God's nonexistence suggested something different. It suggested to me not that they disbelieved in God but rather that they despised God. They strongly disliked him. When I mentioned this thought, the group's response was telling: "It's not so much we hate God as that we hate his followers!"

At this point we could begin talking about what really needed to be discussed. I freely admitted that the bad behavior of some Christians (both real and so-called) earned a deplorable reputation for the rest. However, that fact cannot and does not diminish the weight of evidence in God's favor. I expressed deep regret, as I had to my debate opponent, over the damaging actions and words of fellow believers. Then, in the strongest terms I could find, I urged them not to let any obnoxious persons or bad theology separate them from God's gracious offer of love and redemption.

I share this story simply to propose that atheism and agnosticism represent positions people adopt in response to hurt, disappointment, and anger, mixed in with a strong pride element. People don't start with zero awareness or knowledge of God. As Paul explained to the Romans, awareness of God's existence does not equate with acceptance of his authority (1:21, 28). That awareness leads to choices, and those choices matter.

Compulsion to Worship

Another closely related capacity distinguishing humans from all other creatures on Earth, regardless of intelligence, is worship. Every human worships someone or something. No other creature does. The Hebrew word for worship, *shachah*, appears at a dramatic juncture in the book of Job. In the first chapter, when Job received word that all his wealth had been taken and his ten children, too, he responded with a depth of faith few individuals ever grow into:

> At this, Job got up and tore his robe and shaved his head. Then he fell to the ground in worship and said: "Naked I came from my mother's womb, and naked I will depart. The LORD gave and the LORD has taken away; may the name of the LORD be praised." (1:20–21)

By his actions and attitude Job illustrated the very definition of the Hebrew word for worship, which means "to prostrate oneself before another to do him honor and reverence."[9] His reverence for God taught Job to give thanks and praise in all circumstances (1 Thess. 5:18).

Worship as it is used by Christians today typically involves "singing." The word as used in Scripture and in other cultures, past and present, encompasses much more. In one sense, the dialogue between Job and his friends serves as one of the greatest worship examples in the Bible. Though the five men differed in their understanding of God and his ways, each stayed with the conversation, wrestling with his beliefs, and meanwhile repeatedly extolling God for his greatness, majesty, justice, and mercy. Each man revered him as Creator and ultimate Authority over all creation.

Though not all people worship God, we all worship something, even if that thing is an abstraction instead of an actual idol. Timothy Keller writes in his book *Counterfeit Gods*[10] that everyone esteems something so highly it dictates his or her decisions, attitudes, and actions. But that something, which is part of creation, can never measure up to the Creator himself. The young man Elihu, after listening to the interaction between Job and his friends, felt compelled to remind them to look higher: "Remember to extol his [God's] work, which people have praised in song. All humanity has seen it; mortals gaze on it from afar. How great is God—beyond our understanding!" (Job 36:24–26). Elihu voiced the importance of extolling creation's magnificence not just for its own sake but also as the work of the transcendent Creator. His words hint at human tendencies to become so enamored with the beauty we see that we lose sight of beauty's Source.

The apostle Paul observed that trend in his day. He wrote, "Although they claimed to be wise, they became fools and exchanged the glory of the immortal God for images made to look like a mortal human being and birds and animals and reptiles" (Rom. 1:22–23). Today these images may take different forms, but they surround us nonetheless. Among brilliant scientists, who perhaps seem farthest removed from primitives who bowed to statues of men and animals, we see a strong temptation to view nature with a capital "N," as if the created realm did its own designing and creating. The familiar paean is, "Isn't it amazing what nature has done!"

Two of the world's most famous scientists of the current era illustrate the transfer of worship from Creator to created. Francis Crick, who shared the Nobel Prize for the discovery of DNA's double helix, wrote, "Biologists must constantly keep in mind that what they see was not designed . . ."[11] Evolutionary biologist and best-selling author Richard Dawkins said in his book *The Blind Watchmaker*, "Biology is the study of complicated things that give the appearance of having been designed for a purpose."[12]

The human compulsion to gather for worship—to exult in whatever they deem highest and best—became all the more starkly evident to me during a social gathering at the 2008 skeptics conference. Many society members glowingly described their Sunday afternoon gatherings and other special events, which included sermons on atheism, stimulating conversation about nature's wonders, and opportunities for fellowship with those who share common beliefs. When I said, "It sounds like the society is your church," they had to agree.

Concern about Coming Judgment

Animals, by contrast, do not hold religious gatherings. Nonhuman creatures show concern only for their day-to-day existence and survival. Without the capacity for language and abstract thought, they cannot consider "before" or "after" their life. Not so with humans. We are compelled to wonder about our origins and destiny. We want to know about the origin and destiny of virtually everything in the universe. The question of what will happen after we die jumps back and forth in our thoughts from childhood onward.

Death's certainty and imminence was a central theme in the debate between Job and his friends (7:6–9, 21; 8:9; 9:25–26; 10:20; 14:1–2; 16:22–17:1). They were, as I mentioned previously, realists. Whether we wish to talk about it or not, each of us knows we cannot escape the experience of physical death.

A universal question lurks behind our awareness of looming death. What if it's not really the ultimate end? This question by itself reveals the categorical difference between humans and other creatures. Only beings whose life consists in something more than merely physical and soulish reality would even conceive of such a question. Further evidence springs from the observation of how people live. If we humans belong only to the material world, then the most rational philosophy of life would be to eat, drink, and be merry, for tomorrow we die (see Isa. 22:12–14). The supreme value would be selfish pleasure. However, few of us actually live this way or find such a life truly satisfying, at least not for more than relatively brief periods. There is a reason.

Early on in the debate Job pointed to that reason. Only humans carry within us a sense that we're being examined and evaluated throughout our lives and that we will one day, beyond this life, be held accountable for our lives. Job described this awareness in this way: "What is mankind that you [God] make so much of them, that you give them so much attention, that you examine them every morning and test them every moment?" (7:17–18); "His [God's] eyes are on their [every human's] ways" (24:23). Elihu added, "His [God's] eyes are on the ways of mortals; he sees their every step. . . . He takes note of their deeds" (34:21, 25).

We humans differ from the rest of Earth's animals in that we alone comprehend what judgment means (see sidebar, chapter 14, p. 203). We exercise judgment over self and others, judging intentions as well as actions. We may not always judge rightly, but we do judge. As Jesus declared to large crowds gathered at the temple, "You judge according to the flesh" (John 8:15 NASB) and "Do not judge according to appearance, but judge with righteous judgment" (John 7:24 NASB).

Job and Elihu imply this awareness of pervasive judgment belongs inherently to every human being. The New Testament concurs. Jesus said God's Holy Spirit "will convict the world concerning sin and righteousness and judgment" (John 16:8 NASB). In the apostle Paul's words, "The requirements of the law are written on their [all humans'] hearts, their consciences also bearing witness" (Rom. 2:15). The apostle John received a vision of this coming judgment. He wrote, "I saw the dead, great and small, standing before the throne, and books were opened. Another book was opened, which is the book of life. The dead were judged according to what they had done as recorded in the books. . . . Each person was judged according to what they had done" (Rev. 20:12–13).

Many a human has tried to ignore, dilute, or rationalize away the awareness of coming judgment. However, the universality of conscience affirms "the requirements of the law written on their hearts." This concern over judgment, unique to humans, becomes clear not only in the Bible's words, but also in our observations of nature. Not even the most advanced of higher animals, other than humans, shows any inclination to worship or hint of concern about judgment.

Extension of Physical Life

Even from a strictly physical perspective humans stand apart from all other animals. In terms of the number of heartbeats comprising a life span, humans live far longer than other creatures. Animals at the high end of heartbeat longevity, such as mice, cats, dogs, horses, elephants, and whales, have the capacity for as many as a billion heartbeats within their life spans. Human hearts, on the other hand, can sustain nearly three billion beats in a lifetime.

This significant difference in humans' capacity for longevity demands explanation. The human body's characteristics allowing for such extended activity on all levels (physical, mental, and spiritual) suggests uniqueness of design and purpose. It argues for a qualitative rather than mere quantitative difference between humans and the rest of Earth's creatures.

Job points to yet another reason for humans' longer life spans. Based on personal experience, he concludes that God often intervenes to rescue people from life-threatening danger, preserving their lives for a purpose. Job says to God, "You gave me life and showed me kindness, and in your providence watched over my spirit" (10:12). I once asked a large group of people mostly over age thirty to recall at least one instance when, by the laws of physics and probability, they should have been killed, and everyone had one or more such recollections. I can remember at least a half dozen events in my own life that I survived against high odds. Like Job, I'm drawn to the conclusion that God intervened, or perhaps sent angels, to extend my time on Earth.

Just how tenuous our earthly lives are and how much we all need divine intervention to continue living for any length of time is a theme picked up by Elihu. He expressed God's control over human longevity in these terms: "If it were his intention and he withdrew his spirit and breath, all humanity would perish together and mankind would return to the dust" (34:14–15).

More Than Animals

Humans certainly do share a great deal in common with other species. Our bodies, like many other animal bodies, are made up of DNA, RNA, proteins, flesh, blood, and bones. Our bodies, like theirs, undergo decay, disease, and eventually death. The differences between us, the qualities most familiarly summed up as spiritual, cannot be reasonably explained as reflections of ascending intelligence.

This last point sometimes becomes lost, especially among those who resist the idea and implications of a Creator, and partly in view of earthly animals with whom we humans share much: the *nepesh*, or soulish animals. Like humans, some animal species manifest intelligence, emotions, and will. The people of Job's era lived nearer these creatures, in terms of both daily dependency and physical proximity; and, of course, they had fewer technological distractions. No wonder the ancient book of Job offers the Bible's most extensive treatment of the origin, history, and characteristics of these amazing creatures. The next few chapters look into what Job, his friends, and God himself had to say about them and how it reflects, in some cases, what researchers have just recently begun to confirm—findings that provide a potent challenge to evolutionary ideology.

8

Origin of Soulish and Spiritual Qualities

Canadian university students, as I once was, seem reluctant to listen to an unopposed lecture, regardless of the speaker's reputed competence. They tend to prefer a point-counterpoint presentation, a preference growing on US campuses as well. With that thought in mind, I usually take steps to ensure that when I visit a university campus, especially in Canada, the event is set up as a skeptics forum, similar to those described in previous chapters. One of the first such forums I was involved in took place in London, Ontario, at the University of Western Ontario. What I remember most about that evening was an informal debate that took place long after the formal presentations and the ninety-minute Q&A session were over. About thirty students stayed to spar with me over which animals (other than humans) would be considered the smartest.

Most of the students insisted that the smartest animal must be the chimpanzee, or at least one of the other great apes. They based this deduction not on any comparative studies of various higher animals, but rather on our supposed evolutionary lineage. All had been taught the standard Darwinian model, which maintains that humanity's intellect and other characteristics arose through natural descent from previously existing large-bodied primates. They believed humans evolved their unique characteristics after branching off from a shared, relatively recent common ancestor.

A few students risked suggesting that perhaps dolphins are a bit smarter than chimpanzees. After a few moments of discussion I commented that a couple of animal experts from about four thousand years ago identified certain birds as the brightest, or at least among the brightest, of all species. These experts were Job and Elihu.

Several students immediately grasped the significance of our discussion. No evolutionist ever would claim that human mental faculties naturally arose through recent common descent from a dolphin, and certainly not from a bird. If some bird species do indeed manifest higher intellectual capability (in some contexts) than chimpanzees, gorillas, and orangutans, and if birds are the *only* nonhuman creatures to share particular intellectual characteristics with humans, then naturalistic explanations for the origin of the human mind and spiritual characteristics face a severe, perhaps insurmountable, barrier. This barrier, however, represents just one among several serious challenges confronting naturalistic explanations for Earth's life in all its spectacular diversity. For example, the origin-of-life issue has become far more faceted and complex than most scientists ever anticipated.

Origin of Physical Life

Not surprisingly, every creation account in the entire Bible identifies God, not nature itself, as life's originator. Job's book speaks as directly and emphatically to this point as Genesis or any other relevant Scripture passage. Job said to his friends, "But ask the animals, and they will teach you, or the birds in the sky, and they will tell you; or speak to the earth, and it will teach you, or let the fish in the sea inform you. Which of all these does not know that the hand of the LORD has done this? In his hand is the life of every creature and the breath of all mankind" (12:7–10).

Evolutionists from virtually all theological and philosophical perspectives acknowledge the profound challenge of coming up with a realistic, naturalistic explanation for the origin of even the simplest conceivable life-form. Physicist Paul Davies, who spent two years researching the issue in preparation to write his book *The Fifth Miracle*, noted, "This gulf in understanding [life's origin] is not merely ignorance about certain technical details, it is a major conceptual lacuna."[1] In his opening lecture at the International Conference on the Origin of Life in Oaxaca, Mexico, in 2002, origin-of-life researcher Leslie Orgel admitted, "It would be a miracle if a strand of RNA ever appeared on the primitive Earth."[2]

Such comments express the recognition, confirmed repeatedly in the intervening years, that to engineer the chemical assembly of life's building blocks (amino acids, nucleobases, and pentose sugars) and those building blocks into functional proteins, DNA, RNA, and membranes under controlled laboratory conditions, proves so extremely difficult as to render their natural self-assembly under conditions of the early earth essentially impossible. As origin-of-life researcher Noam Lahav said, "So far, no geochemical evidence for the existence of a prebiotic soup has been published. Indeed, a number of scientists have challenged the prebiotic soup concept, noting that even if it existed, the concentration of organic building blocks in it would have been too small to be meaningful for prebiotic evolution."[3]

The lack of primordial soup and of the necessary chemical building blocks may be the least among the various obstacles facing origin-of-life scientists in search of a naturalistic explanation. The assembling of life's building blocks into proteins, DNA, and RNA requires that the foundational building block molecules be homochiral. That is, the amino acids must be *all* left-handed in their configuration and the pentose sugars *all* right-handed. However, no natural mechanism can be postulated for any period of Earth's history to explain how homochirality might have been generated. Organic chemist William Bonner summed up his twenty-five-year search for a solution to the homochirality problem with this statement: "Terrestrial explanations are impotent and nonviable."[4]

Frustrated, Bonner concluded that homochiral molecules must have been generated somewhere in outer space.[5] Unfortunately for Bonner and others seeking naturalistic pathways for life's origin, the only astrophysical source for generating nontrivial quantities of homochirality resides in the circularly polarized ultraviolet light emanating from black holes and neutron stars. Even this source produces,

Transcendent Creation Miracles

What distinguishes a "transcendent" miracle from other miracles involving precise timing or shaping is a transition from nonexistence to existence—totally apart from previously available material components and the operation of physical laws or dimensions. In the original language of Genesis 1, the verb used for "create" highlights three transcendent creation miracles, as distinct from transformational miracles (see sidebar "Difference between 'Make' and 'Create'" on p. 123). The three transcendent creation miracles are these:

- creation of the universe (v. 1)
- creation of soulish animals (v. 21)
- creation of humans (v. 27)

In these three verses, the Hebrew verb *bara'*, translated "create," appears. In each instance something entirely new and previously nonexistent within the cosmos comes to exist.

at best, only a few percent greater excess of one configuration over the other.[6] Worse yet, other radiation sources emanating from black holes and neutron stars would break down rather than build up prebiotic molecules.

A still greater challenge to the naturalistic origin-of-life scenario involves assembly of the required proteins, RNA, DNA, and membrane structures in such a way as to yield a viable cell. These growing, rather than shrinking, barriers to the possibility of a spontaneous origin of life on Earth (and more could be cited[7]) explain why debaters skeptical of God's existence prefer to pass over the discussion of life's origin.

Origin of Soulish and Spiritual Life

Until recently, the debate concerning life's origin focused primarily on the beginning of physical life. However, recent discoveries have compelled a widening discussion. As Genesis foreshadowed, it must now include at least two additional origins of life—the beginning of life that is *physical and soulish* and the beginning of life that is *physical, soulish, and spiritual* (as described in the previous chapter). Emergence of each of these kinds of life (see sidebar, p. 122) belongs in the current origins discussion. A viable model must account for each.

Some hypothesis must account for the sudden, rather than gradual, forward leaps from nonlife to life and then from one kind of life to the next. The first such leap occurred about 3.8 billion years ago, perhaps even earlier. The second occurred about 150 million years ago (nearly 400 million years after the Cambrian Explosion) in a period equivalent to the fifth and sixth creation days of Genesis 1. The third came at the end of the sixth day, roughly 50,000 to 90,000 years ago.

The Hebrew noun for creatures made in that second creation of life is *nepesh*, characterized by the English concept of "soulishness."[8] As mentioned previously, the term encompasses an array of life-forms that manifest a combination of intellect, emotion, and volition, characteristics utterly new to the animal kingdom. Given these special qualities, such animals can form and nurture more than momentary or superficial relationships with members of their own species, and

Difference between "Make" and "Create"

The Hebrew text of Genesis 1 includes two different verbs to depict the origin of the *nepesh* and *'adam*, the first human. The use of the verb *'asah*, translated "make," refers to God's manufacture of the physical aspects of *nepesh* and *'adam*. These aspects, in general, would not be considered entirely new because similar structures already existed in creatures that appeared earlier. Nevertheless, at least some of the physical makeup of the *nepesh* and *'adam* must be sufficiently distinct and additionally complex to deserve mention of God's direct intervention. From a biblical perspective, the use of the verb *'asah* contradicts the notion that some wholly natural process brought the physical forms of *nepesh* and *'adam* into existence.

The second verb used in Genesis 1 to denote the origin of the *nepesh* and *'adam* is *bara'*, translated "create." This Hebrew word's meaning carries an even stronger connotation of newness or innovation than its English counterpart. It implies transcendent (from beyond space, time, matter, and energy), supernatural causation.

each species in its own specific way shows a unique capacity to relate to humans (who were not yet in existence).

According to Genesis 1, the soulish characteristics of the first *nepesh* were strikingly novel. The biblical account implies that nothing like *nepesh* had existed previously among Earth's creatures. The difference between *nepesh* (such as cats and cockatoos) and previously existing creatures (such as termites and goldfish) would appear to be much greater than one of *degree*. Rather, the difference is one of *kind*. Genesis tells us God intervened from outside of nature (see sidebar, p. 123) to introduce something of great value.

The strong, specific biblical claim concerning the *nepesh* and *'adam* invites scientific testing. Does the standard explanation of the origin of soulish and spiritual characteristics reveal a gap just as mystifying and intractable as the one Davies noted in the scenario for the origin of physical life? Once again, insights from the ancient book of Job apply to a current question.

Animal and Human Soulishness

In 2009, the "year of Darwin," the world celebrated the 200th anniversary of Darwin's birth and the 150th anniversary of his book *On the Origin of Species*. Biologists wrote numerous review papers and articles in 2009 showcasing what research has added to Darwin's knowledge since the time he posited his theory. These publications aimed to make the point that scientific discoveries since Darwin's day have strengthened the case for a naturalistic advance of life. They reported, for example, that the scientific case for a long history of life on Earth is now beyond doubt, and so is the historical record of life's progression from simple, small-bodied life-forms to more complex, larger-bodied life-forms. How many people realize, however, that this scenario exactly parallels what the Bible teaches? The crucial difference, of course, concerns how the history of life took the direction it did. The Bible credits God's creative involvement, not just natural processes, for the big changes scientists observe in the record of Earth's life.

From a biblical perspective, the two biggest changes would be the step-function transition from nonsoulish to soulish life and from soulish life to life that is both soulish and spiritual. In his book *The Descent of Man*, Darwin claimed these changes were relatively minor and easily explained by natural processes alone.

Darwin explicitly stated that the difference between human and nonhuman minds is merely "one of degree and not of kind" and that "there is no fundamental difference between man and the higher mammals in their mental faculties."[9] As proof, he pointed out "there is a much wider interval in mental power between one of the lowest fishes, as a lamprey or a lancelet, and one of the higher apes, than between an ape and a man."[10] (On the magnitude of the mental difference between a fish and an ape the Bible would concur because, as the Bible points out, fish are totally lacking in soulish characteristics.)

Darwin's claims that humanity's intellectual capabilities originated from a recent common ancestor shared with chimpanzees and orangutans remained virtually unchallenged by the scientific community until just this past decade. Whenever this kind of inquiry has been pursued, however, the findings support statements recorded in Job. Three recently published papers—one in *Nature*, the second in *Behavioural Processes,* and the third in *Behavioral and Brain Sciences*—now alert the scientific community to the severe challenges the origins of soulishness, wisdom, and spirituality pose to naturalistic models for life.

Which Is Smartest?

In a recent essay in *Nature*, biologist Johan J. Bolhuis and psychologist Clive Wynne, both of whom accept the Darwinian premise that Earth's species evolved naturally, nevertheless contest the Darwinian principle "that species with shared ancestry will have similar cognitive abilities."[11] In particular, they point out that from an evolutionary perspective "the appearance of similar [cognitive] abilities in distantly related species, but not necessarily in closely related ones, illustrates that cognitive traits cannot be neatly arranged on an evolutionary scale of relatedness."[12]

Bolhuis and Wynne compare and contrast the cognitive capacities of birds with those of primates. Their goal was to test Darwinian models that view apes as humans' closest relatives through fairly recent common ancestry, and birds as very distantly related to humans and also to apes.

Bolhuis and Wynne discovered something different. In numerous instances birds defied the Darwinian prediction. For example, "Caledonian crows outperform monkeys in their ability to retrieve food from a trap tube—from which food can be accessed only at one end."[13] Another experiment demonstrated that "crows can also work out how to use one tool to obtain a second with which they can retrieve food, a skill that monkeys and apes struggle to master."[14] They began to observe that certain bird species exhibit greater powers of the mind than do apes.

Bolhuis and Wynne went on to reveal further mysteries. For example, they observed that a certain "marsh tit stores seeds in tree bark or in the ground and is able to retrieve them several days later," whereas a "close relative" of this bird stores no food at all.[15] Biologists presumed the difference would be explained by a larger hippocampus in the brain of the food-storing tits. However, the evidence did not support this suggestion. Surprisingly, studies showed that food-storing birds performed no better in spatial-memory tasks than did the non-food-storing birds.[16]

Bolhuis and Wynne's research lends new credibility to Job and Elihu's assertions about birds' intelligence (Job 28:10–11; 35:11). In fact, if claims from the book of Job are correct, we can expect to see future studies revealing more evidence that birds' cognitive abilities more closely resemble humans' than they do apes', a profound challenge to assumptions about how those capacities could have been passed naturalistically to humans.

Ability to Foresee

The familiar evolutionary assumption that more recently and highly evolved animals possess only those features manifested at least to a small degree in their progenitors has led to the conclusion that foresight (the ability to look forward in time and visualize a future setting) cannot be unique to humans. Two experimental psychologists at Cambridge University have proposed a new framework for designing experiments to settle the debate about whether or not nonhuman animals possess at least some degree of foresight.[17]

These Cambridge psychologists commented that until now the debate has been needlessly ambiguous. This ambiguity stems from the failure of researchers to design experiments that would distinguish clearly between an animal's ability to engage in mental time travel as opposed to engaging in future-oriented activities that have nothing to do with precognition. An example of future-oriented activity would be an elephant matriarch's leading her herd to a watering hole. Rather than "thinking ahead," she is more likely basing her search on her past experiences in successfully discovering water sources. Additional experiments strongly suggest that while advanced birds and mammals frequently engage in future-oriented behaviors, these creatures do so based on cognitive input *other than* a capacity for actual foresight. Thus far, it appears the ability to travel forward in time mentally and visualize the self in a future context belongs uniquely to humans without a precursor in the animal kingdom.

The Cambridge research duo plans to continue testing their tentative conclusion, taking it to a greater level of certainty (or uncertainty). Based on observed trends, I anticipate their work will contribute to the scientific case for what the Bible has declared all along—that the soulish and spiritual qualities distinguishing certain animals from earlier species and distinguishing humans from earlier animals came from the Creator's intervention in the world of nature.

Capacity for Symbolic Thought

Three psychologists at the University of California, Los Angeles (UCLA), recently published an even more dramatic challenge to the Darwinian paradigm. In an article that appeared in *Behavioral and Brain Sciences* they made a stunning claim, highlighted provocatively in the article's title, "Darwin's Mistake: Explaining the Discontinuity Between Human and Nonhuman Minds."[18] Their article declared the evolutionary notion of cognitive continuity an error. Research results comparing animals and humans indicated "a significant discontinuity in the degree to which human and nonhuman animals are able to approximate the higher order, systematic, relational capabilities of a physical symbol system."[19] They took this conclusion further still, adding that "this symbolic-relational discontinuity pervades nearly every domain of cognition and runs much deeper than even the spectacular scaffolding provided by language or culture alone can explain."[20]

Although this UCLA study addressed the properties of mind that pertain specifically to symbolic thought, the researchers recognized how much more broadly their findings apply. Symbolic thought plays a central role in multiple aspects of what makes humans unique, including aspects described as spiritual. This discontinuity carries potent implications for evolutionary theory, the standard descent of man scenario in particular. The concept of continuity resides at its core. So this research strikes at the heart of the naturalistic paradigm. In this important respect, naturalism does not hold up.

New Directions in Behavioral Research

Darwin deserves credit for looking within nature for a cataloging of observed similarities among soulish beings, as contrasted with non-soulish ones. Such gathering and organization of data is the scientist's first job. Without the abundance of data available today, Darwin gave a best guess at a naturalistic, nontheistic explanation for life's origins and development. From his perspective, the differences between the mental facilities of apes and humans seemed minimal. Would he draw the same conclusions today, given the scientific evidence now available? No one can say, but his successors remain understandably reluctant to let go of those conclusions—for philosophical, theological, and personal reasons, including the currently promoted definition of science as a search for naturalistic answers only.

From their observations and relationships with higher animals, Job and his friends drew a very different set of conclusions. Without access to propositional revelation, or sacred writings, they deduced from nature that God, not nature itself, must be the causal agent behind all three origins of life: physical, soulish, and spiritual. Although still limited in number, research studies today exploring these differences line up harmoniously with biblical teaching on the creation of these special life-forms, including the teaching found in Job.

Another line of reasoning to support the idea that the *nepesh* (soulish animals) arose by supernatural design rather than by natural process springs from observation of the ways these creatures provide for human needs. They have special capacities allowing them to relate to us humans, serving and pleasing us in ways they do not relate to their own species and in ways that do not promote their own survival. Research reveals no natural evolutionary mechanism by which these animals gradually changed over time to adapt to humans. Rather, these creatures possessed the body structures, soulish capacities, and motivation to serve and please humans *before* humans existed. Some insights to how the *nepesh* provide for humans, as well as new findings about their unique behaviors in relating to humans, appear in the next two chapters.

9

To Serve and Please

The popularity of the 1989 animated feature *All Dogs Go to Heaven*, not to mention countless other films since then with cats, dogs, and other four-legged friends in leading—even speaking—roles, hints at the human tendency to view animals in human terms. On shopping trips to pick up supplies for our two cats, my wife and I see displays of pet clothing, strollers, and other accessories that seem an attempt to anthropomorphize (that is, characterize as human) pets, dogs in particular. The bond between a pet and its owner can be so strong and fulfilling, it's no wonder the human begins to think of this animal companion in human terms. After all, each animal does have a distinct personality. However, personality cannot be equated with spirituality.

Animals certainly can and do perform heroic acts, but they also misbehave. They may do grave harm both to property and people, but do they possess moral virtue or commit sin? The distinction becomes crucial to the question of whether there exists a qualitative difference between animals and humans. Many years ago, I faced a heated debate on this point with some students at a major South African university. They passionately defended the idea that dogs can be considered evil in the same way as humans can.

This discussion took place just before apartheid's end. Fear and animosity had reached a palpable pitch in the region. The rate of violent crime had escalated. Many people depended on guard dogs, more aptly described as attack dogs, for their personal protection. These young people had personally witnessed several bloody incidents in which dogs had injured or killed people (including children) who posed no real threat.

At the time, I could not cite the research studies described later in this chapter. They hadn't yet been made. So I focused my response on how animals bond with and reflect their human owners or handlers—not forgetting how in nature they respond to perceived danger. I commented on Genesis and Job's message that God created soulish animals, both birds and mammals, with the capacity to bond emotionally to members of their own species as well as to humans, but *without* an innate sense of right and wrong.

I urged them to judge the aggressive, vicious behavior of dogs in light of two possibilities: (1) their actions express their innate desire to please the humans who provide for them; and (2) their actions demonstrate their innate motivation to preserve their own life. "Could it be," I asked, "that these dogs you saw were acting as their owners had trained them and wanted them to—if not simply reacting to perceived threat?" I added, "How consistent is the pattern that good dogs belong to good people and bad dogs belong to bad people?"

Animals' Motivations

The individual animals within virtually any species possess at their core a noticeable drive to do whatever possible to extend their life—both its duration and its quality. For the *nepesh* animals, as compared with other animals, this drive expands to include protecting the life of their offspring. For a number of species, this motivation is so strong that a parent will sacrifice its own longevity and quality of life for its progeny's sake.

The *nepesh* are endowed with powerful instincts to nurture, serve, and please members of their own species, and these instincts seem to carry over into their relationship with humans. They manifest the same motivations but often in different ways. For example, some *nepesh* species exhibit the desire to draw a reaction from or entertain the humans they're attached to. They seem to like showing off how clever they are and the amazing things they can do. Stories also abound of animals that have risked and sacrificed their own safety and well-being, in some cases their very lives, for the sake of the humans who care for them.

The *nepesh* also are endowed with varying degrees of curiosity and playfulness. Some *nepesh* species display intense interest in exploring and investigating their environment. Cats come immediately to mind. The curiosity and playfulness of the *nepesh*, however, have limits. Their interests extend about as far as their immediately detectable environment (which can be large), including potential food sources, potential resources for constructing beds, nests, dens, or lodges, and potential items for play and entertainment, but no further.

Humans' Motivations

The curiosity of humans shows no apparent limits. Humans want to explore, study, investigate, dismantle, reassemble, and understand everything in their environment and beyond, in the realm of their thoughts. There is nothing within the entire universe—from the physical properties and functioning of the extremely large to the physical properties and functioning of the extremely small—that humans do *not* want to identify, comprehend, and explore. Humans are so compulsively curious that many will deliberately risk their physical well-being in attempts to satisfy their curious yearnings—not to mention their motivations to play.

Humans share with the *nepesh* certain drives, which I've characterized as the desire to serve and please others. In humans, however, these motivations, just as with the qualities of curiosity and playfulness, reach out more widely. Like *nepesh*, humans invest time, energy, and other resources in nurturing, serving, and pleasing their own kind. Unlike *nepesh*, humans willingly extend this investment to those they've never met and with whom they're connected only by our shared humanity, regardless of differences in age, gender, ethnicity, and a host of other characteristics. This response seems most evident in times of calamity.

Just as soulish animals reach out to form relationships with humans, we humans seek to form relationships with *nepesh* as well. However, our reaching out goes much further. We will invest in caring for needs and pleasures of *nepesh* with whom we have no expectation of either personal contact or gain. Most supporters of the Humane Society and World Wildlife Fund never meet or know the animals whose lives they preserve and protect. What's more, humans will even invest in providing for and protecting non-*nepesh* life, such as bacteria, insects, and plants, as well as for nonlife, the inanimate resources of Earth. God's command to Adam and Eve in the Garden of Eden to manage Earth's resources for the benefit of all life seems to be backed up by an innate motivation to do so. We love nature's beauty and vitality and desire to protect and preserve it—for the sheer aesthetics, even beyond personal gain.

The most extreme difference between *nepesh* and human motivation to serve and please may be seen in our drive to worship, specifically the desire to serve and please God, the Creator, or whomever/whatever we deify as most worthy of our attention. As noted in chapter 7 (pp. 112–13), this yearning for relationship with the ultimate Source of all that's good and right and glorious, the Someone who gives meaning to human existence, may become diverted, but it cannot be denied.

Some crucial questions arise at this juncture. If these motivations to serve and please, protect and preserve belong innately to *nepesh* and even more expansively to humans, why is our world in so much trouble? Why is its wealth so unevenly distributed? Why have so many species of life become endangered or extinct as a result of human activity? Why do we abuse the environment, deplete resources, and harm our fellow humans?

In the whole history of humanity, no one—not even the most brilliant or wise or insightful human—has proposed a better answer to such questions than the highly unpopular, politically incorrect, biblical answer: *sin*. Only humans, not animals, have a capacity for sin, as both Scripture and science tell us. While *nepesh* respond to their instincts and innate relational motivations, humans from the time of Adam and Eve onward constantly face an inner battle between two sets of instincts and motivations. On the one hand, we have some sense of what's good and right. On the other, we find ourselves helpless to perfectly follow where that sense points us. In his letter to the Romans, the apostle Paul described this struggle between the innate "law of the mind" and the innate "law of sin and death." We humans seem to have inherited this struggle not from previously existing creatures but rather from the first of our kind, the first human pair.

Job may have been the first human to articulate "for the record" the one and only source of hope in the midst of this struggle. He discerned that it does not reside in any great quality or capacity within us. Nor does it come from any other humanly devised source within the universe. Job came to understand where it comes from by studying the world around him in humility of heart. If we will humble ourselves, we too can learn a great deal from observing the *nepesh*.

Interference

The effects of sin have become easily visible in our interactions with two groups of birds and mammals: those that have experienced harmful contact with humans and those that have not. The difference in their response tells the story. Rather than seeking contact with humans, the *nepesh* creatures that have been impacted negatively either run away in fear or attack out of fear. Those that have been treated well by humans or have never interacted with humans tend to draw near. Their reaction provides a sort of mirror for humanity, not only of our encounters with other people and animals but also of our response to the Creator of the universe. Sin interferes and holds the power to destroy relationships, including our success in serving and pleasing.

In my midtwenties I determined to test what I learned from Job about God's endowment of soulish animals with an inborn desire to serve and please humans. In my experience, animals tended to shy away from humans, unless they were dependent on humans for basic needs. So during a vacation I backpacked to a place deep within British Columbia's mountains where, according to park rangers I consulted, no humans had likely ventured for at least twenty years or more. When I found a spot that looked good for camping, I set up my pup tent and waited, watching to see how the local *nepesh* wildlife would react to my presence. I had eaten earlier as I walked so as not to attract them with food.

I arrived at this site around 8:00 p.m. (darkness comes much later in summertime at northern latitudes). By about 10:00 p.m., an assembly of birds and small mammals gathered around my tent to observe this strange newcomer to their territory. That night I slept with the tent open, and when I awoke the next morning I was surprised to discover a ground squirrel inside just inches from my face. I expected my furry visitor to run off when I sat up, but the curious character stayed put. Then I noticed outside my tent a porcupine keeping watch. This creature also stayed still when I moved. As I emerged from the tent to stretch, I saw that my entourage from the night before had now grown larger and closer. Some came near enough for me to touch.

Though I refrained from offering food, I enjoyed many close encounters over the next few days. Birds landed on my shoulders or on my knees as I sat down to rest. A mountain goat brushed up against me, inviting me to pet it. By the time I returned to civilization, my experiences had convinced me that God indeed endowed a special set of creatures, soulish animals, with a desire to relate to humans—some to serve, some to please, and others to do both.

Created to Please

In pondering the idea that birds and mammals desire relationships with humans, it occurred to me that before we humans existed these animals already possessed the qualities they needed to relate with us, to serve us and please us in unique and specific ways. This observation challenges evolutionary explanations for life, but it fits harmoniously with the biblical claim, especially as emphasized in Job, that God's creative process involved preparing Earth with all its features and life-forms for humanity's benefit.

The evolutionary challenge arises from the fact that the *nepesh* precede humans. Therefore, their innate capacities to serve and please—if real, specific, and unique to their relationships with humans—cannot be attributed to adaptation or some other natural process or mechanism. Scientifically testing these innate capacities would either support or deny the plausibility of both evolutionary and biblical creation models for life's development. An especially revealing test would be to determine whether the capacity to serve and please correlates closely with the degree of emotional bonding between the soulish creature and its human caregiver.

Snowball

Only in the past few years have researchers begun to conduct the necessary studies on the degree to which birds and mammals are motivated to serve and please humans. Much credit goes to the internet and, as unscientific as it may seem, to the video-sharing website YouTube. Since YouTube's inauguration in 2005, its participants have posted several thousand video clips of birds and mammals performing a wide range of behaviors, including some rather astonishing feats—whether spontaneous and real or staged and manipulated.

One major instigator of a research program on the capacity of *nepesh* creatures to serve and please humans was a cockatoo named Snowball. This entertaining character achieved fame through a YouTube video showing it dancing to the Backstreet Boys' song "Everybody."[1] Snowball struts its stuff, bobbing its head, high-kicking its legs, and unfurling feathers in rhythmic response to the musical beat.

Snowball attracted the attention of a neuroscience research team from the Scripps Research Institute and the University of California–San Diego. The researchers initially suspected that Snowball's performance was a response to visual cues from humans in the same room and not an innate ability to dance to a musical beat. To test their assumption, the neuroscientists traveled to the Indiana bird sanctuary where Snowball lived. There they performed a battery of tests. They removed possible cue givers from the room and altered the tempo of Snowball's favorite music, speeding it up and slowing it down at random. To their amazement, Snowball adjusted dance steps and head bobs to the changing beat.[2] Their published findings reveal that a nonhuman animal—in this case, the cockatoo—possesses the brain structure and circuitry to detect a musical beat and to synchronize body movements in response to the beat.

As a follow-up to this breakthrough study, a research team from Harvard, MIT, and Brandeis searched the YouTube database for

Pedro

Upon reading the conclusions of Aniruddh Patel's team, I flashed back to my own experiences with a vocal mimic during my teens and early twenties. My family kept a conure (a small green parrot) named Pedro. For reasons only Pedro knows, the bird bonded more closely to me than to my parents or sisters. Pedro would hop on my shoulder anytime possible, snuggle in behind my ear for a while, and then go to work on me. This "work" included carefully clipping off any facial whiskers I had missed with my razor and "flossing" my teeth, picking up particles I'd missed with my toothbrush, even from my back molars.

Pedro also trained me to preserve the cleanliness of my shirts. Apparently sensing my dismay at finding a deposit on my shoulder, the neatnik would gently tug on my ear lobe when the urge to release came. Once I realized the signal, I would take Pedro to the nearest perch for a moment before his return to my shoulder. My family informed me I was the only human in Pedro's life to become trained in such a way.

Pedro especially liked watching me play bridge. To the chagrin of my bridge opponents, the squawker would cheer and dance in response to my quiet delight each time I won a hand. I remember my mother saying, "It's bad enough to lose to our son at bridge, but it's worse to have to endure his bird's gloating."

My friends called Pedro a music critic. Whenever my sisters turned on their favorite rock 'n' roll station, this feathery snob would throw a loud screeching tantrum. If I switched to a classical station, the tantrum quickly gave way to swaying and bobbing. Pedro was especially demonstrative whenever he heard a piece by Bach.

These memories told me that Pedro, like Snowball, reflected the depth of the *nepesh*-to-human bond. Both the San Diego and Boston research teams would concur that their findings cannot be used to say that Snowball, or cockatoos in general, are Backstreet Boys fans while Pedro, or conures in general, are Bach aficionados. Rather, their results show that a vocal mimic, in its desire to please the human with whom it has bonded, has a capacity to detect and reflect the pleasure (or displeasure) that human takes in a variety of things, including music.

evidence of other species with a capacity to dance to a musical beat.[3] They found thirty-four examples in addition to Snowball, including other cockatoos, parrots, and even an Asian elephant. Their investigation revealed that the capacity to dance to a musical beat resides only within creatures described as "vocal mimics"—animals capable of imitating sounds produced by humans or by human activity, including spoken words, vocal and instrumental music, and noise from machines.

The leader of the San Diego–based research study, Aniruddh Patel, observed that dancing to a beat requires a human connection. He noted that parrots haven't been shown to dance to a beat in the wild, "even to the songs of their courtship displays."[4] Apparently, the stronger the emotional bond between the vocal mimic (bird or Asian elephant) and its human owner, the more spectacular its ability to dance to its owner's favorite music (see sidebar, p. 138). The work done by Patel and his team shows that at least some soulish species possess certain capabilities they express only when relating to human beings.

Each of the two research teams made an effort to infer an evolutionary explanation for the musical and dancing abilities of vocal mimics and humans. The great problem they encountered, however, springs from the consistency with which the evolutionary paradigm hypothesizes that humans derive by natural process from the great apes, or from a fairly recent common ancestor far distant from either birds or elephants. Yet none of the nonhuman primate species show any capacity for either vocal mimicry or dancing to musical beats. How, then, did this aptitude for music and dance pass through the evolutionary tree to *Homo sapiens sapiens?*

Another challenge to naturalistic evolutionary models comes from the fact that this capacity to dance to a musical beat offers vocal mimics no detectable survival advantage. So no evolutionary model would predict it as an anticipated evolutionary outcome. The fact that this type of behavior never shows up in the wild underscores the point. On the other hand, the unique abilities of vocal mimics fit perfectly with the biblical claim that God designed and created soulish animals with humanity in mind, endowing them with special capacities to serve and delight humans.

Do *Nepesh* Sin?

The entrenched belief that humans represent a rung on the ascending evolutionary ladder comes with the corollary that humans possess only those features present—at least to some degree, however small—in the animals that preceded us. On that basis, some scientists and others conclude that a capacity for sin and evil cannot be unique to humans. The evidences most frequently cited in favor of this assumption include the "guilty look" and the vicious dog syndrome.

With respect to dogs described as mean or vicious, people tend to forget that canines have been domesticated from the wild. The instincts by which dogs survive in the wild do not simply evaporate when these animals come to live among loving humans. When people forget this fact, they expose themselves and others to potential harm. Multiple cases can be cited, however, in which a dog's injurious behavior represents the animal's defensive reaction to past mistreatment *or* its desire to serve and please its owner. Many dogs have been trained to protect their owner's turf. If such a dog detects an intruder or a threat, the response can range from loud barking to more aggressive behavior, depending on the animal's training. When a guard dog senses a visitor poses no threat to its owner, the owner's family, or the owner's property, typically its behavior turns from intimidating to warm and friendly.

Some pet dogs, however, seem always in attack mode. Such dogs tend to belong to people who seem always in attack mode. To say that these dogs are evil or sinful would assign to them a capacity for abstract thought and discernment that their brain structures simply do not support. Rather, they demonstrate the strength of their desire to please their malicious, perhaps deeply fearful, owners. If their owners reward or take pleasure in vicious behavior, that's what these dogs reflect. In the context of a puppy raised from birth, the old proverb rings true: "You can learn a lot about a man by observing the behavior of his dog."

Another argument for attributing moral discernment to dogs springs from their frequently observed "guilty look." In some canine breeds, forbidden behavior gives rise to a particular facial expression and even body language humans tend to interpret as expressions of genuine guilt. A recent study by Alexandra Horowitz of Barnard

College, New York, put this guilty-look hypothesis to a thorough test.[5] Her experiment included fourteen domestic dog breeds and a variety of trials in which the dogs had opportunity to disobey their owners' command to not eat a particular treat.

Horowitz found that the guilty look had nothing to do with whether the dogs had disobeyed their owners by partaking of the treat. Rather, her experiments showed that admonishments by the dogs' owners caused the dogs' expressions to change. In fact, obedient dogs that had refrained from eating the prohibited treat and yet were scolded by their misinformed owners exhibited the guilty look just as noticeably, or more so, than did the disobedient dogs. Horowitz concluded that the guilty look represents a response to the owner's behavior and not to any comprehension of a misdeed.

In other words, the dogs showed not the slightest awareness of right and wrong in the moral sense. The so-called guilt seen in a dog's facial expression and body language reflects the degree to which it stays attuned to its owner's pleasure or displeasure. If I were to guess why the guilty look appears among domestic dogs and not in other species of soulish animals, I'd give two reasons. First, I'd be hard-pressed to think of any such creature with a greater desire to please humans or capacity to reflect their feelings. Second, dogs seem capable of an unusually wide range of facial expressions and body language.

Do *Nepesh* Read Thoughts?

Belief that humans, as products of evolution, possess more highly refined versions of soulish characteristics (intelligence, emotion, and volition) seen in their primate progenitors meets an additional hurdle when explaining certain uniquely human qualities of mind, qualities that differ in kind and not merely in degree. Scientists have identified one of these qualities as the "theory of mind," and they assumed it existed among multiple soulish species.

Theory of mind refers to the ability of an individual to consider another individual's thoughts and to discern with at least some degree of success what another mind knows, what another mind may be thinking, what emotions that mind may be generating, and what motivations prompted decisions, expressions, or actions. This capacity normally and measurably develops in humans from early childhood onward. Further tests are needed to determine whether this capacity exists to any discernible degree in primates. Meanwhile, researchers have begun to test for the theory of mind among canines. Why? Dog owners through the centuries have told innumerable tales of their pets' mind-reading abilities.

Prompted by this abundance of anecdotal evidence, four Canadian psychologists devised a set of experiments to determine whether this mental capacity among dogs is real or merely perceived.[6] In these tests researchers presented the dogs with two containers: one with food and one without. In experiments 1 and 2, a trustworthy human pointed to the food-filled container and a deceptive human pointed to the empty container. The experiments were then repeated using inanimate cues (black and white pointers) to show the dogs which container held food. The dogs' success (or lack thereof) in determining which humans to trust equaled their success (or lack thereof) in figuring out which cues to trust.

The research team argued that if the dogs truly possessed theory of mind, they would have performed significantly better in ferreting out the trustworthy or deceptive humans than in discerning the trustworthy or deceptive inanimate cues, but they did not. The study's conclusion points to the fact that, as much as we humans would like to believe dogs can read our thoughts or judge the intentions and character of the humans they come in contact with, in reality they are reading our own subtle (or not-so-subtle) cues.

Even without sharing in our unique human capacities for moral judgment and discernment of thoughts and motives, dogs and other soulish creatures please us uniquely and immeasurably. They enrich our lives and teach us what pure loyalty, trust, and devotion look like. In addition to the pleasure they provide, they manifest qualities that serve not only their own survival needs and quality of life but also provide for our human needs, even though we humans arrived on the scene later.

Created to Serve

Of all the passages in the Bible describing animals and their relationship to humans, Job 38–39 provides the most extensive treatment. This ancient book brings attention to the manner in which certain species of soulish animals have been designed and equipped to serve as well as delight humans. Job mentions the role of creatures within each of the three broad categories Genesis 1 identifies as part of God's sixth-day creative activity, prior to the creation of humans and apparently as part of his preparation for humanity's needs upon arrival.

The three categories of sixth-day animals, which are all land mammals, include (1) short-legged mammals, such as rodents and hares; (2) long-legged mammals easily tamed, such as goats, sheep, and cattle; and (3) long-legged mammals not easily tamed, namely the wild mammals. History reveals that all three of these groups played a crucial role in launching and sustaining human civilization. Even now, though the nature of human civilization has changed in dramatic ways since its launch, these three groups still play crucial, albeit markedly different, roles. In other words, these three sets of creatures identified by Moses and described in Job were apparently designed in advance to meet humanity's needs both at the beginning of human civilization and today, at what some researchers consider the peak of human civilization. Research reveals more every day about their unique service to humanity—past, present, and future.

Short-legged Mammals

Rodents and hares, warm-blooded animals with a high ratio of body surface to body mass, can potentially lose body heat to their environment at a much faster rate than do many other animals. What keeps these creatures alive is their ability to grow fur—lots of fur. The colder their environment, the more fur they grow. Rodents and hares exceed all other fur producers by a huge margin.

In contrast, the human body is beautifully designed for hot climates. A tall, slender stature gives humans a high ratio of skin area to body mass. Humans' bipedal mobility diminishes exposure to sunlight. The human body is also endowed with an efficient cooling system: perspiration. As long as we humans can keep ourselves hydrated, we can stay sufficiently cool to function even in Earth's hottest climate zones.

The human body, however, seems poorly designed for cold climates. Although Neanderthals (a nonhuman primate species) managed to thrive in cold regions—helped by their short limbs, barrel-shaped torsos, and enormous nasal cavities—archeological evidence shows that humans were able to quickly displace them. Humans found ways to live in climate zones up to fifteen degrees colder than the coldest temperatures Neanderthals could tolerate. Evidently, early humans' ability to clothe themselves made all the difference.

That's where rodents and hares came in. The warming possibility they offered to humanity was ideal. Whether wild or tame, these creatures reproduced in abundance and could survive on virtually any food source. They covered a wide habitat range, and their fur could be easily obtained. Sewing pelts together into suitable garments for head, body, and feet required only a modest level of technology. The thickness of rodent fur varied with climatic temperature in a manner virtually perfect for human needs. To a significant degree, credit for the launch of global human civilization goes to rodents and hares.

Even with the advance of technology and the introduction of sophisticated clothing sources, the harvesting of rodent and rabbit fur remained a thriving enterprise for centuries. Furrier farms dotted the countryside across Canada and Russia. Only in the last few decades has the introduction of synthetic fabrics replaced humanity's demand for animal fur.

Today, however, rodents serve humanity in a way completely unexpected or unimagined by previous generations. Rodents contribute dramatically to ongoing medical advances. Because rodents' DNA proves remarkably similar to human DNA, these creatures can serve in our stead for the development of many new therapeutic procedures and medical treatments. Given their short generation time, rodents allow researchers to make breakthroughs in months or years that would take decades or centuries if experiments were restricted to humans or apes. In addition to the ethical and economic advantages offered by rodents, the medical advantage cannot be overstated. Researchers can run tests on tens of thousands of rodents under highly controlled conditions (without concerns over their test subjects' cheating) and thus produce much more definitive results—all the while avoiding and alleviating human suffering.

Different rodents serve as proxies for different human maladies. The armadillo, for example, is our stand-in for the study of leprosy. It's the only species other than humans at risk for this disease. Thanks to the availability of armadillos for research, physicians have been able to develop successful treatments for leprosy in humans.

One of the great plagues of our time takes various forms that are collectively labeled *dementia*. Alzheimer's and other types of brain deterioration have become almost epidemic among the elderly. Neuroscientists, however, recently noted with much astonishment that the molecular pathways the human brain uses to form long-term memory are virtually identical to those of rodents' brains.[7] This similarity allows researchers to work with mice, genetically engineering these molecular pathways in an effort to understand and treat memory problems. So far, four teams have discovered that by inducing slight differences at the molecular level, they can achieve remarkable improvements in the ability of mice to learn and remember.[8] These improvements, while detrimental to normal mice and humans,[9] hold great promise for the millions who suffer from debilitating memory loss.

Rodents and hares serve humanity in other ways, too. We've learned about vitamin C supplementation from studying guinea pigs. We're learning more about certain human cancers and cardiovascular disease from studying these same ailments in the various species of rodents where they also occur. The multiple benefits these creatures provide to humanity strongly suggest God designed them specifically for our good. It would be fair to say that because of the rodents and hares God created, we humans enjoy longer life and a higher quality of life than we could without them. In turn, our greater longevity and wealth help accelerate technological advances, allowing us to spread the impact of God's truth and love more efficiently and effectively to the ends of the earth.

Livestock

A second set of creatures mentioned on the sixth creation day also benefits humanity in crucial ways. The Hebrew word for "livestock," *behemah*, refers to (relatively) long-legged herbivores. Compared with carnivorous mammals, these soulish animals would be considered easy to tame. Some, such as goats, literally beg to be tamed. Through all human history these animals have served human needs in countless ways. For example, oxen, goats, cattle, sheep, pigs, horses, donkeys, llamas, yaks, and camels provide us with transportation, farm labor, dairy products, meat, leather, and even musical instruments (horns and flutes made from their horns). These robust creatures graze on a variety of plants, withstand extreme temperatures, and live together in herds typically undisturbed by the presence of other livestock species.

Some of the larger livestock animals in particular—horses, donkeys, llamas, and camels—can speedily move humans and their goods across vast distances and treacherous terrain. Oxen can power machines to grind grain and pump water, as well as to plow fields. Elephants can help do some heavy lifting. All these creatures have proved amazingly adaptable. Anywhere on Earth where organized agriculture is possible, livestock can thrive. These creatures, like rodents and hares, played a significant role in helping early humans launch and sustain global civilization.

There is no other group of creatures we take for granted more than livestock. Among the rest of Earth's life-forms we find no adequate substitute for them. Who can imagine creatures more aptly designed to meet humanity's nutritional needs? Without livestock, organized agriculture might never have gotten a foothold. Without the launch of organized agriculture, global civilization might never have developed, bringing technology along with it. Humanity remains, to this day, largely dependent on these creatures.

Wild Animals

The third group of soulish creatures mentioned on day six of creation includes a colorful array of carnivorous land mammals. "Wild animals," in this context, would even include the various feline and canine species that have since become common household pets. These animals may be much more difficult to tame than livestock and rodents, but they certainly make delightful human companions.

Unlike livestock, which must spend nearly all their waking hours consuming and digesting food, wild animals can ingest their nutritional needs for the day—or longer—in a matter of minutes. This capability, along with intelligence and a capacity for training, including "potty training," means such animals can socialize with us, live closely with us, and form deep attachments to us. Pound for pound, they are more agile, more dexterous, and stronger than their herbivore counterparts, qualities that enable them to provide us with endless entertainment.

Without a doubt, the taming of these wild mammals presents its challenges. Unless raised from infancy, some may take several months or more of consistent effort before they can be trusted around us, and even then that trust has its limits. The upside, however, is that these animals tend to bond tightly and specifically to just one or a few individuals. This loyalty factor along with a strong desire to serve and please their human caregivers means these mammals not only entertain us but also provide some remarkable acts of service to us. Guide dogs for the vision and hearing impaired, police dogs, search-and-rescue dogs, and sympathy cats represent some familiar examples.

More than all other animal species, long-legged, land-dwelling carnivores show us truths about ourselves that we might otherwise overlook. They often mirror our behavior. This mirroring can affirm positive tendencies in us, and it can expose negative tendencies that need correcting. In this respect, these "wild" mammals prove just as vital to humanity's well-being today as at civilization's launch.

Preserve and Protect

Genesis 2 further highlights the importance of these three types of land mammals. Before God created a mate for the first man, he allowed Adam to interact with and name all the birds and land mammals in Eden. Perhaps God wanted Adam to appreciate how each of these species would bring joy to his life. God also may have wanted Adam to understand how crucial these mammals would be for the fulfillment of the task soon to be set before him—the task of managing Earth's resources for the good of all and spreading that goodness around the whole world.

Sadly, the story reminds us what happened—and is happening still—when the first humans decided they could manage on their own. Half of the 21,000 bird species and 8,000 mammal species residing on Earth when humans arrived have been driven to extinction. The very creatures God specially designed to meet humanity's needs and to bring us delight have been wiped out primarily by human exploitation. Consequently, humanity's potential to serve God by caring for each other and the rest of Earth's life and resources has suffered loss. In light of this devastation, caring for the ten soulish creatures named in Job 38 and 39 takes on even greater importance.

10

Top Ten *Nepesh*

"I've read the book of Job more than once, but I've never come up with what y'all talked about today. Why is that?" The question drew several nods and inquisitive looks from the small cluster of Bible class students lingering on the sidewalk in front of a Texas church where I had just spoken. What better opening could a teacher want?

This unplanned session allowed me to explain my belief that everything in the pages of Scripture deserves careful consideration. Nothing can be deemed inconsequential without further study. The Bible is packed like a single suitcase carrying a lifetime's wardrobe—tightly compressed, to say the least. God communicates volumes in remarkably few words. So we can expect to find layers of meaning in many or most passages. That's the perspective I brought to the text of Job. When I arrived at chapters 38 and 39, I asked myself these questions:

- Why does the author mention these ten animals in particular?
- What do these ten animals share in common?
- What connects these animals to the larger context of Job 38 and 39?
- What does God want us to learn about him from his mention of these animals?

Attempts to answer these questions generated the content for my presentation. As part of my sidewalk follow-up talk, I encouraged these avid learners to notice even the tiniest biblical details and ask themselves, "Why is this here?" In the book of Job, as elsewhere in Scripture, that question leads to some *almost* hidden treasures.

Job's Top Ten List

While Genesis 1–2 identifies three major categories of soulish creatures now recognized for their specific benefits to humanity, Job 38–39 singles out ten varieties of *nepesh* for special attention. At first glance, the animals listed appear unrelated, certainly an odd assortment. Some are wild, some are easily domesticated; some are familiar, some most people have never come in contact with; some have four legs, some have only two, and some have wings. To discern what binds them together presents an intriguing challenge.

When Job said to his friends, "Ask the animals, and they will teach you, or the birds in the sky, and they will tell you" (12:7), he could well have been referring to these ten. By taking a closer look at them and at what they have meant to humanity through the ages, we gain a fresh glimpse of God's gracious providence that compels us to bow humbly before him.

The Lion (Job 38:39–40)

Until about 10,000 years ago, the lion was the most widespread of all Earth's large land mammals (besides humans). These big, highly social cats lived in most of Africa, across Eurasia from western Europe to India, and in the Americas from the Yukon to Peru.[1] Cave art depicting lions dates back 32,000 years, and lions appear as symbols of nobility and courage in ancient Sumerian and Babylonian literature. Early Egyptian royals may have been the first to make pets of them. Figurative references to lions, both positive and negative, appear in many parts of the Bible outside the book of Job,[2] and the lion became a metaphor for the Messiah himself, "the Lion of the tribe of Judah" (Rev. 5:5).

The king (and queen) of beasts earned its title and attention by its size, strength, agility, and hunting prowess, not to mention the male's deafening roar. With an ability to prey on even the largest land mammals, lions often are pictured as fearsome killers. Few people today, however, realize the important role they've played in enhancing both the population and vitality of the large herbivore herds on which they prey.[3] Unlike human hunters, lions go after the weak and sickly, not the strongest and healthiest. In doing so they optimize the health and fitness of the larger group and, in turn, benefit the humans who depend upon those herbivores for their well-being (see chapter 9, pp. 146–47).

Lions deserve their royal title in a different respect, as well. If raised by humans from birth, they rank highest among the *nepesh* in their capacity to give and receive affection. Sadly, people have often exploited lions for this very reason. Before laws were passed to prevent the practice, people bought adorable, endearing lion cubs and then abandoned them when size and strength became problems. While I'm in complete sympathy with such laws, I can also be grateful for an amazing opportunity to make firsthand observations of a pet lioness, whose young caregiver, a college student, committed to care for her for life.

The two came to the Caltech campus nearly every day during my time as a researcher there. When the young man attended lectures, the lioness napped near the professors' feet, quickly winning their hearts. Any friend of the student became her friend as well. What a heart-stopping sight to see this majestic creature lolling on the lawn with a half dozen or more preschoolers romping around her and even climbing on her. She seemed to take delight in their touch. The only time she became difficult to manage was at the end of the day. If any playmates and friends remained nearby when the time came to hop into the van, she balked. And she could be as difficult to budge as any mule.

The 1965 movie *Born Free* (based on the book of the same title) gave millions a glimpse of the lion-to-human bond. The film tells the real-life story of Elsa, one of three orphaned lion cubs raised to adulthood by Joy and George Adamson in Kenya. When the two older cubs found homes in European zoos, Elsa stayed at home. Whether Joy ate, worked at her desk, met with community leaders and business associates, or drove her jeep to pick up supplies, Elsa remained at her side. Eventually, however, the Adamsons were forced to make a choice between sending Elsa to a zoo and returning her to the wild. The story's title tells what choice they made. Though heartbroken, Joy persisted in training the reluctant Elsa for survival in the wild, and after several months the lioness left her humans' home in the company of a wild male lion. The Adamsons left for England. The high point of the story comes with the couple's return a year later. Hearts leapt and tears overflowed as they found Elsa, her mate, and three cubs all alive and thriving—and especially as Elsa lavished affection on her not-forgotten friends.

Such close bonding happens with greater rarity between humans and male lions. Like the males of virtually all cat species, lions establish and protect a certain territory. They tend to mark that territory by spraying, even dousing humans in their vicinity. So the story of a lion named Christian drew significant attention when it surfaced several years ago and more recently with its posting on YouTube. Two young Englishmen raised the cub. As he grew, they gained permission to exercise him in a nearby churchyard, hence the name. When Christian outgrew their flat and their food budget, which had swelled to the equivalent of $500 per week, the men contacted the Adamsons for help. When Christian was ready, they returned him to the wild.

A video clip titled "Christian, the Lion, Reunion" documents what happened more than a year later when the men journeyed to Africa hoping to find and check up on their beloved big cat. The dramatic footage (about six minutes long) shows Christian charging toward the two, leaping up to "hug" and "kiss" them, and then escorting them back to his den where he introduces them to his cubs and his female companions, allowing the men to pet one and all. Astonishingly, the wild adult and juvenile lions showed no hesitation to receive human affection.

Lions, among the most feared of all mammalian predators, manifest a profound capacity to form deep and enduring relationships with humans. This paradoxical nature of lions represents an evolutionary enigma. How can it be accounted for, apart from the work of a Creator intent on revealing something of his own nature? C. S. Lewis saw the picture clearly and created a character named Aslan.

The Raven (Job 38:41)

The title character in Edgar Allen Poe's best-known poem joins the lion in Job's special list of creatures. The raven, a courier in the biblical accounts of Noah and Elijah, deserves mention for its first-rate intelligence. Of all the *nepesh*, the raven comes closest to humans in its capacity for problem solving and tool use. This smart bird outperforms chimpanzees and other primates in both types of tasks (see chapter 8, p. 126).

People who have made pets of ravens tell stories of how entertaining they can be. They seem to enjoy mastering puzzles and picking locks—and, as mentioned previously, showing off their skills to humans. Keeping them in a cage seems nearly impossible. But who would want to lock them up for long? Ravens' personalities make them much too engaging for long-term confinement.

The raven's intellect is a strong argument against human descent from preexisting primate species or from a recent common ancestor. No evolutionist would posit that humans descended from the corvidae (category featuring intelligent birds such as jays, crows, and ravens) or that humans and corvidae shared a recent common ancestor. Yet some of the raven's brain structure is nearly identical to that of the large primates. Again, this argues against an evolutionary explanation, since from an evolutionary perspective they are unrelated, possessing no possible recent common ancestor.

The most important service ravens provide to humans has nothing to do with their capacity to engage or entertain, but it significantly impacts the quality of human life from the dawn of civilization to the present day. Ravens take full advantage of our human deficiency in cleaning up after ourselves.

Humans throughout all ages have left messes after their cookouts. Ravens are the one species thoroughly prepared to clean up. Although both crows and ravens are omnivorous, ravens feed predominantly on meat. So whether they get wind of a prehistoric roast over the campfire or a modern-day barbeque, ravens recognize an opportunity in the offing. They gather even as the party begins to observe at close range the disposition of the scraps, fallen crumbs, and partly cleaned bones. Once the humans depart, they move in quickly to clean up, helping to restore the campsite or barbeque scene to its previous condition.

Ravens provide an additional service for humans traveling at high rates of speed. They take care of our road and rail kill, quickly disposing of potential hindrances and hazards left on our transportation arteries. They show no fear of our noisy machines and vehicles, yet they possess the keen intellect, quick reflexes, and strong muscles to avoid becoming road kill themselves. In creating ravens, God anticipated humanity's need for assistance in the sanitation department.

The Goat (Job 39:1–4)

Of all land mammals on Earth today, none seems easier to tame than the goat. Many times on my hiking adventures, wild goats have followed me along the trail until I stopped. Then they took the opportunity to chew on my shirttails or pack straps. When I reached out to pet them, they did not back away. The ease with which goats can be tamed may explain why archeological evidence affirms that goats were the first animals to be domesticated.[4]

Could it be that the Creator planned in advance to assist humanity in rapidly launching organized agriculture? Some mammals can provide more wool or hair than goats, some can provide more milk, more meat, and thicker leather, and some grow larger horns, but goats serve as a one-stop agricultural shop. They provide adequate supplies of all these resources, and what better way to introduce humanity to the full spectrum of animal agricultural enterprises? What's more, goats are easy to feed. They eat almost any kind of shrub, ground cover, or plant waste. Nor are they fussy about climate and terrain. Flat or hilly, mountainous or lush, forested, grassy, or desert—whatever the landscape, they don't mind.

The ease with which goats allowed humans to launch agriculture productivity paved the way for humans to domesticate other mammals and birds for agricultural purposes. Intensive cultivation requires the help of mammals for labor. So we have goats to thank for lifting us out of the hunter-gatherer economy of prehistoric times and setting us on the path toward today's globally dispersed, highly developed civilization.

Though humans no longer depend quite as heavily on goats for sustaining agriculture, goats now fill another vital role for which no one had imagined an economically viable alternative. Goats have become our front-line forest, brush, and grass fire prevention unit. With today's high human population and widely distributed assets, the task of limiting damage, loss, and death from natural and humanly caused fires has grown ever more challenging. The standard technique for limiting such destruction is the firebreak.

Creating firebreaks using bulldozers and brush-clearing ground crews carries a high cost and often yields less-than-desired results. These methods rarely do an adequate job of stripping vegetation, and the rugged, steep terrain presents a danger to both workers and equipment. Big machines simply cannot reach certain areas. For goats, however, no terrain is too rugged or too steep, and goats are supremely thorough in consuming fire fuel. They will consume anything flammable. The only expense for this firebreak crew is the goat herder's salary. Meanwhile, the goat herder saves the cost of feeding his herd.

Dry, fire-prone regions aren't the only areas served strategically by goats. Damp regions of the American South, as well as Hawaii, Oregon, Washington, and British Columbia have been plagued by the spread of a non-indigenous Himalayan blackberry. This rampant, weedy vine forms impenetrable, prickly thickets. Once it takes hold, it can choke out all other plants in its vicinity and even block animals' access to food and water. Until recently this thorny pest was judged impossible to eradicate. Where bulldozers and other attempted solutions failed, however, goats have succeeded. Just after berry season, trained goats sent into the infested area will strip the vines of every last leaf. As the vines regrow leaves, the goats immediately eat them. After several cycles of regrowth and consumption, the vines lose their ability to produce new leaves. They die and the goats can be relocated. Whatever a farmer plants to replace the blackberries will thrive on the decayed, well-fertilized remains of the vines.

Goats may one day be able to help restore other lands invaded by foreign plant species. Again we see how this creature provides strategic assistance to humanity both in the emergence of civilization and in the ongoing maintenance of global resources. When we arrived on the scene, goats were here waiting to serve us.

The Deer (Job 39:1–4)

As far as goats lean toward the serving side of the top-ten spectrum, deer lean toward the pleasing side. Even in the aesthetic sense, they bring delight to humans. Although deer, like goats, can be domesticated, deer farms remain a rarity. Running speed makes these creatures elusive, difficult to herd and corral, and leaping ability makes fencing them impractical. More significantly, domesticated deer cannot compete economically with sheep, cows, goats, and pigs in production of milk, meat, and leather. Their value to humans lies elsewhere.

Deer possess an advantage over some other long-legged herbivores in their capacity to flourish in and around virtually any human habitation. They thrive in completely wild environments and yet have no fundamental need of a wild habitat. They prosper in the wild but also in proximity to cultivated fields, meadows, towns, and cities. This adaptability means humans need not travel far to find deer.

Although wild and elusive by nature and imposing in size, deer pose no physical threat to humans, not even to children. The flavor of their meat along with all their other features makes deer the ideal game animal. Today, the survival and economic imperative to hunt has all but disappeared from the earth. Nevertheless, game hunting remains popular. The hunt's sporting nature—the various skills it demands and challenges it poses—provides a unique pleasure for many people. To this day avid hunters rank deer as their favorite animal to hunt.

The Donkey (Job 39:5–8)

Most mammals, once tamed and domesticated, have difficulty transitioning to life in the wild, and rarely can one revert back after that transition is complete. Elsa the lioness and Christian the lion both required months of arduous training to make the change from domestic life to living on their own without human support. When that switch took place, it was permanent, despite these animals' sustained affection for the humans who raised them.

The donkey, another creature on Job's top-ten list, stands out as a striking exception to this rule. For a donkey, the transition from domestication to wild living and back again appears seamless. It can be made repeatedly. This capacity to transition proves beneficial to both the donkey and its owner, given the donkey's self-protective instincts.

Donkeys manifest a high level of alertness to danger. This awareness of potential perils helps keep both the donkeys and their owners safe, in more ways than one. If a ridden donkey approaches a hazard of any kind, it comes to a halt and refuses to budge, protecting both itself and its rider from harm. A biblical example of such behavior appears in Numbers 22, the story of Balaam, whose donkey tried to prevent him from a (spiritually) dangerous visit to Balak (Num. 22:21–34). If a donkey's owner and his neighbors come under attack, the donkey flees to safety, where it stays till the danger passes and the owner comes looking.

One need not worry about the well-being of a donkey that has lost contact with its owner. This creature can immediately shift to fending for itself, even in severe conditions. A donkey can live on its own for several weeks, months, or longer and survive no worse for wear. Then, after living as a feral creature, it can easily reunite with its original owner or even with a new one. In fact, the donkey seems more than willing to return to its former domestic state. It can make this transition back and forth several times in its life, if necessary.

Donkeys have been valuable to humans throughout history as providers of both work and transportation. Their strength and sturdiness enables them to pack heavy loads, propel wagons, grind grain, pull plows, tug water lifters, and drag timbers. Their sure-footedness makes them excellent for riding or carrying heavy gear through treacherous terrain. Perhaps more than any other creature, donkeys have facilitated the spread of humanity and civilization around the world.

The Wild Ox (Job 39:9–12)

As a provider of work, no creature has been more vital to humanity than the various breeds of bovine mammals, or cattle, the domesticated progeny of the wild ox included in Job's list. In fact, the passage itself essentially challenges humanity to tame this creature and discover the benefits of its incredible strength. Wherever people live, cattle now live, too.

The effort to domesticate oxen has proven worthwhile. Oxen serve as humanity's premier work animal, especially for farming. When tamed from birth, an ox will submit to a yoke and plow and till a farmer's field. It will pull a heavily loaded wagon. It can be harnessed to a machine to grind grain or lift water. Unlike other domesticated animals, oxen seem *eager* to perform heavy labor for their owners. The very structure of an ox suggests it was specially designed to perform heavy tasks. Even today, except in the most highly industrialized and technologically wealthy nations, oxen still serve as the primary source of heavy agricultural labor.

Oxen are big enough and strong enough that only the largest predators—such as grizzlies, lions, tigers, and crocodiles—pose a threat, and then only if a weakened or juvenile animal gets separated from the herd. So farmers and ranchers need not worry as much about protecting their cattle as they do about protecting sheep, goats, and pigs, for example. In that respect, cattle seem relatively easy to maintain. Dairy cows require a certain amount of care, but they provide humanity more milk, cheese, and butter than all other animals combined. A single champion Holstein cow can deliver more than eighty quarts of milk per day. Cattle hold status as the champion meat producer among all domesticated animals and serve as our primary leather source as well.

Several millennia ago humans began to breed cattle in such large numbers that cattle became, in terms of sheer biomass, Earth's dominant domesticated animal. In fact, the biomass of domesticated cows has long outweighed that of all other domesticated animals combined. Meanwhile, unknown to the humans responsible, this prolific breeding has extended the duration of global civilization.

The discovery that cows have helped save modern civilization came from ice core studies. As rings tell a tree's story—not just its age but also conditions affecting its growth—so, too, layers in Earth's oldest and thickest ice packs reveal the history of the planet's atmospheric conditions. Each layer traps some air bubbles, and scientists can now analyze these bubbles because they have access to cylindrical "cores" extracted from ancient ice fields. One such core is nearly two miles (three kilometers) long and offers a detailed record of the past million years of Earth's climate history.

This deep drilling into the ice of Antarctica and Greenland has yielded some surprises.[5] The primary motivation for studying ice cores was to determine when the next ice age should begin. As it turns out, we're overdue. According to the pattern observed in the core—a pattern established by three of Earth's astronomical cycles—the next ice age should have begun several thousand years ago.[6] So researchers have turned their attention to discovering what kept, and still keeps, the cooling at bay.

Deforestation of Eurasia to make way for intensive crop cultivation and pastureland about 6,000 to 8,000 years ago contributed to raising levels of planet-warming atmospheric carbon dioxide from 245 parts per million to 285 parts per million. Fewer trees meant fewer carbon dioxide "sponges." Then, a few thousand years later, extensive irrigation for rice farming and greatly increased cattle breeding—for greater quantities of milk and meat per animal—raised planet-warming atmospheric methane (a much more potent greenhouse gas than carbon dioxide) from 450 parts per billion to 700 parts per billion.[7] The cow's digestive tract, designed to metabolize cellulose in grasses, produces prodigious quantities of methane gas.

This ice core research points to a series of amazing "coincidences" that worked, apart from human awareness, to benefit humanity's survival and sustain civilization's advance. Though humanity came on the scene 50,000 to 90,000 years ago,[8] massive deforestation did not begin until about 10,000 years ago—about 5,000 years prior to when the cooling cycle would normally have begun. Then, for still undetermined reasons, humans switched from primary dependence on easy-to-domesticate goats and sheep to dependence on the more difficult-to-domesticate oxen, further sustaining the warming trend. Then, humans bred cows for more efficient milk production and increased the release of methane gas in the process. Shortly thereafter, humans launched a difficult farming enterprise, extensive irrigation for rice production. All these changes occurred with just the right timing and amplitude to stave off Earth's next ice age. How is that possible? I'm inclined to conclude that divine providence, rather than dumb luck, leans to humanity's side—past, present, and future.

The Ostrich (Job 39:13–18)

Job 39 says of the female ostrich, "God did not endow her with wisdom or give her a share of good sense" (v. 17). Science now tells us that of all the bird species, the ostrich has the smallest brain relative to body weight. In fact, the ostrich's brain is no bigger than one of its eyes. Yet good reasons can be found for this creature's inclusion in Job's top-ten list.

The ostrich's small head offers some advantages. Its light weight means the head can be mounted atop an exceptionally long neck. This long neck lifts the ostrich's keen eyes high enough above the ground (eight feet) to spot danger from afar, and thus many species of mammals rely on ostriches to act as sentinels. The ostrich's small head and slender neck also contribute to the bird's enormous leg-to-body-mass ratio. This ratio permits ostriches to outsprint antelopes going 40 mph and to run for hours at sustained speeds of 32 mph.

The Job passage also notes that ostriches, unlike other birds, run away from their eggs. This behavior does not mean, however, that ostriches lack care for their young. On the contrary, once the eggs hatch, parent ostriches will defend their brood even against a lion. A single well-aimed kick from an ostrich can actually kill a lion. So what does such behavior mean?

Ostriches live in savannas and deserts. They cannot fly. They have no choice but to lay their eggs out in the open. When predators pose no noticeable threat, the female ostrich (colored light brown) will sit on the eggs during the dawn and dusk hours while the male ostrich (usually black) sits on the eggs at night. However, when the bright sun foils the ostriches' camouflage or when packs of hyenas and jackals come around, the ostriches' presence would invite danger to themselves and their eggs. In this case, their strategy to run or to stay far away from the eggs makes sense. It helps keep the predators away. As for the smaller predators, the parent ostriches need not worry. The shells of their eggs are so strong that a 200-pound man could stand on one without breaking it.

The strength and size of ostrich eggshells served early humans in a special way. In searching for prey, early hunters found themselves at a competitive disadvantage. Compared with other large mammals, they lacked speed and strength, and their senses of sight, hearing, and especially smell proved significantly inferior. Their one physical advantage—the ability to stay cool in the heat—required almost continual access to water. That's what ostrich eggshells provided.

Hunters would collect eggs from unguarded nests, use a tool to make a small hole in the top of the egg, and extract the albumin and yolk. Once emptied, each ostrich egg (a significant food supply in itself) could store about a quart (or liter) of water in a nearly unbreakable container. When these water supplies were placed in strategic locations throughout their hunting grounds, the hunters gained the needed advantage. By hunting during the hottest part of the day and keeping themselves hydrated, they could run their prey to heat exhaustion while avoiding attack from large predators. Despite being slower and weaker than their prey, humans could hunt successfully, thanks to their wits and the availability of ostrich eggs. Ostrich feathers helped also. They served as fans to prevent heat stroke and to cool fevered brows.

Today, ostriches again offer help for human survival. As mentioned in chapter 4, their meat offers excellent nutritional quality, and its low levels of saturated fat and cholesterol make it ideal for those who suffer from diabetes or cardiovascular disease. A transition from beef to ostrich meat may even help slow the alarming increase in these and related ailments, not to mention the average global temperature. As an additional benefit, ostrich could become the least expensive of all meats and thus more widely available to the poor. Agriculture experts calculate that if ostriches are bred to appropriate levels, their meat could be sold for half the price of turkey meat, the current low-cost champion.

The Horse (Job 39:19–25)

The majestic equine species, their flowing manes and tails streaking across continents for tens of thousands of years, have lived in close companionship with humans since about 4,000 BC, when their domestication began. The variety of ways people have related to horses since taming the first wild ones indicates the creatures' high ranking in both service and pleasure among the top ten animals on Job's list. To this day horses assist humans significantly in both work and play.

Horses seem ideally structured for personal transportation. Unlike the donkey, a horse keeps even the tallest human rider from dragging their feet on the ground or low-lying brush. Unlike the camel, the horse holds the rider low enough that a fall is less likely to result in serious injury. Even more so than the donkey or the camel, the horse provides a stable mount for the human rider. Strong enough to carry a person (plus personal gear) long distances, fast and maneuverable enough for both sport and necessary escape, and loyal enough to face deadly foes when asked, the horse deserves the esteem it has been granted through the ages.

Although grazing herbivores, horses need not spend all their waking hours eating and digesting. With the right kind of food supplied by their owners, horses can take care of their nutritional needs during an hour in the morning and an hour in the evening. The remainder of the day they can devote to other activities.

Like humans, horses perspire. So with adequate water they can work with or carry humans in the heat of the day. Some will even tolerate wearing clothes for warmth. With appropriate covering, horses can stay outdoors in all but the coldest of arctic conditions. Almost anywhere humans wish to go, horses can and will go, too.

Job 39 highlights two of the horse's most notable features—courage and loyalty (vv. 20–25). A horse will bond to its human companion so strongly as to sacrifice its health and even its life for that person. Horses willingly carry their riders headlong into danger, if asked. Unlike any other nonhuman animal, the horse seems to relish the risky ride into battle (39:21–25). Horses charge into the fray with swords flashing and clashing or with shells exploding all around them. They show no fear in conveying police officers into a rioting crowd.

This deep connection to humans also manifests itself in a totally different way. Not only do horses assist in search and rescue work, but these gentle giants also serve as therapy animals. They bring joy and confidence to those, both young and old, who must endure confinement to a wheelchair. Whether being ridden or just petted, horses bring calm and comfort to people suffering mentally and emotionally. They also serve us as the source of certain medications.

The horse's unique characteristics potently challenge evolutionary theory. Horses and donkeys are so similar biologically they can, if forced, mate with each other. So evolutionists naturally propose the two animals descended from a common ancestor. Yet in their soulish attributes, horses and donkeys seem direct opposites. Donkeys do fine as loners while horses live in tightly bonded social groups. Donkeys run from trouble while horses show readiness to charge into battle with their riders—a response that seems to defy the survival-of-the-fittest principle.

The Bible contrasts the two creatures dramatically in accounts of their service to Jesus Christ. As Jesus Christ entered Jerusalem to offer himself as an atoning sacrifice for humanity's sin, he rode a donkey—a symbol of peace (Matt. 21:1–11). When Christ returns to Earth to bring an end to sin's expression once and for all, he will come, by the apostle John's prophetic account, riding a horse—a symbol of war (Rev. 19:11–21).

The diverse characteristics that make horses ideal for serving and pleasing humanity existed in horses *before* humans existed. These traits cannot be considered mere adaptations to cohabitation with humanity. They seem more likely the result of exquisite design.

The Hawk and the Eagle (Job 39:26–30)

The list of Job's special *nepesh* ends, as it begins, with the inclusion of intelligent, skillful predators, in this case two birds of prey. Both the hawk and the eagle rank high in avian IQ, as measured by their innovation in feeding habits. Both also share a capacity to form strong bonds with humans and a willingness to serve humans' needs. Hawks and eagles have been known to hunt game and then, rather than eat what they've caught, offer it to their human friends. This characteristic of the hawk and eagle held survival importance for early humans because these raptors could find game in regions where food is extremely scarce. At certain times and places, humans would likely have starved to death without the assistance of hawks and eagles.

These creatures have the keenest senses for detecting prey. In addition to excellent hearing, they possess the best eyesight of any member of the animal kingdom. Their visual acuity (ability to resolve detail) exceeds that of humans by eight times. They can spot an animal the size of a small rabbit from two miles away. This acuity comes from an indented fovea (portion of the retina), which magnifies the central portion of their visual field, and is further enhanced by color detection capability. Whereas humans detect three basic colors and all their blends, hawks and eagles detect five. This exceptional color sensitivity allows them to sight even the best-camouflaged prey.

Hawks differ from eagles, of course, in size and flight expertise. Hawks' shorter wings and longer tails enable these birds to twist and turn rapidly in flight. This aerodynamic feature equips them to chase prey at high speed through forests. Eagles' broader wings and shorter, wider tails allow these birds to glide almost effortlessly on rising air currents. This sustained soaring ability allows some eagles to forage for prey over an area as large as one hundred square miles in a given day. These characteristics mean hawks serve ideally as falconry birds in forested terrain or where game is plentiful, and eagles serve ideally where game is scarce and the terrain is open. Both birds have the capacity to obtain significantly more food in a day than their sustenance requires.

Job 39:30 points to one more service hawks and eagles provide for humanity, a service somewhat related to that performed by ravens. As carrion consumers, these two creatures assist in the disposal of decaying flesh in the aftermath of natural disasters, including the disaster of human warfare.

Historical Support

In terms of their contribution to launching and sustaining human civilization and providing uniquely rewarding relationships, the ten creatures referenced in Job 38–39 constitute a "hall of fame." To imagine what our life today would be like without them seems all but impossible. Some slivers of insight, however, come from the history of life on three continents.

As humans migrated to North and South America and Australia, some undecipherable blend of their activities and natural phenomena resulted in the extinction of three-fourths (or more) of the large-bodied bird and mammal species there, including some of the ones on Job's list. At the same time these animals flourished across Africa, Europe, and Asia. Lacking horses, donkeys, and cows, in particular, some of the earliest peoples of these western continents and Australia did manage to survive for thousands of years. However, they never developed the civilization level that characterizes parts of the world where these animals abounded. While other variables certainly apply, this contrast cannot be overlooked.

More than any other book of the Bible, Job illuminates the value of the soulish creatures to humanity's physical and emotional well-being. But their value extends further still. Our interactions with these animals provide far-reaching spiritual lessons as well, lessons deserving of ongoing, in-depth exploration.

11

Lessons from the Animals

People often find it hard to believe that living as close to Los Angeles as I do—less than an hour (or three, depending on traffic) from downtown—I get to enjoy seeing wildlife nearly every day. Because my home is nestled against the San Gabriel Mountains, wild creatures—skunks, opossums, raccoons, hawks, and owls—sometimes show up in my yard. And many more—deer, coyotes, bears, and bobcats—I see on the trails where I run.

I wish I had more contact with animals. As you may have noticed, people who live in close association with animals, domesticated or wild, tend to develop a keen awareness of how to relate to them and how to learn from them. That goes for farmers, ranchers, herdsmen, veterinarians, trainers, villagers, and rural folks. When Job says, "Ask the animals and they will teach you," these people don't scratch their heads and wonder *How?*

Animal Communication

Nonhuman animals speak without words. They teach us by allowing us to know them and interact with them. They teach by example and illustration, subtly at times, but never with masks. In one sense, Job and his friends held an advantage over many of us who now read their story. They lived closer to the *nepesh*. They depended on the *nepesh* for their daily sustenance. They interacted with both tame and wild *nepesh*, and not with just a few species but a large and diverse mélange. Today, most of the world's population lives some distance, whether geographically or otherwise, from soulish animals. Widespread urbanization has created concrete jungles where most humans' contact with *nepesh* creatures is limited to highly bred domesticated dogs and cats (though some have exotic pets) and a few wild animals on display in regional zoos or preserves. To Job and his peers, God's handiwork and divine nature seemed voluminously and ubiquitously evident. However, most humans today live too far from nature to notice the evidence, to "ask the animals" or be taught by them.

In my work as a Christian astronomer and public advocate for fact-based faith, I have met many nontheists, anti-theists, and agnostics over the past thirty years. Though I cannot speak for all of them, I can say most have lived in or near urban environments. Thus far, not one has either farmed or worked primarily in the wilds of nature for a living. A few have been biologists doing highly specialized field research, but only after becoming well established in academia, where naturalism holds sway.

Job and his friends would likely have considered the idea that humans evolved from animals laughably absurd. Their familiarity with the soulish animals allowed them to appreciate the unique and amazing abilities these creatures display but also to discern the fundamental distinctions between *nepesh* and humans. Elihu worshiped a Maker "who gives songs in the night, who teaches us more than he teaches the beasts of the earth and makes us wiser than the birds in the sky" (Job 35:10–11).

Teaching Us about God

All forms of life, like glorious works of art, provide insights into the heart of the Artist who created them. Scenes of nature's grandeur viewed through virtually any lens—human eye, camera, microscope, and telescope—fill us with wonder. However, the response that comes from observing and handling *nepesh* claims a category all its own, an intensely personal one. Beauty and intricacies of design may be resplendent in flowers and stars, but only *nepesh* reveal the infinite variety and mystery of behaviors made possible by soulish, relational capacities.

We can learn from these creatures in two ways: by observing them in their natural habitats and relationships, and by interacting with them directly. Even the most superficial observation of animals in the wild reveals some insight into God's character and values. Each soulish species in its own unique way nurtures its young and trains them for independent adult life, whether this process takes a few weeks, as in the case of shrews, or many years, as with elephants and whales. Each is endowed with a specific advantage over other species in acquiring its nutritional and other survival needs. The cheetah runs faster over short distances; the lemur climbs with ease to reach seeds and nuts; the giraffe's long neck and tongue allow it to pluck leaves from thorny branches nearly twenty feet off the ground; and the owl's night vision enables it to hunt under cover of darkness. Each has its own reproductive cycles and rituals, and those that live in herds or social groups possess innate means of establishing order and protecting the entire community.

Each species also possesses some specific defense mechanism(s) to protect itself from natural predators. Whether the variety of camouflage patterns, from spots to stripes and from subtle colors to bold, or the diversity of shapes and sizes, from tiny, flexible frames to massive, sturdy ones—the list of variations seems almost endless, and each seems fixed at optimal levels to ensure a species' adaptability and longevity apart from human interference.

When humans begin to interact with these creatures, even more wonders come to light. Almost immediately we realize how such animals respond to reward. The more we learn about the rewards they value and enjoy, the closer our relationships with them can grow. From Scripture we learn that God expects us to see him as our rewarder. The writer of Hebrews said our faith is built on the belief that God exists *and* "that he rewards those who earnestly seek him" (11:6). As we look to the animals, we see evidence to support both these beliefs.

The ten *nepesh* described in chapter 10 represent just a sampling of the countless ways God expresses his care for humanity through the soulish animals. His love seems apparent both in the degree to which these creatures are willing and able to serve us and bring us exquisite pleasure, and also in the variety of ways they do so. The *nepesh* testify of God's extravagant generosity to us.

Because they have no capacity for sin, soulish animals can illustrate a purity of devotion we humans long for—both to receive and to give. Tamed animals show a level of trust and loyalty that makes us want to deserve their faith. When humans invest in the challenges of building such trusting, loyal relationships, God reveals a glimpse of his perfect patience, persistence, and wisdom in building a relationship with each of us. A person who begins to comprehend the power and love of God revealed in the soulish creatures has already taken the first crucial step toward accepting God's offer of relationship. The *nepesh* show us that whatever "wildness" in us separates us from God, God is powerful enough, patient enough, wise enough, and caring enough to overcome it.

Teaching Us about Ourselves

Human "wildness" shows up in our innate tendency to go our own way, doing what we want or what we deem best rather than what God shows us to be right and good. Soulish animals can help us recognize the limits of our "taming" ability, limits that should engender a measure of humility. Perhaps we humans are not so great and powerful as we often believe ourselves to be.

God reminded Job and his friends that no human can tame either pride or speech. God alone has the power to tame them. Only God can "look at all who are proud and humble them" (Job 40:12). Speaking through James in the New Testament, God said, "No human being can tame the tongue. It is a restless evil, full of deadly poison" (James 3:8).

When we humans attempt to humble others, we tend to do harm in the process. We humiliate in ways that either tear down and destroy a person or propel a person in self-defense toward greater expressions of pride or self-exaltation. Only God has the capacity to cause the precise internal and external circumstances that will bring a person to appropriate humility. Only God possesses the love and wisdom necessary to deal with human pride in a consistently constructive manner.

The same problem crops up in our efforts to say the right thing. Job's book makes that point with abundant clarity. If Eliphaz, Zophar, and Bildad came to Job for the right reason, to offer comfort and support, their words accomplished the opposite effect. They accused Job of secret sin and wickedness. They exalted their own virtue and wisdom over his. They deepened and prolonged Job's suffering.

Where a lack of control does obvious damage, overcontrol harms people more subtly. By clamping down on our own or others' words, we may fail to express or to hear what needs to be communicated. Feelings that need to be expressed turn inward, and problems requiring attention get ignored. The only person ever to speak with perfect timing and words was Jesus of Nazareth. He spoke hard words and tender words, whatever the relationship and circumstances called for. He spoke directly as needed and in stories as needed, perfectly attuned to his hearers' hearts and utterly without guile. No orator the world has ever seen can compare.

Sadly, we humans have difficulty accepting our powerlessness and utter dependency on God in these areas. Meanwhile, even the proudest animals will trust and depend upon us once we have proven ourselves trustworthy. Beyond showing us how we've run amok, *nepesh* also offer us valuable lessons in how to live, lessons about serving and delighting each other and thus serving and delighting the One who cares for us and created us in his image.

Teaching Us How to Live Together

Developing a rewarding relationship with a soulish animal, one in which the creature comes to us rather than cowers or flees, requires sensitivity to that animal's needs and consistent effort to meet those needs. In other words, it requires building trust. The same element plays a crucial role in successful relationships among humans. And so we do not miss this point, God provides a striking illustration among birds.

In a recent study of 267 bird species, four British zoologists discovered a strong correlation between trust, as exhibited in monogamous relationships, and socially beneficial cooperation.[1] Although the majority of bird species are thought to be monogamous, mating behavior as well as levels of collaboration differed greatly among the studied species, from one extreme to the other. However, a significant pattern emerged. The higher the degree of mating fidelity within a species, the greater the efficiency and complexity of cooperative behavior. Conversely, the higher the level of mating promiscuity, the lower the collaboration level.

The zoologists concluded that division of labor demands a high degree of trust among the community's individuals, and mating behavior helps establish that trust. The team made one further observation that deserves mention. The species with higher levels of fidelity and collaboration also displayed higher survival rates and greater quality of life for individuals within the group.

If we look to the birds for instruction, as Job says, we find that God's plan for marriage represents more than some arbitrary moral rule or convention. Monogamy contributes to the productive and peaceable division of labor that makes a high-technology global civilization function at its best. Behind each of God's moral laws we find practical, beneficial reasons for obeying.

Birds and mammals provide a host of life lessons, by demonstration, to those who take the time to study. The great horned owl, for example, sacrifices its comfort and ease to ensure that when its hatchlings emerge, it will be able to supply them with adequate food to survive. Canada geese show care for the weak and injured. If one is hurt, another, usually its partner, will protect it from predatory attacks and provide nourishment until healing is sufficient to continue their journey. The river otter provides remarkable lessons for parents and teachers alike. Because young otters initially fear water, the parent makes a game of scampering through the woods with the little ones on its back. Once the offspring get used to this game, the adult begins to slip briefly into the water. After the little otters grow familiar with the water rides, the adult occasionally submerges and lets its young briefly experience floating. In this step-by-step, fun-filled way, the young otters learn to swim.

Teaching Us the Way Back to God

Of the many lessons humanity can learn from soulish creatures, two stand out above the rest. First, we see that sin gets in the way of relationship success. Just as sin diminishes our capacity to fully benefit from our relationships with the *nepesh*, that same sin damages our ability to relate to God.

Second, in their example of relating to us, we see in the *nepesh* our own capacity for something more, something higher, something beyond our own limits. That "something" is not a thing at all, but a Being, in some way like ourselves but perfectly good. As much as *nepesh* appear designed and motivated to respond to us humans and bond with us, likewise we humans appear designed and motivated to respond to God. In our pride, however, we handle that motivation in strange ways. We may attempt to tame ourselves through a set of disciplines or rituals to make us worthy of God's care. Or, having seen or experienced examples of that empty effort, we may decide living by our own wits brings more momentary excitement and pleasure than living to serve and please God ever could—at least not *now*.

Teaching Us Humility

If we allow them, the *nepesh* can help us recognize the folly of attempting to make our own way into God's good graces or of finding a temporary substitute for relationship with him. Soulish animals shine a spotlight on humanity's capacity for both greatness and wretchedness, a most humbling view if we fully take it in.

Whatever potential for glory and magnificence we possess clearly came not from ourselves or by inheritance from our parents or from some earlier life-form. According to the laws of the universe, an "effect" cannot be greater than its "cause." Whatever potential we own that exceeds that of our splendid animal companions on this earth must be attributed to our Creator (and theirs). As Elihu says, "The Spirit of God has made me; the breath of the Almighty gives me life" (33:4).

Despite our best efforts (and not even counting our worst), the harm we humans have caused each other and all Earth's life-forms reveals the degree to which we have ignored our Creator and lived autonomously. What clearer illustration could we want of our need for his loving authority beside and inside each of us? For those individuals who need more humbling, God provided a couple of uniquely fearsome *nepesh* to tackle that task.

12

Answers to Dinosaur Questions

On a balmy evening near San Diego, the church sanctuary overflowed with adults and kids, mostly junior high age and up, to hear my talk called "Science and the Bible: How the Latest Scientific Discoveries Affirm Scripture's Reliability." As I wrapped up my message, I was delighted to see long lines forming behind two microphones placed in the aisles to accommodate the audience's questions. (My friends tease me about accepting speaking engagements for the sole purpose of getting to the program's Q&A portion.)

At the microphone to my right, a woman introduced herself as a biology teacher and posed the evening's first question. "Why," she asked, "did you fail to mention the dinosaurs described in Job 40–41 and all the new evidence showing that dinosaurs and people lived together before the time of the flood?" The gauntlet floating not so gently toward me raised a few eyebrows and definitely some tension. However, having read about this "evidence" and having studied Job 40–41, I was glad for the opportunity to take up the issue.

The identity of the "behemoth" and "leviathan" described in Job 40 and 41 has become a matter of debate among Christians only in the last few hundred years. Prior to the nineteenth century this topic received scant attention. To consider *why* that's so seemed a good starting point. My answer began with that question.

Dinosaurs in Job?

The specific passage that has convinced some Christians, including the biology teacher, that dinosaurs and humans cohabited is Job 40:15–41:34. The two creatures described there seem far too terrifying, they say, to equate with any kind of animal that still roams the landscape today. Perhaps seeing dinosaurs portrayed in the *Jurassic Park* movies solidified their belief that only dinosaurs could have engendered the degree of terror aroused by the behemoth in Job 40 and the leviathan in Job 41. What animal alive today could possibly fit a literal reading of Job's descriptions? What animal could be anywhere as monstrous and fearsome?

One key problem with the dinosaur interpretation lies in timing. It implies dinosaurs lived long after well-established dates of their extinctions. It also overlooks that knowledge of dinosaurs is relatively recent. Not until 1819 had any fossil bones been found and identified as belonging to giant lizard-like creatures.[1] Even for specialists, knowledge of dinosaurs can be traced back only a couple of centuries. So for this passage to convey its intended impact to Job's contemporaries—and to many centuries of hearers and readers of his story between then and the early 1800s—it most likely refers to creatures these people would have recognized.

To untangle questions over interpretation of a Bible passage, the reader must establish the context and point of view. Job 40–41 records the second portion of God's response to the dialogue between Job and his friends. In the first portion, recorded in Job 38, God challenges the men to consider his transcendent power demonstrated in his creation of the heavens and the earth and in his preparations to create advanced life. He gives what amounts to a poetic preview of the first five creation days summarized in Genesis 1. From the last few verses of chapter 38 and onward into chapter 39, God turns his hearers' attention to the transcendent power, wisdom, and care displayed in his creation of the *nepesh*, particularly in the species he designed to take part in sustaining and enriching human life and civilization.

Dinosaurs would have no place within this context. Nothing researchers have discovered about them suggests they possessed characteristics uniquely associated with *nepesh*. When asked where they fit in the Genesis 1 or Job 38 creation accounts, I suggest they fit best in the context of day five life-forms. As large as they were, they deserve no special mention because dinosaurs vanished from Earth, according to abundant physical evidence, long before most of the *nepesh* species arrived and even longer before humans. Given that Genesis and Job focus on key miracles God performed to prepare a home for humanity, dinosaurs do not make the cut. They do not rank high enough in the list of most important creation miracles.

Job 38–39 emphasizes the value God places on all life, and on human life above all other. God singles out ten creatures specially designed for humanity's benefit and reminds Job and his friends to learn from them—lessons about God's greatness, about human greatness, and about the source of human greatness. The use of rhetorical questions throughout this communication indicates the intent to persuade, to make a point with emotional impact, and to open up the hearers' minds to something they have yet to grasp. This pattern continues into Job 40–41, where God's voice brings attention to two more creatures for special consideration.

Eliphaz had earlier exhorted Job (5:17–23), saying that if Job would submit to God's correction and discipline, "the wild animals would be at peace" with him. He was right to point out that sin interferes with harmony between humans and animals, but he missed the point that not all *nepesh* creatures made for humanity's benefit prove equally receptive to taming (see chapter 9, pp. 145–47). Here in Job 40–41, the behemoth and leviathan take center stage to illustrate just how extremely difficult some can be. By comparison, however, humbling or taming a human takes even greater strength and skill, supernatural power and wisdom.

The words "illustrate" and "comparison" lead directly to the question of literary genre, another important facet of the interpretive process. The book of Job exemplifies the structure of an epic poem, a form characterized by figurative language and colorful imagery. These poetic conventions serve its purposes: impact and memorability.

To interpret Job's metaphors and similes woodenly would be inappropriate. The question of genre, then, brings us back to considering

❋ what animals alive today could possibly fit the poetic depictions of Job 40–41, what animals could be as fearsome as the passage suggests. Given the detail provided and in light of the context, reasonably accurate identifications emerge.

What Is the Behemoth?

The behemoth has a tail that "sways like a cedar" (40:17), and "its bones are tubes of bronze, its limbs like rods of iron" (40:18). What's more, "it ranks first among the works of God" (40:19). This reference to a tree and to ranking first initially sets the modern reader's imagination moving in the dinosaur's direction. The only land animal ever to possess a tail the size of the cedar is a dinosaur, and the dinosaur definitely ranks tops among land animals in terms of size. Yet a closer look at the metaphoric language and the mysterious reference to ranking show other possibilities, especially for those who have no picture of a dinosaur already stored in their mental photo gallery.

In reality no creature, living or extinct, fits the literal picture painted by English translations of the Hebrew text. No animal has ever possessed bones of bronze or limbs of iron. But bronze and iron certainly convey hardness and strength. Such imagery says more about the impression this creature makes upon the hapless human who may experience a close encounter with it. From a human vantage point, the behemoth may as well have brass bones and iron limbs for all the protection any common defensive (or offensive) weapon of Job's era would provide against it.

Multiple clues in the passage describing the behemoth (40:21–23) indicate it spends time primarily in marsh, stream, and river surrounded by reeds and lotus plants. Its danger to humans lies in its ability to remain hidden in this watery environment. Apparently the behemoth can stay so well concealed that by the time a boat or swimmer discovers its presence, disaster unavoidably awaits. However, this terrifying creature seems remarkably sedentary, not an aggressive stalker of prey.

In fact, Job 40:15 says, "Look at Behemoth, . . . which feeds on grass like an ox." A few verses later we read that "the hills bring it their produce, and all the wild animals play nearby" (40:20). If the behemoth were a raging, meat-eating predator, these wild animals would most likely play somewhere far away. The mention of grass and produce confirms the impression that this creature feeds on plants, not on flesh.

Putting these details together, we can conclude that the behemoth is a threat to humans, not because it considers humans as prey, but because this creature is highly territorial and enormously strong. As Job 40:23 asserts, regardless of the extent to which the river rages, it is not alarmed: "it is secure, though the Jordan should surge against its mouth." The mention of the Jordan River provides further interpretive assistance. To date no remains of herbivorous dinosaurs have been found in the Jordan River valley.

One creature seems to fit best with this cluster of details—an herbivore (in the *nepesh* category) that spends its time in marshes, streams, and rivers, lies hidden in its watery habitat, possesses indomitable strength, vigorously defends its territory, and poses severe threat to humans, but only if they venture into its vicinity—and that's the hippopotamus. Through the centuries prior to discovery of dinosaurs, the identity of behemoth as a hippopotamus held sway among the majority of Hebrew and English Bible scholars because of its match with both the literal and figurative language of the text.[2]

The tail metaphor, however, seems a significant misfit at first glance. The hippopotamus has a rather unspectacular tail, certainly undeserving of comparison with a cedar, at least in size. But the passage refers to movement, not dimensions. The Hebrew word translated as "tail" is *zanab*. The range of definitions for *zanab* may include "tail," "end," and "stump."[3] Exactly what *zanab* means in the Job 40 context becomes clearer upon investigation of the manner in which the hippopotamus poses a grave threat to humans.

As an herbivore, the hippopotamus shows no desire to prey on humans. However, it wants no other large creatures or craft, including humans and their vessels, to invade its watery hangout. Hippopotami typically cause injury or death to humans when a boat, raft, or canoe unwittingly enters a section of river they occupy. These creatures submerge their massive bodies, all but nostrils, beneath the surface all day long, and for good reason. They do so not to lie in wait for invaders but rather to survive. This behavior allows them to keep cool enough to avoid heat stroke.

The problem for humans in a boat, raft, or canoe is that the nostrils become recognizable only when their craft gets close, within a few yards (or meters) of the hippopotamus. Where one hippopotamus soaks, others can usually be found nearby. Being territorial guardians, the hippos rise up against the encroaching watercraft and capsize it. Given the creatures' awesome size and strength, their reaction often results in injury or drowning for the boat's occupants.

The tactic employed by an adult hippopotamus to overturn a watercraft is a swaying maneuver involving its huge, heavily muscled thighs and rump. This maneuver may well explain the description of the behemoth's swaying tail in Job 40:16–17: "What strength it has in its loins, what power in the muscles of its belly! Its tail [*zanab*] sways like a cedar; the sinews of its thighs are close-knit." The loins, belly, thighs, and rump (or "tail" or "end") all play a part in the motion by which hippopotami capsize boats and terrify humans. What appears at first glance as a mismatch in the behemoth-hippopotamus comparison represents no problem at all. In fact, Job 40:15–24 provides one of the most detailed and accurate descriptions of hippopotamus anatomy and behavior humanity possesses from the ancient world.

God's main point, however, in this description of the behemoth has more to do with demonstrating humanity's limitations in taming certain *nepesh* creatures. No human has ever been known to tame an adult hippopotamus. Some have achieved success in taming a hippopotamus separated from its mother soon after birth and raised mostly apart from contact with other hippopotami, but these successes can be counted on one hand. Even then, the human caregivers must exercise considerable caution to avoid accidental injury by these powerful creatures.

What Is the Leviathan?

The second fearsome creature described in God's challenge to Job and his friends all the more emphatically evokes dinosaur images in the minds of twentieth- and twenty-first-century Bible readers. According to Job 41, the leviathan wields "fearsome teeth," a mouth like "doors," a back covered with "rows of shields," a chest "hard as rock, hard as a lower millstone," and an underside like "jagged potsherds." So impenetrable is the leviathan's natural armor that humans' swords, spears, javelins, clubs, slingstones, and arrows essentially bounce off, providing no effective protection against this *nepesh*.

Metaphoric language abounds in leviathan's depiction, even more so than in behemoth's. The passage also makes an explicit connection between the leviathan's ferocity and the topic of human pride. Job 41 says, "Any hope of subduing it [leviathan] is false; the mere sight of it is overpowering. No one is fierce enough to rouse it. . . . When it rises up, the mighty are terrified; they retreat before its thrashing. . . . Nothing on earth is its equal—a creature without fear. It looks down on all that are haughty; it is king over all that are proud" (vv. 9–10, 25, 33–34). Any close encounter between a human (lacking modern equipment) and a leviathan is portrayed as potentially deadly for the human. Unlike the behemoth, the leviathan is carnivorous. It poses an even more dangerous and terrifying threat because a human runs the risk of being eaten.

Once again, as in the description of the behemoth, metaphors and similes dramatically express the emotional impact of a human's close encounter with a leviathan. Flames and sparks of fire stream from the leviathan's door-like mouth, while smoke and flashes of light pour from its nostrils only in the figurative sense (41:18–21). These word pictures create an impression of how a human would feel when close enough to detect the leviathan's breath. In such a situation, the person faces the terrifying prospect of imminent death in the jaws of a ferocious beast.

The leviathan's chest, likened to a millstone, would seem a granite barrier to any human attempting to ward off attack with the use of a spear or club (41:24). Again, this creature makes even the mightiest person feel utterly weak and helpless in its presence. When it awakens, humans retreat.

Like the behemoth, the leviathan spends much time in the water. When it swims, "it leaves a glistening wake behind it" (41:32). When it attacks, it "makes the depths churn" (41:31). On the shorelines, it leaves a distinctive "trail in the mud" (41:30). One dare not "open the doors of its mouth," which is "ringed about with fearsome teeth" (41:14). The leviathan has powerful limbs and a graceful form (41:12). All these more literal descriptive statements combine with the figurative splashes to help the reader identify this creature.

Centuries before the discovery of dinosaurs, Bible scholars consistently identified the leviathan as either a crocodile or alligator. The various features make for a close match. Both species have jaws nearly as large and flat as doors, and although the muscles used to open them are relatively weak, the muscles used to close them can snap shut with deadly force. A man can hold the crocodile's or alligator's mouth shut with just one hand, but if that hand were to loosen and let those jaws open, both the hand and arm could suddenly become a snack.

Alligator and crocodile tails leave wide and unmistakable trails in shoreline mud and sand, as the Job passage describes. Both creatures glide gracefully and rapidly through water, propelled by that powerful tail. Their capacity to hold their breath for over ten minutes makes these animals especially dangerous. They can lie submerged and motionless in muddy depths, unseen to humans along the shore or in a nearby boat, and then launch themselves in a blinding flash from that submerged, still position. Any animal or person who comes near can be snatched and killed.

The leviathan fears no other creature, as the Job text relates. It earns the title of king in its own right—another reason to identify it as a crocodile. More than once a crocodile has ambushed a mature lion and dragged it into the water, whereupon fellow crocodiles help dispatch and consume the lion in short order. The only animal the crocodile refrains from molesting is the hippopotamus—for good reason. The hippopotamus provides the crocodile with easy prey. Because the territorial hippopotamus upends any boat or large creature that floats too near, crocodiles wait just outside that invisible territorial boundary line, knowing the hippopotamus's behavior may well serve up a hearty meal.

Until recently, scholars disputed the claim that alligators and crocodiles could be considered soulish animals. Researchers initially reported that these creatures sometimes eat their offspring rather than care for them. Recently, however, field biologists have corrected this erroneous report. Both species do, in fact, nurture their young.

Because newly hatched alligators and crocodiles are highly vulnerable to predation, alligator and crocodile mothers protect their hatchlings by gathering them up in their huge mouths, aware that no other predator would dare come close to that ring of fearsome teeth. When the threat has passed, the little ones crawl safely out.

Alligators and crocodiles may be the least soulish of the soulish animals. As with the hippopotamus, adult crocodiles and alligators defy taming. Even when raised by a human from the time they emerge from the egg, these creatures seem nearly impossible to tame. The only modest successes recorded thus far have required the young be raised by humans from hatchling stage on, totally apart from other alligators and crocodiles, with at least an hour of handling each day.[4]

Living miles and millennia distant from the behemoth and leviathan, anyone who reads Job today may reasonably wonder, *Why would God devote so much of a rare direct communication with humans to elaborating on the description and behavior of a couple of wild animals—especially ones we'll probably never encounter?* My own response to this wondering comes from the conviction that whatever receives attention in Scripture's pages deserves thoughtful reflection. This particular Job passage drives home, in colorful, evocative imagery, some significant truths about God and us. The One who created these wild beasts rules over all life and understands them in ways no human can. He has the power and wisdom to tame any creature at will. Humans do not. These two creatures powerfully dramatize our need to depend upon God for the power and wisdom essential for managing Earth's life, especially and most importantly for managing, or taming, our own lives.

Back to the Dinosaur Question

Because dinosaurs capture so many people's imaginations, especially children's, and because people often ask where dinosaurs fit into the biblical creation chronology, having a few facts about them at our disposal can be helpful. Research indicates dinosaurs first appeared shortly after a massive extinction event called the Permian catastrophe, roughly 251 million years ago. They came in three waves, each defined by its era as well as certain distinctive characteristics. The first wave, Triassic dinosaurs, roamed the earth from 251 to 200 million years ago; Jurassic dinosaurs ruled from 200 to 144 million years ago; and the last generation, the Cretaceous dinosaurs, dominated from 144 to 65 million years ago.

My suggestion dinosaurs belong within the context of the fifth creation day comes from the Genesis 1 description of that era's events. That day begins with the creation of swarms of small-bodied sea animals. From a natural history perspective, this wording seems an obvious reference to the Cambrian explosion. The day concludes with the introduction of Earth's first birds and larger sea animals. These two events suggest a time window for day five that opens roughly 543 million years ago and closes somewhere between 60 and 140 million years ago. This timing places the dinosaurs in the midst of creation day five.

Early in the exchange with his friends, Job commented, "In his hand is the life of every creature" (12:10). The psalmist echoes, "In wisdom you made them all; the earth is full of your creatures" (104:24). These Bible passages proclaim God's personal responsibility for every species of life that has ever existed, each one of which in some way serves a God-ordained purpose(s). One way or another, all past life played a role in preparing the planet for humanity. Some species served specifically to provide the resources we humans would need to launch and maintain global civilization, ultimately a high-technology civilization.

A familiar cartoon illustrates one possible dinosaur role. It shows an apatosaurus reclined on a couch telling his psychiatrist about a strange, symbolic dream haunting him night after night. Hinting that the dream may have something to do with his patient's destiny, the psychiatrist asks, "What symbols do you see in this dream?" The patient replies, "10W30." While dinosaurs were not the primary source of Earth's petroleum reserves, they did contribute substantially to Earth's biodeposits. They also helped regulate the chemistry of Earth's atmosphere. Reading Psalm 104 with a scientist's eye, I infer that God's plan involved sustaining the maximum possible biomass and biodiversity throughout life's history on Earth. Geologists tell us that from 250 to 65 million years ago, Earth's shallow seas and wet climate favored large reptilian creatures. In that era, dinosaurs suited God's plan to fill Earth with as great an abundance and diversity of life as conditions allowed. The presence of those creatures meant that when humans arrived they would have at their disposal the best atmosphere for their needs and the richest supply of biodeposits.

More to Teach

Job and his friends recognized that animals, especially *nepesh* animals, can teach us innumerable, invaluable lessons about life and the Creator of all life. Animals show us how richly the Creator has provided not only for our basic survival but also for our pleasure, joy, and quality of life. Animals allow us to see, by comparison, the unique glories of humanity and what it means to bear the image of God, and also to see the awful effects of human autonomy and rebellion against the Creator's authority. As Job makes clear, God uses animals to put us in our place, revealing both our greatness and our wretchedness.

Animals bring us face-to-face with the paradox of a loving God who allows his creatures to sin and to experience sin's effects. Job brings us face-to-face with the question of who suffers and why. If God holds absolute control over all creation, why would evil be allowed an entrance? The next chapter explores how the dialogue in Job can help us find insights and answers to this age-old question, the stumbling block on which the faith of many has crashed.

13

Answers to the Problem of Suffering

"Dad," said the frantic voice on the other end of the line, "I need money for my rent, and I need it today!" This call, familiar to most anyone whose daughter or son lives away at college, came as I was scrambling to meet a deadline, but my son's "emergency" could not be postponed. So I dropped everything, drove to my bank, withdrew cash, and raced to a different bank to deposit this cash into the landlord's account for immediate access.

Anticipating a potential wait at one or both banks, I grabbed my latest issue of the *Astrophysical Journal*. I hate wasting reading time, and bank lines often provide it. This day's visit did not disappoint. As I perused an intriguing article, the man behind me asked, "What *are* you reading?" He had never seen an eleven-hundred-page technical "magazine" with hundreds of graphs and equations. I told him I was checking the journal for articles relevant to the book I was working on.

The man expressed even more shock to discover my book-in-progress concerned Job. "How can today's astrophysics possibly relate to the book of Job?" he wondered aloud. As I began to explain the connections between the two, a few more people from the line moved closer. After a couple more minutes, some of the bank employees left their desks and wandered near. As more customers entered the bank, they noticed the small cluster and joined it. I ended up giving an impromptu talk on Job and science right there beside the rack of deposit slips.

That day God underscored for me how the questions discussed by Job and his friends so closely resemble the questions people wrestle with today. If God invested vast resources, time, and genius into making and preparing the universe, Earth, and Earth's life for humanity's existence and benefit, then why would he allow our life to be fraught with so much pain—physical, emotional, relational, and other? How can all the "bad" stuff serve any "good" purpose? The book of Job sets forth some helpful insights for addressing these age-old questions.

Lavish Creation

Observing Earth's beauty, abundance, diversity, and grandeur, people of all generations and cultures have been struck by the extravagance of it all. The Creator provided humanity with so much more than a place to merely survive. He presented us with a place to thrive. Every one of our senses—physical, soulish, and spiritual—has been graced with rich rewards. Even with limitations on their knowledge, technology, and experience, Job and his contemporaries perceived that God had invested generously in his creation. The diverse characteristics and capabilities of Earth's panoply of creatures, including humans, proved to them that God cares. As Eliphaz, Job, and Elihu declared, God's glory and goodness reverberated all around them (5:9–11; 9:8–10; 10:12; 36:22–37:24).

From a twenty-first-century perspective, God's investment in the creation process appears all the more astonishing. Little more than a hundred years ago life scientists viewed living cells as nothing more than blobs of featureless jelly. Astronomers viewed our Milky Way Galaxy as the entire universe. What a difference a century or two can make!

Today, scientists recognize that cells house thousands of discrete molecules. Some match the functionality and complexity of the most elegant instruments humans have ever designed and constructed. In terms of their efficiency of operation and output, these molecules exceed mankind's best accomplishments. The intricate manner and astonishing efficiency with which they work collaboratively toward achievement of complex goals far exceeds the operation of human-designed systems. No city operates as smoothly as a living cell and its constituent parts.

Astronomers now have plumbed the universe's theoretically observable limits. Within those limits they see about two hundred billion medium-sized and larger galaxies. These bodies and the dwarf galaxies that accompany them contain a total of about 50 to 60 billion trillion stars. All this stuff, however, constitutes only about 1 percent of the universe's mass. The actual universe is far more vast than the observable universe. The universe we observe is the universe of the past because light takes time to travel from distant astronomical sources to our telescopes. Because the universe has continuously expanded since the cosmos burst into existence, the current universe must be significantly larger than the universe seen through our telescopes. The universe's geometry tells us the universe at this moment must be more than a hundred times more extensive than the universe we can observe. Thus, the actual universe must be at least a million times more massive than 50 billion trillion stars.

Even nontheistic astronomers acknowledge the universe's strategic design to accommodate the eventual possibility of humans. This reality, called the anthropic principle, has gained wide acceptance. Theistic astronomers agree that the Creator has been fashioning the universe for a very long time. While humans entered the cosmic scene just tens of thousands of years ago, God has crafted and shaped the universe on our behalf for some 13.7 billion years.

From a human perspective, God's creative activity in preparation for our arrival seems radically overdone. Yet God cannot be accused of waste. Whatever he does fulfills a purpose. When the Pharisees and teachers of the law asked Jesus for a miraculous sign just for the sake of a power display, he refused, despite his capacity to raise a man from the dead (Matt. 12:38–39). As much as he longed for a healing from God and acknowledged God's power to perform it, Job ultimately recognized that God would do nothing to interfere with the greater good he held in store. He does miracles to achieve his purposes, and that's all.

The mind-boggling age and extent of the universe and the unfathomable intricacies of even the tiniest entities within it all proclaim that God has mind-boggling and unfathomable plans and purposes for it—and for humanity. Just as Job initially struggled to grasp any possible good purpose behind the afflictions and losses he suffered, humans today still struggle to grasp any good purpose behind the sufferings life inevitably brings—far more to some than to others—without apparent rhyme or reason.

Absolute Sovereignty

Job and his friends expressed no doubts about the Creator's absolute sovereignty. They stated their assumption that very good reasons *must* exist for every event and circumstance that occurs—both good and bad. As Job declared at the beginning of his trials and afflictions, "The LORD gave and the LORD has taken away; may the name of the LORD be praised" (1:21).

Early in the dialogue with his comforters, Job devoted an entire speech to describing God's limitless power, his capacity to achieve anything he wants at any time and anywhere (Job 9). Whether it be moving mountains, fine-tuning the physics of the sun and stars, guiding the circumstances and events of a person's life, or bringing trouble to some and blessings to others, God can and, in fact, does take responsibility for it all. From Job's perspective, no circumstance or event anywhere within or beyond the cosmos occurs outside of the Creator's control.

In chapter 23 Job expounds further on God's foreknowledge and sovereignty: "He knows the way that I take. . . . He stands alone, and who can oppose him? He does whatever he pleases. He carries out his decree against me, and many such plans he still has in store" (23:10, 13–14). Job understood God's sovereignty as continual, not occasional. He proclaimed, "What is mankind that you make so much of them, that you give them so much attention, that you examine them every morning and test them every moment?" (7:17–18).

Perfect Love

Job and his friends also expressed their belief in God's loving-kindness. Elihu spoke of God's generous provision for our physical nourishment, declaring that God "provides food in abundance" (36:31). Virtually every people group on Earth celebrates together around food. God offered it in great quantity and in varieties of flavor, aroma, and texture. While he could have delivered our nutritional needs without such frills, instead he made a complex menu to delight all our physical senses. (Sadly, human mismanagement of God's rich provision has led to the tragedy of widespread starvation.)

Eliphaz acknowledged God as the source of all humanity's needs, including the need for safety and comfort: "The lowly he sets on high, and those who mourn are lifted to safety" (5:11). Because of God, he adds, "the poor have hope" (5:16). Everyone benefits from God's protection: "From six calamities he will rescue you; in seven no harm will touch you" (5:19).

Even in the depths of his anguish and torment Job could say with conviction, "You gave me life and showed me kindness, and in your providence watched over my spirit" (10:12). Looking to the future, Job anticipates, "You will long for the creature your hands have made" (14:15). Despite his intense suffering and the confusion it brought him, Job trusted God's motives toward him. His trust finds an echo in Paul's affirmation that "in all things God works for the good of those who love him, who have been called according to his purpose" (Rom. 8:28). Afflictions and sufferings befall everyone. God "sends rain on the righteous and the unrighteous" (Matt. 5:45), and sometimes instead of watering their crops the rain floods their land and destroys all they own. But God promises that whatever happens, his intent is to bring about a greater good—whether in material terms or in spiritual and eternal blessings.

Perfect Creation

A God who is absolutely sovereign and perfectly loving would make no mistakes in his creative work. Despite skeptics' reports of bad designs in nature, one after another of these so-called blunders has been shown, on closer examination, to serve some beneficial purpose. The craftsmanship of the biblical God has been and will continue to be vindicated. However, we're still left to account for and deal with the obvious imperfections of life in this world—disease, injustice, natural disaster, human cruelty, and death—not to mention our own incapacity to live and love perfectly. How can this seeming contradiction be reconciled?

Job and his friends grasped the idea that this world, this life, is not humanity's ultimate destination. They spoke with confident hope of a superior life yet to come, life beyond physical death. In the midst of his trials, Job professed assurance of the reward awaiting him: "Though he slay me, yet will I hope in him" (13:15); "I will wait for my renewal to come" (14:14). This pivotal truth poured from Job's lips when he proclaimed, "After my skin has been destroyed, yet in my flesh I will see God; I myself will see him with my own eyes—I, and not another. How my heart yearns within me!" (19:26–27).

Logic dictates that if a superior life awaits—an existence above and beyond this earthly reality—the world as we know it must be inferior, imperfect. In that case, how can we trust in the perfect power and love of its Creator? Can the sovereign God of the Bible actually be God if mere humans can envision a better world than the one he crafted?

A consideration of purpose plays a crucial role in determining the perfection of any system or design. An optimally fuel-efficient automobile might be deemed imperfect if the vehicle cannot transport passengers from one location to another in a timely manner. A perfectly comfortable vehicle might prove imperfectly costly. In other words, perfection and purpose correlate. On that basis, the imperfect universe in which pain and suffering impact every human life may still be considered the perfect work of a perfect God—if it perfectly fulfills his good purpose. Here, then, are the crucial questions we must ask about our world:

1. Does humanity's time and experience in this world represent an essential step of preparation for something better?
2. Does the level or duration of humanity's exposure to discomfort, pain, and suffering exceed what's necessary to accomplish that preparation?

Multipurpose Creation

Christianity's two-creation model provides the appropriate context for answering these questions of purpose. According to the biblical model, the current creation exists for more reasons than merely to provide humans with a beautiful, comfortable, well-stocked home. It cannot and will not ever fully contain God (1 Kings 8:27), whose stated goal is to live with us and be our God (Rev. 21:3). It cannot and will not last forever. While it does allow humans to engage in complex and fulfilling relationships and to discern the existence and divine nature of the Creator, it fulfills other, greater purposes, too.

The universe serves as a theatre in which God exposes the sin problem, preserves free choice, and brings about an end to sin and sin's effects—evil, suffering, pain, and death. What's more, it establishes conditions whereby God can guarantee permanent freedom from sin and ultimately unshackle human free will from the restraints imposed by the cosmic space-time dimensions and physical laws.

The Bible holds the promise of another creation for those who choose to live forever with God under his divine authority. This "new creation" will become theirs immediately after the great white throne judgment described in Revelation 20:11–15. The perfection we humans now dream of—and more—will become an unending reality. Our roles as well as our relationships with God, each other (even Job and his friends), the angels, and any other beings God chooses to include will provide perfect satisfaction.[1]

Temporary Exposure to Sin's Effects

The biblical doctrine of two creations, each perfect in its own right, essentially undercuts the most frequently touted "evidence" for atheism, or nontheism. In his book, *God: The Failed Hypothesis*, particle physicist Victor Stenger writes, "The problem of evil remains the most powerful argument against God."[2] Indeed, the problem of evil remains the *only* "positive" (that is, non-negative) argument against God's existence (see sidebar, p. 195).

Nontheists spell out what they consider "the logical problem of evil" in this way:

1. If an all-loving, all-knowing, and all-powerful God exists, such a God would have chosen to keep pain, suffering, and all

expressions of sin (which grows into evil) from coming into existence.

2. These bad things do exist.
3. Therefore, such a God does not exist.

This argument assumes that a good God would essentially lock the gate to the Garden of Eden. He would keep humans away from the possibility of sin and its resultant pain and suffering at all times and all places. But is this assumption sound? An assumption so far-reaching and significant must not slip by unchallenged. With so much at stake, it deserves careful consideration.

If sin and its effects continued forever, impacting everyone without any possible escape or relief, then a person might have an argument against God's goodness and power. But what if these things are merely temporary? What if our temporary exposure to them actually serves a higher good than would otherwise be possible?[3]

Examples of temporary pain that eventually leads to great good abound within human experience. Olympic athletes willingly undergo painful training in order to reach their highest potential and bring honor to their country. A student suffers under the demands of a tough professor to gain the opportunity for a rewarding career. A child receives temporarily unpleasant discipline from loving parents as part of character training that fosters success in relationships and contributes to society's good.

One reason the problem of evil has persisted as an argument against God may be that we struggle so mightily to identify what eventual good could possibly justify the magnitude of sin's horrific impact. In Stenger's words, "No one can conceive of a reason God could have for allowing so much suffering."[4] He adds, "We have the undeniable empirical fact of considerable suffering in the world and have no reason to believe that the great bulk of that suffering is necessary."[5]

Stenger's comments lead to the question: *How much suffering is necessary—and necessary to accomplish what?* If suffering serves the purpose of exposing humanity's fatal flaw and the need for help from above, then perhaps we need still more, not less. Twentieth-century history sadly reveals how difficult it is to expose humanity's fatal flaw. More than a hundred million people were brutally murdered

Common (Negative) Arguments for Atheism

To reject God by denying his existence doesn't exactly equate with a firm, logic-based belief in God's nonexistence, but rejection and denial characterize the reactions of most people I've met who adopt the atheist label. These are some of the reasons they typically give for their response:

- Family, friends, clergy, or strangers who should have been kind and caring instead inflicted pain. God can't exist (or be good) if he lets that happen.
- Christians, or people who claimed to be Christians, have committed terrible deeds or exhibited character flaws worse than those of nonbelievers. So nonbelief is just as good as belief.
- Those who believe in God seem less intelligent or have less education than those who disbelieve. Faith reflects stupidity or ignorance.
- Religious beliefs appear entirely subjective, based on emotion, fables, fears, and falsehoods. Believers tend to be incoherent or inconsistent or both.
- Prayer does no more good than talking to the ceiling. People pray for good things and nothing happens. So there must be no one listening or worth asking.

Such rationalizations do not excuse rejecting the evidence for God nor do they make sense. God calls people to worship and follow *him*, not other people. Because believers sometimes may behave badly or ignorantly, be ill-equipped to defend their faith, or fail to receive what they pray for lets no one off the proverbial hook.

The tendency toward selective "evidence" can be strong in us all. However, many atheists tend to rely on it heavily, if not exclusively. They point to the worst examples from the past, such as the Crusades or the Inquisition, and to often-disgraced Christian leaders in the present, as prime representatives of what belief in God accomplishes.

Each of these arguments against faith represents a logical fallacy, showing that logic is not the core issue in people's rejection of God. As my friend Kenneth Samples points out, it may be helpful to turn attention to the question of goodness rather than evil. It presents every bit as great a philosophical challenge. He suggests testing the case for belief in God by using the best examples among believers, not the worst, and by evaluating the strongest evidence and best reasoning, not the worst. His words echo those of Peter, who exhorts believers to prepare themselves to give reasons for their hope, and to do so with gentleness, respect, and the integrity of a clear conscience (1 Pet. 3:15–16).

in that one century alone at the hands of despots who built their regimes on the notion of humanity's adequacy to govern the world for the good of all.

Inadvertently or otherwise, Stenger implies a completeness of knowledge neither he nor any other human has a basis to claim. The fact that he cannot envision a sufficient reason within the physical confines of the universe does not constitute proof that no such reason for suffering exists. No doubt Job found himself unable to imagine any good that could possibly outweigh his suffering and loss. I've even met people who carry resentment toward God on behalf of Job because they dispute the worth of the final outcome of Job's suffering. However, Job must be allowed to speak for himself on the matter. If he considered his pain and loss and despair worth enduring for the experience of hearing from God, who are we to contradict him?

Then again, Job received a significant outpouring of blessings and riches to replace what he had lost, including the restoration of his health, wealth, and family. But such earthly compensation rarely follows severe loss and hardship. What about pain and suffering where potential benefits lie beyond physical reach? Can anything hold sufficient value or reward to make this suffering worthwhile?

Cost and Benefits of Free Will

Given that God is our Creator and the source of all goodness, wisdom, power, and love, it makes sense that rebellion against his authority—in other words, sin—would become the root cause of all that we recognize as less than or contrary to these ideals. Rebellion takes many forms. It may be as subtle as simply ignoring God or as blatant as lashing out violently to harm others. But without the freedom to exercise this choice, what would be lost?

Any action by God to shield humans eternally from any possible temptation to rebel against his authority would severely limit, if not eliminate altogether, humanity's expression of free will. It would render us little more than robots. This loss of freedom would diminish what we recognize and experience as goodness and love. Such an absence of free will would drastically restrict both the quality and quantity of love humans could give and receive. What would life be without the reality of goodness? As part of his plan to make life meaningful, God made free choice a reality. He placed an object of temptation in the Garden of Eden. Then he opened Eden's gate to the most powerful tempter of all.

True freedom of human will implies that some people can actually choose to assert their own will over God's will. In Eden God purposely granted the first humans that opportunity. He certainly could have kept temptation away from humanity for all eternity. He could have kept the tree of forbidden fruit out of Eden. He could have blocked Satan from ever accessing either the Garden or the planet.

Many people wish God had done these very things. Throughout all human history, people have questioned why we can't just return to the paradise Adam and Eve enjoyed before they exercised their choice to rebel. The first human couple and their offspring had the potential of living forever with much joy, little pain, and little or no affliction. Such a life may seem the best life conceivable; however, the God who created life says otherwise. In the words of the author of Hebrews, "God had planned something better for us" (11:40). God's plan was and is that we would have the potential to "be made perfect" with our free will and capacity to love still fully intact.

God's purpose for us humans includes the *expansion* of our capacity to experience freedom and love. To achieve such a purpose requires humanity's exposure to sin's temptation because genuine love demands real choice, just as real choice allows for real evil. In his transcendent wisdom, God implemented a plan that brings multiple benefits and blessings from our temporary exposure to temptation and the effects of sin:

- Humans who choose (by the power God provides) to surrender to God's authority in the face of ultimate temptation receive God's promise that nothing can ever again draw them away from him.
- Humans who pass this test of choice and receive God's promise need not be tested again and are ready to experience life totally apart from sin and temptation.

- Once free from sin's pull *and* presence, humans can express their freedom in expansive new ways.
- This new level of freedom allows humans to experience love and joy without limits.
- This new freedom allows humans to fulfill roles they cannot yet imagine, in relation to each other, to angels, and to God himself.

The wonder of God's plan, which undoubtedly holds in store even more glories than these, grows greater with the recognition that he bears its enormous cost. Human sin caused him more pain than any one person has endured. Furthermore, the elegance of God's plan may be seen in his willingness to customize life's test for every individual, giving each person the maximum opportunity to pass it.

Some skeptics may still dispute that the pain of going through life in this creation to gain an unshackled free will that remains forever secure against the threat of evil is too much. But Job and his friends understood, at least in part, that the test for each person is mercifully passable—and mercifully brief. As Job expressed it, "My life is but a breath" (7:7). He likened his life to "a cloud [that] vanishes and is gone" (7:9). He said of his days on Earth, "They skim past like boats of papyrus" (9:26). In other words, Job and his friends recognized, even without the perspective of twenty-first-century science, that exposure to sin and its effects is astoundingly brief. In a creation roughly 13.7 billion years old, humanity has been around for just 0.0004 percent of that time. An individual's exposure to temptation and suffering lasts no more than 0.0000006 percent of cosmic history. That's not to say that a day in anguish or agony can ever feel brief. It can seem like an eternity until it passes.

Only with Help

From a New Testament perspective, God intervenes to calibrate the intensity of the test any human endures. Not many have faced the degree of temptation and suffering that Job experienced, but we all experience them to varying degrees. Meanwhile God offers his strength, guidance, and comfort to each individual, helping that person not only make it through but also pass with flying colors. The apostle Paul writes, "God is faithful; he will not let you be tempted beyond what you can bear. But when you are tempted, he will also provide a way out so that you can endure it" (1 Cor. 10:13). Further, "We also glory in our sufferings, because we know that suffering produces perseverance; perseverance, character; and character, hope. And hope does not put us to shame, because God's love has been poured out into our hearts through the Holy Spirit, who has been given to us" (Rom. 5:3–5).

The book of Job illustrates how God worked in Job's life, sustaining him through the worst of the worst. It also reminds us that in the midst of our suffering we humans tend to complain that the suffering is more than we can handle. Students in the middle of a difficult course often complain it is too hard; only later do they recognize that the knowledge, skills, and training gained outweigh the struggle. So, too, we who have not yet completed our lives on Earth may complain that the pain and suffering seem too much, especially when at their most intense. But if we take time to ponder the good purposes being accomplished for time and eternity and stretch to imagine what life will be like in God's perpetual presence amid the splendors of the new creation, we begin to see (at least in part) why a good God would allow sin and suffering and evil to exist in this creation.

Not Our Home

With Elihu's support, Job embraced vital truths that carried him through his experience of torment and anguish to a place of peace and praise. Even at his lowest point, Job maintained his affirmation of God's sovereignty and of God's loving, rewarding nature. He believed God held good gifts in store for his future. Such gifts, Job and Elihu acknowledged, could never be fully received and experienced in the present creation. They discerned that this world was not their home. Like the author of Hebrews recorded centuries after them, Job and Elihu admitted "that they were foreigners and strangers on earth. . . . They were longing for a better country—a heavenly one. Therefore God is not ashamed to be called their God, for he has prepared a city for them" (Heb. 11:13, 16).

From their reading of God's world by the light of his Holy Spirit, Job and Elihu perceived that they were candidates for God's redemption, not by any merit of their own but by God's gracious intervention on their behalf. They may not have known all the details, and they didn't know the name of their Redeemer, but they certainly knew his identity. The next chapter describes how Job and Elihu discerned, for the benefit of all, the Good News that overcomes the bad.

14

Answers to Our Greatest Need

Over the last two decades of my work with Reasons To Believe, I've flown more than half a million miles. Many of those miles involved travel "disasters" that to this day give me nightmares. But some bring back good memories. In fact, virtually all resulted in amazing opportunities to share reasons to believe in Jesus Christ as Creator and Savior. Now, I almost welcome travel mix-ups. (I say "almost" because I still lack Job's maturity when it comes to dealing with life's trials.)

My travel experiences have underscored for me how God works in all manner of circumstances and unexpected changes, even the good ones. Just before take-off on a cross-country trip, a flight attendant approached me to ask if I'd be willing to trade places with another passenger. She said a mother was hoping to sit beside her disabled daughter. Of course I said yes and got up to move, expecting to land in a middle seat between two Goliaths, as has happened more than once. Instead, the attendant escorted me all the way up to seat 1B.

A wealthy business owner from Montreal sat beside me in my unfamiliar first-class surroundings. The fact that I was born in Montreal gave us a quick connection. The fact that my father designed the glass shield for the hockey rink in the Montreal Forum created a deeper bond, especially when he heard my dad knew hockey legends

Maurice "Rocket" Richard and Bernie "Boom Boom" Geoffrion. This businessman was a huge hockey fan. Before long I discovered this pleasant, impeccably dressed man suffered from an all-too-common North American syndrome—the good life. His business prospered. He enjoyed good health. He owned a beautiful home, plus a summer cottage on a wooded lakeshore, along with three vehicles and a boat. His family life couldn't be better, he said, and his favorite team was on its way to yet another Stanley Cup.

Eventually he asked what I do for a living, and when I told him, his response was surprisingly honest: "I've never really given much thought to God." I asked if perhaps all the good things in his life might be distracting him from considering what's most important. Without any hesitation he said, "Yes." Then he added, "I know I'm going to die someday, but I never let myself think about death or about what lies beyond." As gently as I could, I told him God cared for him so much that if he persisted in allowing life's good things to come between him and his eternal destiny, God might begin removing some of those good things.

The color instantly drained from his face. He confessed that his wife of thirty years had just begun to express, for the first time in their marriage, some dissatisfaction with their relationship. As far as he understood, she was trying to tell him that his inability to demonstrate any sense of meaningful purpose in his life had begun to trouble her. She disliked the shallowness of their existence. He went on to say that a few other people besides me had tried to talk to him about God. But, he explained, he never took the God issue seriously because none could give him any concrete evidence for their belief in God. When I told him science had played a huge part in my coming to faith in Christ, he asked, "Can you give me any solid scientific evidence for God's existence?"

Ninety minutes later, he told me he was adequately convinced God is real. With two other passengers now leaning in our direction to eavesdrop, the Montreal business owner asked me to explain exactly what a person needs to do to get his life right with God. What he needed first and most of all, I said, was humility. It takes a humble heart to read and receive the message in God's two books. "Which *two* books do you mean?" he asked with a quizzical look. I told him

Why Not Good Works versus Bad?

Eliphaz, Bildad, and Zophar belong to a long list of religious leaders, including many Christians, Jews, and Muslims, who for centuries have contended that a "weighing in the balance" of good deeds versus bad deeds ultimately determines our eternal destiny. Many people around the world today still think such a scenario represents Christianity.

This view of salvation (or condemnation) leads to minimizing sin and its damaging effects, and at the same time exaggerates both the quantity and quality of good works. The question of how God judges became the focus of a debate between the prophet Ezekiel and Jewish religious leaders of his day.

Ezekiel declared the common perception of judgment day as the balance scale scenario to be only *partly* correct (18:4–32; 33:10–20). He explained what God does with the "record" of people's lives. It all depends on their response to God's grace, whether they accept or reject his offer to replace their prideful heart with a heart to obey. Once a person accepts that exchange, "none of the offenses they have committed will be remembered against them" (18:22). On the other hand, if a person repeatedly refuses to repent and receive God's gift, then "none of the righteous things that person has done will be remembered" (18:24).

In essence, only one pan remains on the proverbial scale. When people turn from trusting their own righteousness to trusting in God's righteousness, God deletes the record of their transgressions. It's gone. So for those who accept God's offer, made available personally in Jesus Christ, judgment day resembles a joyous awards ceremony (1 Cor. 3:12–15). When people opt to trust in their own goodness as if it's "good enough," God deletes their accomplishments record. It's gone. All that remains is the account of their malevolence. So for those who reject God's offer in Christ, judgment day means facing up to a nightmarish reality (Rev. 20:13).

Ezekiel's explanation drew a huge outcry from the religious leaders. They complained, "[T]he way of the Lord is not just" (18:25, 29). Yet an earlier prophet had already warned them that their self-righteous deeds looked more like "filthy rags" (Isa. 64:6) because such acts represented efforts to bring glory to self rather than to God. They reflected pride, not humility. Thus, they could not be considered good at all. As Ezekiel reminded them, God in his kindness had determined not to count such "righteous deeds" against those who remain unrepentant and ungrateful. He implored the people, "Repent and live!" (18:32).

Among those who bow before God, no room for pride remains. They understand that whatever good they accomplish is motivated, empowered, and set up by God. As the apostle Paul wrote, "For we are God's handiwork, created in Christ Jesus to do good works, which God prepared in advance for us to do" (Eph. 2:10).

God has revealed himself to humanity in both the words of Scripture and the works of nature. He replied, "Please tell me what the book of nature says."

I spent the next twenty or thirty minutes reviewing what a highly successful, deeply humble businessman named Job had discerned about God from studying the world around him. Job not only perceived vital truths, I explained, but also submitted to truth, and to God. I mentioned how Job's contemporary, Elihu, also listened to God's quiet voice and came to understand the basics of God's plan. Then I reviewed for him what Paul taught in the book of Romans about God's offer of eternal life with a capital "L."

"It's no accident that stewardess brought you to sit beside me," he said. I'm not sure what happened in the hearts of the other two listeners, but I watched this one Montreal business owner eagerly receive God's gracious offer. Meanwhile, I received something special from God. In addition to a heart overflowing with joy, I received a striking reminder that even someone who appears totally disinterested in spiritual things may be more open than we think at first glance.

Job's Refutation of Bad Theology

Early in their exchange with Job, Eliphaz, Bildad, and Zophar did their best to persuade Job that his calamities and afflictions resulted from God's having weighed him in the balance scale and found him wanting. They expressed certainty that despite his admirable accumulation of good deeds, words, and attitudes, something sufficiently weighty had been added to his pile of bad deeds, words, and attitudes to tip the scales against him. To them, that unidentified sin explained why God brought disaster and suffering upon Job. Their exhortation may sound familiar: repent of the bad, focus on doing more good, and God will remove your miseries and restore your good health and good fortune (8:1–7; 11:10–20; 15:4–35; 22:4–30).

Job adamantly rejected his friends' exhortations as false. He held no illusions about his imperfection before God, but he also assured them his conscience was clear. At the same time Job identified the arrogance of their theological perspective, which implied that since he was suffering horribly and they were not, they must be in better standing with God.

Job did agree, as I mentioned, that he fell short of God's moral perfection (9:14, 28–29), just as every person does (9:2; 14:4; 15:14). However, he claimed to be "blameless" (9:21; 12:4; 31:6), and God himself acknowledged Job's blamelessness (1:8; 2:3). By the use of that term he indicated not that he had never done wrong, but rather that he had taken necessary steps to make things right with those he had wronged. On that basis, he argued, his suffering did not come as a consequence of specific sin(s), while his friends insisted that it must be.

Job's Recognition of His Helplessness

Job drew a different conclusion about God's justice and mercy than his friends did. In his humility, Job appears to have developed keen self-awareness as well as God-awareness. Job expressed his conviction that God's standard of moral purity could be discerned by anyone willing to examine his or her heart, where it is indelibly written. He also recognized that the conscience, embedded within the human spirit, reacts when a person breaks God's law—even if a person's experience and culture has managed to distort one's conscience.

"Does he [God] not see my ways and count my every step?" (31:4)

"If I sinned, you [God] would be watching me and would not let my offense go unpunished." (10:14)

"For I know you will not hold me innocent. Since I am already found guilty, why should I struggle in vain?" (9:28–29)

"What are mortals, that they could be pure?" (15:14)

"How can mere mortals prove their innocence before God?" (9:2)

These words come from "a man who fears God and shuns evil," a man of whom God said (and repeated), "There is no one on earth like him; he is blameless and upright" (1:8; 2:3). The message clearly emerges that if Job's righteousness is inadequate, then everyone's righteousness falls short. No quantity or quality of good deeds can fully

Job's Discernment of God's Redemptive Plan

1. My Creator exists.

"[God] alone stretches out the heavens." (9:8)

"Your hands shaped me and made me." (10:8)

"In his hand is the life of every creature and the breath of all mankind." (12:10)

2. My Creator possesses limitless power and wisdom.

"His wisdom is profound, his power is vast." (9:4)

"He performs wonders that cannot be fathomed, miracles that cannot be counted." (9:10)

3. My Creator cares for me.

"You gave me life and showed me kindness, and in your providence watched over my spirit." (10:12)

4. My Creator is good and perfection is his standard.

"You [God] examine [mankind] every morning and test them every moment." (7:18)

"If I sinned, you would be watching me and would not let my offense go unpunished." (10:14)

"He knows the way that I take." (23:10)

5. I fall hopelessly short of the Creator's goodness.

"How can mere mortals prove their innocence before God?" (9:2)

"How then can I dispute with him?" (9:14)

"I know you will not hold me innocent. Since I am already found guilty, why should I struggle in vain?" (9:28–29)

"Who can bring what is pure from the impure?" (14:4)

"What are mortals, that they could be pure?" (15:14)

6. Because the Creator is powerful, wise, and loving, he formed a plan to redeem me.

> "I will wait for my renewal to come. You will call and I will answer you; you will long for the creature your hands have made." (14:14–15)

> "Even now my witness is in heaven; my advocate is on high. My intercessor is my friend as my eyes pour out tears to God; on behalf of a man he pleads with God as one pleads for a friend." (16:19–21)

7. If I entrust my life to the Redeemer, I will be rescued by him.

> "I could only plead with my Judge for mercy." (9:15)

> "Though he slay me, yet will I hope in him." (13:15)

> "My offenses will be sealed up in a bag; you will cover over my sin." (14:17)

> "Give me, O God, the pledge you demand. Who else will put up security for me?" (17:3)

8. If I receive the Creator's offer, my rescue will be assured.

> "I know that my redeemer lives, and that in the end he will stand on the earth. And after my skin has been destroyed, yet in my flesh I will see God; I myself will see him with my own eyes—I, and not another. How my heart yearns within me!" (19:25–27)

> "When he has tested me, I will come forth as gold." (23:10)

9. If I reject the Creator's offer, my condemnation will be assured.

> "If you say, 'How we will hound him, since the root of the trouble lies in him,' you should fear the sword yourselves; for wrath will bring punishment by the sword, and then you will know that there is judgment." (19:28–29)

compensate for human waywardness, for that core rebellion against God, however subtly a person may express it (see sidebar, p. 203).

The conscience speaks even into the hearts of those who have no direct access to God's special *written* revelation. As Paul said, "The requirements of the law are written on their hearts, their consciences also bearing witness" (Rom. 2:15). Job lived prior to the availability of the written word. Yet he clearly comprehended his incapacity to deliver himself from the mire of moral imperfection. Overwhelmed by the thought of it, he lamented, "If only there were someone to mediate between us, someone to bring us together, someone to remove God's rod from me, so that his terror would frighten me no more. Then I would speak up without fear of him, but as it now stands with me, I cannot" (Job 9:33–35).

Job's Discovery of God's Redemptive Offer

After giving voice to his feeling of hopelessness, Job sifted through the tangle of his thoughts and beliefs. He rejected existential despair. He affirmed that his Creator cared for him. He saw God's care as a reality in his own life and in the bounty evident throughout creation. In his words, "You gave me life and showed me kindness, and in your providence watched over my spirit" (10:12). Job also acknowledged the Creator's transcendent power. He testified, "His wisdom is profound, his power is vast. . . . He performs wonders that cannot be fathomed, miracles that cannot be counted" (9:4, 10).

In the midst of his pain and grappling with what he knew and understood, Job recognized and expressed these vital truths: (1) However righteous a person may be, he cannot justify himself to God on his own merit; (2) God has the capacity to accomplish what no mere human can, even to resolve our seemingly hopeless moral dilemma; (3) God yearns for us as a father longs for his child, enough to do for us what we cannot do for ourselves, no matter the cost.

Job followed these truths to their logical conclusion when he announced to his friends, "I will wait for my renewal to come. You [God] will call and I will answer you; you will long for the creature your hands have made" (14:14–15). He added, "Even now my witness is in heaven; my advocate is on high. My intercessor is my friend . . . ; on behalf of a man he pleads with God as one pleads for a friend" (16:19–21). In this declaration, Job foreshadowed the paradoxical and yet essential doctrine of one God in three persons. He voiced the need for someone to arbitrate between them, to "lay his hand upon us both" (9:33 NASB). Yet, who could lay a hand on God? The only possibility would be someone "Who, being in very nature God, did not consider equality with God something to be used to his own advantage" (Phil. 2:6). Only God, Job reasoned, would have both the moral perfection and sufficient power to pay the redemption price. He pleaded, "Give me, O God, the pledge you demand. Who else will put up security for me?" (17:3). It seems clear God revealed to Job, by the Holy Spirit's enabling, that God must be singular in one context but plural in another.

Job's Assurance of Salvation

Not only did Job ascertain the means by which God *could* rescue him from his plight, but he also expressed firm confidence that God *would* rescue him, without fail. In a passage made famous by Handel's *Messiah*, Job proclaimed:

> I know that my redeemer lives, and that in the end he will stand on the earth. And after my skin has been destroyed, yet in my flesh I will see God; I myself will see him with my own eyes—I, and not another. How my heart yearns within me! (19:25–27)

The apostle Paul may have had Job's words in mind when he wrote, "I know whom I have believed, and am convinced that he is able to guard what I have entrusted to him until that day," that is, the end of days (2 Tim. 1:12).

Many centuries before Paul, Job articulated the core elements of the Gospel, which had yet to fully unfold along history's timeline (see sidebar, p. 206). God gave this ancient man an outpouring of insight and faith in the midst of excruciating circumstances, and Job's story registers null and void all complaints and excuses people may offer for missing God's message or failing life's test.

Elihu's Discernment of God's Redemptive Offer

1. My Creator exists.

"The Spirit of God has made me; the breath of the Almighty gives me life." (33:4)

"If it were [God's] intention and he withdrew his spirit and breath, all humanity would perish together." (34:14–15)

"All humanity has seen it [God's work]; mortals gaze on it from afar." (36:25)

2. My Creator possesses limitless power and wisdom.

"How great is God—beyond our understanding!" (36:26)

"The Almighty is beyond our reach and exalted in power." (37:23)

3. My Creator cares for me.

"God is mighty, but despises no one." (36:5)

"He is wooing you from the jaws of distress to a spacious place free from restriction, to the comfort of your table laden with choice food." (36:16)

4. My Creator is good and perfection is his standard.

"It is unthinkable that God would do wrong, that the Almighty would pervert justice." (34:12)

"Can someone who hates justice govern? Will you condemn the just and mighty One?" (34:17)

"[God] takes note of [mankind's] deeds." (34:25)

"In his justice and great righteousness, [God] does not oppress." (37:23)

5. I fall hopelessly short of the Creator's goodness.

"Should God then reward you on your terms, when you refuse to repent?" (34:33)

"He makes them listen to correction and commands them to repent of their evil." (36:10)

6. Because the Creator is powerful, wise, and loving, he made a way to redeem me.

> "For God does speak—now one way, now another—though no one perceives it." (33:14)

> "He may speak in their ears and terrify them with warnings, to turn them from wrongdoing and keep them from pride, to preserve them from the pit." (33:16–18)

> "Spare them from going down to the pit; I have found a ransom for them." (33:24)

> "God does all these things to a person—twice, even three times—to turn them back from the pit, that the light of life may shine on them." (33:29–30)

7. If I entrust my life to my Redeemer, he will surely rescue me.

> "[A] person can pray to God and find favor with him, . . . [Then] they will go to others and say, 'I have sinned, I have perverted what is right, but I did not get what I deserved. God has delivered me from going down to the pit, and I shall live to enjoy the light of life.'" (33:26–28)

Those Who Have Never Heard

A troubling question posed not just by atheists and agnostics but also by many believers in God focuses on the fate of people who have missed out (or will miss out) on hearing the whole redemptive story as it played out in the person, sacrifice, and triumph of Jesus of Nazareth. As widely distributed as the Bible has been, not everyone has had opportunity to read or come into contact with its detailed message. In that case, how could a just God hold them accountable for not responding to his offer of rescue?

Job illustrates that the written word is not the *only* revelation that speaks about God, his attributes, and his purposes for humanity. God also speaks through nature, the conscience, prayers, dreams, and visions.

Nature and conscience have communicated ubiquitously. As Paul said in the opening page of Romans, "For since the creation of the world God's invisible qualities—his eternal power and divine nature— have been clearly seen, being understood from what has been made, so that people are without excuse" (Rom. 1:20). Later in his letter, Paul directly addressed the argument about those who have never heard. He wrote, "But I ask: Did they not hear? Of course they did: 'Their voice has gone out into all the earth, their words to the ends of the world'" (10:18). Paul here quoted a phrase from Psalm 19. The full passage reads,

> The heavens declare the glory of God; the skies proclaim the work of his hands. Day after day they pour forth speech; night after night they reveal knowledge. They have no speech, they use no words; no sound is heard from them. Yet their voice goes out into all the earth, their words to the ends of the world. (Ps. 19:1–4)

Psalm 97:6 reiterates the point: "The heavens proclaim his righteousness, and all peoples see his glory."

Elihu's Reiteration of God's Offer

Job faced an unfair battle—four against one: his three friends whom he could see and hear, plus Satan. While Job held his own early on in the exchange of speeches, eventually his three friends wore him down with their incessant attacks on his character and convictions. They offered anything but comfort. As the debate came to an end, Job exclaimed in weary frustration, "Oh, that I had someone to hear me!" (31:35).

At this point, the young man Elihu, the likely dialogue recorder, broke his silence. Although he offered no more compassion than the others, he did refute the distorted theology of Job's friends and reiterated the most important points Job expressed. Elihu's words offer an independent demonstration of how powerfully and clearly nature's record and any human's conscience can communicate the message of redemption. Elihu apparently discerned the same truths Job gathered (see sidebar, p. 210).

Easy to Discern, Difficult to Receive

Job and Elihu premiered the overarching themes and message of Scripture long before God's written revelation came into being. Perhaps they heard stories passed on from earlier times, from descendants of Noah and his family or from Abraham's forebears. Yet the bulk of their learning must have come from life experience, both internal and external, and from God's Spirit answering their hunger for truth. One wonders if the absence of distractions from modern technology helped them pay closer attention.

The desire for personal autonomy finds countless avenues for expression these days, as much (if not more) among those living the good life as among those who struggle for daily survival. The temptation differs in no way from one person to the next. Our tendency to surrender ourselves to something or someone other than God himself pulls us with a force that can be resisted only if we call out for help. If and when we do call, we then face temptation to dictate the terms of the help he provides. We attempt to negotiate a conditional surrender. Given the cost of receiving God's free gift, many people choose to exchange the truth of God for a lie (Rom. 1:25) and thus fail "to retain the knowledge of God" (1:28). But whatever anyone may gain in such a bargain falls woefully short of what's lost. God wants to remind us of that promise through Job.

15

Help with the Hard Part

Now that you know I take work with me even to the bank, you can imagine how I prepare for layovers between connecting flights. For these inevitable waits, I reserve special assignments that can be handled via laptop or phone. During one such layover, I met with my editor (also my wife) via cell phone to discuss my response to a skeptic's attack on Genesis 1:1. As Kathy and I talked, my colleague and fellow traveler Kenneth Samples spotted a man two or three seats away leaning heavily in my direction and attempting to tune into my half of that phone discussion. The moment I hit the End Call button, he leaped into conversation with Ken and me.

The man introduced himself as a Stanford computer sciences professor who had written a few blogs on the topic of science and faith. To him, the content of Genesis 1 seemed impossible to reconcile with the order of events revealed in the scientific record, and the biological evidence demanded an evolutionary explanation for the origin and development of life. He said he wasn't sure how, but he assumed people of faith could find some way to "work around these issues."

Then he asked me if I had written any articles on the relationship between science and the Bible. Unable to suppress a wry grin, Ken leaned back in his chair. I told the computer scientist I couldn't say how many articles, but I had published a few books on the topic. That led to more questions about my educational background, which led to further astonishment. "How can you, as an astronomer, say no conflict exists between science and Genesis?" he asked.

The professor's intrigue heightened when I said Job 38–39, in particular, provides important keys to interpreting Genesis 1. Among other insights Job offers, the book elaborates on the degree to which God intervened to shape Earth and its diverse life-forms. Before the first boarding call interrupted, the three of us had about twenty minutes to discuss the value of integrating *all* the biblical creation passages with *all* relevant scientific disciplines—particularly those dealing with the chronology of the universe, Earth, and Earth's life. We parted company, and our new acquaintance took his seat near the front of the plane as Ken and I took ours in the second-to-last row. Soon it was our turn to be surprised. Once the pilot turned off the Fasten Seat Belt sign, the Stanford professor came walking toward us. We continued our conversation for the rest of the journey, and it did not end even when we exited the plane. We continued to talk all the way to baggage claim.

The intensity of this man's interest and questioning reminded Ken and me how strongly some people yearn to fit spiritual truth with scientific fact. Many people remain convinced and deeply troubled that this integration cannot be done. When they discover, however, a worldview that brings together our best understanding of the Bible with our best understanding of the natural world, they often experience a tremendous sense of liberation. I say "often" rather than "always," because a person's response may vary based on certain preconditions.

Pursuit of Truth

Whatever one may say about Eliphaz, Bildad, and Zophar, as well as that Stanford professor, they cannot be called apathetic. They were not lukewarm. They actively engaged in seeking answers. When they found better answers than the ones they first espoused, they showed willingness to trade their old answers for improved ones. "Improved" represents the limit of what we humans can attain. The words "perfect" and "complete" do not apply, because we are finite creatures with finite knowledge. The pursuit of truth never ends. At no time can anyone afford to stop digging for deeper insights and answers.

In the epilogue to the book of Job, the writer records God's words addressed to Job's friend, Eliphaz: "I am angry with you and your two friends, because you have not spoken the truth about me, as my servant Job has" (42:7). Perhaps the simplest summation of the error committed by Eliphaz, Bildad, and Zophar would be this: they underestimated God and overestimated themselves. They misconstrued God's ways. They underrated his love and mercy. They miscalculated the extent of his power and wisdom. Eliphaz, Bildad, and Zophar presumed God would respond in a mechanistic way to each person's goodness or badness. Trouble equated with God's punishment. Blessing equated with God's approval.

Job disagreed. Job's friends believed a person could live righteously enough to deserve God's approval. Job understood that no amount of righteousness he could muster would measure up to God's holy standard. Job recognized that all humanity falls short. As he stated to his friends, "How can mere mortals prove their innocence before God? . . . Who can bring what is pure from the impure?" (9:2; 14:4). Job understood he could not achieve purity on his own. God and God alone could make up the gap. As Job looked honestly at the world around him and within him, he discerned the message that if he trusted wholly in God's providence and mercy, God would surely make a way to rescue him from his hopeless condition. Job clearly met the conditions set forth by the author of Hebrews: "Anyone who comes to [God] must believe that he exists and that he rewards those who earnestly seek him" (Heb. 11:6).

Hidden Purposes of Suffering

When James (Jesus's brother) wrote to encourage fellow believers in the midst of their suffering, he pointed to Job as the paragon of patient perseverance (James 5:10–11). Being well versed in the Tanakh (Hebrew Scriptures), James's readers would have known why he singled out Job. When most people today hear the name Job, they envision his physical suffering—loathsome skin sores, wracking pain, and an unrelenting fever—along with his grievous loss of family and wealth. But James's contemporaries would have recalled the magnitude of both these and more horrors, as described in Job 30.

Not only Job's wife but the rest of society turned on Job when he fell from the pinnacle of prosperity to a refuse heap. He endured rejection and ridicule from the most respected community members as well as from the lowliest. Scoundrels who could not be trusted among Job's sheep dogs abused him with words—and worse:

> But now they mock me, men younger than I, whose fathers I would have disdained to put with my sheep dogs. . . . And now those young men mock me in song; I have become a byword among them. They detest me and keep their distance; they do not hesitate to spit in my face. . . . They throw off restraint in my presence. On my right the tribe attacks; they lay snares for my feet. . . . Terrors overwhelm me; my dignity is driven away as by the wind, my safety vanishes like a cloud. (excerpts from Job 30:1–15)

No one, not even God himself, blamed Job for so openly expressing his anguish. Amid his confusion and despair, Job questioned why the Creator whom he loved and trusted would turn on him, attack him, tear him to pieces, and yet keep him alive. But Job refused to give up his deepest convictions about God's character. He would not curse God, as his wife urged (2:9).

The impact of Job's encounter with God could not have been more profound, and those who read the story cannot afford to miss or minimize it. After hearing God's voice and gaining a glimpse of God's glory, Job responded,

> You asked, "Who is this that obscures my plans without knowledge?" Surely I spoke of things I did not understand, things too wonderful for me to know. You said, "Listen now, and I will speak; I will question you, and you shall answer me." My ears had heard of you but now my eyes have seen you. Therefore I despise myself and repent in dust and ashes. (42:3–6)

Although the suffering must have been unimaginably intense, Job considered the outcome, an encounter with God, magnificent and totally worthwhile—even *before* receiving any of God's restorative gifts and blessings to him.

Job's humility and steadfast faith astound me. The attitude he demonstrated finds expression again centuries later when the apostle Paul reminded the believers in Corinth, "Our light and momentary troubles are achieving for us an eternal glory that far outweighs them all" (2 Cor. 4:17). To the believers in Rome he wrote, "I consider that our present sufferings are not worth comparing with the glory that will be revealed in us" (Rom. 8:18).

Both Job and Paul tell us that human suffering must not be considered gratuitous. Their suffering, however intense, bore inestimable fruit in their own lives and has since benefited the lives of billions of people, and angels too, in ways they could not have foreseen. Their pain was real, and their pleadings honest. But from them we also learn that faith and trust in God yield benefits and rewards far beyond what we can possibly think or imagine.

God's Desire to Give Insight

Time and again we all face questions we cannot understand, "things too wonderful" for our minds to comprehend. Job's concession cannot be construed to suggest we should give up pursuing answers and insights. We must never presume God wants us to remain ignorant. On the contrary, the book of Job reveals God's desire to answer our questions and make himself known—at the moment he deems best.

God's answers and insights may bounce off the knuckles of shaking fists or be smothered in the dust of our running away. But Job neither cursed nor hid. He acknowledged that every aspect of his life remained an open book before the Almighty (7:17–19). God literally sees everything. So why pretend? Like King David, Job deserves credit for his honesty. "The patience of Job" occurs as a cliché in many languages. No wonder. What other man in recorded or literary history so admirably exemplifies this particular "fruit of the Spirit" (Gal. 5:22)? Many a person under less distress has thrown in the towel and looked for a way out.

Job wanted to know God more deeply, to understand God's ways. Like Jacob and David, he wrestled with God in an earnest pursuit of answers, and in doing so Job refrained from setting a time limit on God's reply. He persisted. Job accepted the wait, though it must have felt like forever. In doing so, Job showed utmost reverence for God.

Waiting in reverence for answers from God means rejecting the temptation to malign God's character, as if he were aloof, hidden, and unwilling to answer our cries. Given God's promise to those who love him and remain true to his calling on their lives, the only reason for God's silence in response to a person's pleadings would be to achieve a greater good than an immediate answer could accomplish.

Joy of Discovery

My younger son David is now twenty-two. Despite his advanced age he still relishes a good Easter egg hunt. Every year his friend's grandfather takes the opportunity to hide eggs on his property in places he deems impossible to find, and then challenges David to search for them. Thus far, no matter how thoroughly the eggs have been camouflaged or concealed, David has located every one. Meanwhile, I've noticed this grandfather takes just as much delight in watching David find the eggs as David does in the finding of the eggs.

To me this picture reflects God's experience and our own in the discovery of spiritual treasures. God wants us to know the joy of diligently searching for insights and finding them, even in the strangest of places or when we least expect it. Just as David would care nothing for the eggs if Tom simply stacked them all in a bowl on the dining room table, you and I would quickly become bored and disinterested if the answer to every conceivable question could be looked up alphabetically in some kind of digital encyclopedia.

God designed his revelation to humanity, both the book of Scripture and the book of nature, to resemble a treasure hunt. In both books, invaluable truths abound. Some seem relatively easy to find while others require persistent effort, diligent investigation, and contemplation across many years. God wants us to relish the joy of discovery. Having created us, he also knows that making a breakthrough to understanding indelibly seals the memory of that new insight into our mind. It also motivates us to apply that insight to the way we live and relate to him and others.

Emulate Job

The book of Job opens with God's challenge to Satan: "Have you considered my servant Job? There is no one on earth like him" (1:8). No matter what happened to Job, whether calamity, suffering, slander, ridicule, or other torment, whether afflicted by enemy or friend, God could say of Job, "He still maintains his integrity" (2:3). When God evaluated the words spoken between Job and his friends, he gave Job credit for speaking what was right (42:7). More than a thousand years after Job, another prophet of God declared, "He has shown you, O mortal, what is good. And what does the LORD require of you? To act justly and to love mercy and to walk humbly with your God" (Mic. 6:8).

The story of Job beautifully illustrates how each of us can go about our search for insights and answers to our endless questions. Job provides a pattern: (1) speak of God what is right; (2) rather than cover up wrongs, make them right; (3) give God the honor and reverence he is due; (4) resist temptation to do sin; and (5) maintain integrity in the face of adversity and pain. In other words, emulate Job.

The Maker of the universe allotted 13.7 billion years for the development of a spectacularly provisioned creation. After fashioning a finely tuned planet and filling it with creatures of all kinds, the Creator placed humans on the scene, unique in comparison with all other creatures. The Master of creation charged them (and us) with the task of extending Eden throughout the earth. Then, even after they exercised their freedom in an act of rebellion, carrying us right along with them, God graciously continued to guide and help them. He continues to guide and help us today, so long as we are humble enough to ask. He provided a record of his work in creation, including a written record, so that we humans could continue to fulfill our mandate, know our Maker, and prepare for the new creation to come.

Fulfilling the mandate is no easy task given the presence of sin and its awful effects. Along with the pleasures and joys of creation, we must endure the pain and suffering that comes with sin—for a time but not forever. The necessary condition for genuine love (free will) remains in us, and as we exercise it to accept God's rescue from sin, he sets us free to eventually regain much more than paradise lost.

Meanwhile, he gives meaning to everything we experience and discover in the current, sin-marred creation, and in doing so prepares us for our future role in that new sin-free, suffering-free creation. This plan calls for patience on our part because we can't yet see that new creation with physical, human eyes. Again, we must emulate Job. For all who do, a day will come when the Creator will say to our face, "Well done, good and faithful servant! You have been faithful with a few things; I will put you in charge of many things. Come and share your master's happiness!" (Matt. 25:21).

Acknowledgments

The introduction to this book gives a glimpse of some of the difficulties, challenges, and blessings I met with in the writing process. And yet most of the people who were vital to the project never received mention by name. I'd like to identify and thank them here and now.

My colleagues at Reasons To Believe—Fuz Rana, Dave Rogstad, Kenneth Samples, and Jeff Zweerink—carried an extra load of work as I needed more time to write. Thanks, guys, for your practical help in addition to moral support. Once I pulled together a first draft, rightfully called a "rough" draft, I placed it in the capable hands of my friend and former editorial team member (now working independently) Linda Kloth. Your enthusiasm for the material and your excellent guidance in how to organize it and connect the pieces made an immense difference, Linda. Your editorial sculpting made (my wife) Kathy's efforts to refine and polish the manuscript not only manageable but also, as she says, truly enjoyable. As always, Kathy, I thank you for making my words and ideas shine with greater vibrancy and clarity. You were my steady companion through the troubles and trials that enriched my understanding of and appreciation for God's message in and through Job, the man and the book.

Marj Harman, thank you for ensuring the accuracy of quotations and references, and thanks to you, Sandra Dimas, for your thoughtful feedback and copyedits. The two of you encouraged me more than you can know by your comments "in the margins." Thanks too for helping me with the graphics.

Diana Carrée, my faithful and tech-savvy assistant, you facilitated this project's completion in countless ways, helping both Kathy and me stay on track and meet our deadlines. You are amazing.

Every book with my name on it takes a team effort to produce, and I thank God for the team he has given me, both here at RTB and also at Baker. Robert Hosack, Wendy Wetzel, Paula Gibson, and others too numerous to mention, you are also valuable members of my team. Thank you for blessing me with your confidence in the value of the message God has given me to communicate.

Appendix

Major Biblical Creation Accounts

Reference	Theme
Genesis 1	Creation chronology: physical perspective
Genesis 2	Creation account: spiritual perspective
Genesis 3–5	Human sin and its damaging effects
Genesis 6–9	God's damage control
Genesis 10–11	Global dispersion of humanity
Job 9	Creator's transcendent creation power
Job 34–38	Physical creation's intricacy and complexity
Job 39–42	Soulish creation's intricacy and complexity
Psalm 8	Creation's appeal to humility
Psalm 19	Creation's "message"
Psalm 33	God's control and sovereignty over nature
Psalm 65	Creator's authority and optimal provision
Psalm 104	Elaboration of physical creation events
Psalm 139	Creation of individual humans
Psalms 147–148	Testimony of the Creator's power, wisdom, and care in nature
Proverbs 8	Creator's existence before creation
Ecclesiastes 1–3	Constancy of physical laws
Ecclesiastes 8–12	Limits to human control of nature
Isaiah 40–51	Origin and development of the universe
Romans 1–8	Purposes of the creation

1 Corinthians 15	Life after life
2 Corinthians 4	Creator's glory both in and beyond creation
Colossians 1	Creation's extent
Hebrews 1	Cosmic creation's temporality; role of angels in creation
Hebrews 4	Role of God's rest
2 Peter 3	Creation's end
Revelation 20–22	God's new creation

Notes

Chapter 1 Answers for Today's Issues

1. John E. Hartley, *The Book of Job*, The New International Commentary on the Old Testament (Grand Rapids: Eerdmans, 1988); Roy B. Zuck, ed., *Sitting With Job: Selected Studies on the Book of Job* (Eugene, OR: Wipf & Stock, 2003); Mike Mason, *The Gospel According to Job* (Wheaton: Crossway, 1994); Robert Sutherland, *Putting God on Trial: The Biblical Book of Job* (Victoria, BC: Trafford, 2004); Layton Talbert, *Beyond Suffering: Discovering the Message of Job* (Greenville, SC: BJU Press, 2007).

2. Hugh Ross, *Beyond the Cosmos*, 3rd ed. (Kissimmee, FL: Signalman, 2010); Hugh Ross, *Why the Universe Is the Way It Is* (Grand Rapids: Baker, 2008).

Chapter 2 Gathering of the Greatest Minds

1. Charles F. Pfeiffer and Everett F. Harrison, eds., *The Wycliffe Bible Commentary* (Nashville: Southwestern, 1962), 464.

2. James Orr, gen. ed., *The International Standard Bible Encyclopedia*, vol. 4 (Grand Rapids: Eerdmans, 1956), s.v. "Teman"; Charles F. Pfeiffer, Howard F. Vos, and John Rea, eds., *Wycliffe Bible Encyclopedia*, vol. 2 (Chicago: Moody Press, 1975), s.v. "Teman."

3. Henry H. Halley, *Halley's Bible Handbook With the New International Version* (Grand Rapids: Zondervan, 2000), 28–29, 43; Merrill F. Unger, *Unger's Bible Handbook* (Chicago: Moody Press, 1966), 3–4.

4. Matthew Henry, *Commentary on the Whole Bible*, ed. Leslie F. Church (Grand Rapids: Zondervan, 1961), 514; Orr, *International Standard Bible Encyclopedia*, 3:1680; Pfeiffer and Harrison, *Wycliffe Bible Commentary*, 459–60.

5. Pfeiffer and Harrison, *Wycliffe Bible Commentary*, 459.

6. Menahem Mansoor, *Biblical Hebrew Step by Step*, 2nd ed. (Grand Rapids: Baker, 1980), 1:8, 23.

7. Pfeiffer and Harrison, *Wycliffe Bible Commentary*, 459–60; Henry, *Commentary on the Whole Bible*, 514.

Chapter 3 Answers to Timeless Questions

1. Ross, *Beyond the Cosmos*, 23–48.

2. Given the potential for people to live past nine hundred years in the days before Noah's flood and the lack of birth control technology, the human population could have ballooned to many billions even before Adam attained his seven hundredth year. The best explanation for the low human population that persisted during the pre-flood era would be for murder to be the primary cause of death. For mathematical details of the pre-flood population and murder rate, see my book, *The Genesis Question*, 2nd ed. (Colorado Springs: NavPress, 2001), 101–6.

3. Ross, *Why the Universe Is the Way It Is*, 147–91.

4. Hugh Ross, *More Than a Theory* (Grand Rapids: Baker, 2009), 204–7.

5. There are many reasons independent of the goal to provide a home in the universe for humanity for why God chose the laws of physics that he did. These reasons are described and explained in my book *Why the Universe Is the Way It Is*.

6. Amélie Davis and Xiao-Hai Yan, "Hurricane Forcing on Chlorophyll-a Concentration Off the Northeast Coast of the U.S.," *Geophysical Research Letters* 31 (September 14, 2004): L17304, doi:10.1029/2004GL020668.

7. D. M. Murphy et al., "Influence of Sea-Salt on Aerosol Radiative Properties in the Southern Ocean Marine Boundary Layer," *Nature* 392 (March 5, 1998): 62–65.

8. Nicholas R. Bates, Anthony H. Knap, and Anthony F. Michaels, "Contribution of Hurricanes to Local and Global Estimates of Air-Sea Exchange of CO_2," *Nature* 395 (September 3, 1998): 58–61.

9. Carol Miller, "Wildland Fire Use: A Wilderness Perspective on Fuel Management," *USDA Forest Service Proceedings* RMRS-P-29 (2003): 379–85, http://www.fs.fed.us/rm/pubs/rmrs_p029/rmrs_p029_379_386.pdf; Peter D. Moore, "Fire Damage Soils Our Forests," *Nature* 384 (November 28, 1996): 312–13; A. U. Mallik, C. H. Gimingham, and A. A. Rahman, "Ecological Effects of Heather Burning. I. Water Infiltration, Moisture Retention and Porosity of Surface Soil," *Journal of Ecology* 72 (November 1984): 767–76; Gail W. T. Wilson et al., "Soil Aggregation and Carbon Sequestration Are Tightly Correlated with the Abundance of Arbuscular Mycorrhizal Fungi: Results from Long-Term Field Experiments," *Ecology Letters* 12 (May 2009): 452–61, doi:10.1111/j.1461-0248.2009.01303.x.

10. Ross, *More Than a Theory*, 204–7.

Chapter 4 Answers to New Questions

1. I dealt with several of the better-known attempts to identify bad designs in nature in my book *More Than a Theory*, 203–4.

2. Peter W. V. Gurney, "Is Our 'Inverted' Retina Really 'Bad Design'?" *Creation Ex Nihilo Technical Journal* 13, no. 1 (1999), http://www.trueorigin.org/retina.asp.

3. A. M. Labin and E. N. Ribak, "Retinal Glial Cells Enhance Human Vision Acuity," *Physical Review Letters* 104 (April 16, 2010): id. 158102; Kristian Franze et al., "Müller Cells Are Living Optical Fibers in the Vertebrate Retina," *Proceedings of the National Academy of Sciences, USA* 104 (May 15, 2007): 8287–92; Michael J. Denton, "The Inverted Retina: Maladaptation or Pre-Adaptation?" *Origins & Design* 19, no. 2 (Winter 1999), http://www.arn.org/docs/odesign/od192/invertedretina192.htm.

4. R. Randal Bollinger et al., "Biofilms in the Large Bowel Suggest an Apparent Function of the Human Vermiform Appendix," *Journal of Theoretical Biology* 249 (December 21, 2007): 826–31.

5. Steven V. W. Beckwith et al., "The Hubble Ultra Deep Field," *Astronomical Journal* 132 (November 2006): 1729–55; Ross, *Why the Universe Is the Way It Is*, 30–32.

6. Hugh Ross, *The Creator and the Cosmos*, 3rd ed. (Colorado Springs: NavPress, 2001), 23–26.

7. Stephen W. Hawking, *A Brief History of Time* (New York: Bantam Books, 1988), 169, 175.

8. A small sampling are the following passages: Proverbs 16:1, 4, 9, 33; 21:1; Romans 8:28–30; 9:11–18; Ephesians 1:4–11; 2:10.

9. Ross, *Creator and the Cosmos*, 123–24.

10. An up-to-date review of the space-time theorems and of their philosophical implications may be found in my book *Beyond the Cosmos*, 24–32.

11. Ross, *Why the Universe Is the Way It Is*, 30–41, 209–11.

12. Richard S. J. Tol, "Why Worry About Climate Change? A Research Agenda," *Environmental Values* 17 (November 2008): 437–70, doi:10.3197/096327108X368485; Richard S. J. Tol, "The Stern Review of the Economics of Climate Change: A Comment," *Energy & Environment* 17 (June 2006): 977–81.

13. Judith L. Lean and David H. Rind, "How Natural and Anthropogenic Influences Alter Global and Regional Surface Temperatures: 1889 to 2006," *Geophysical Research Letters* 35 (September 16, 2008): L18701–L18707, doi: 10.1029/2008GL034864; Thomas R. Karl et al., eds., "Temperature Trends in the Lower Atmosphere: Steps for Understanding and Reconciling Differences," A Report by the Climate Change Science Program and the Subcommittee on Global Change Research, Washington, DC, April 2006, http://www.climatescience.gov/Library/sap/sap1-1/finalreport/sap1-1-final-all.pdf; Wikipedia, s.v. "Global Warming," last modified January 13, 2011, http://en.wikipedia.org/wiki/Global_warming.

14. Vincent di Norcia, "Global Warming Is Man-Made: Key Points in the 2007 Fourth Report of the International Panel on Climate Change," December 17, 2009, http://dinorcia.net/GloblWarmgIPCCReportSummary.pdf.

15. Ibid.; Peter M. Cox et al., "Acceleration of Global Warming Due to Carbon-Cycle Feedbacks in a Coupled Climate Model," *Nature* 408 (November 9, 2000): 184–87.

16. William F. Ruddiman, Stephen J. Vavrus, and John E. Kutzbach, "A Test of the Overdue-Glaciation Hypothesis," *Quaternary Science Reviews* 24 (January 2005): 1–10.

17. Ibid.; William F. Ruddiman, "How Did Humans First Alter Global Climate?" *Scientific American* 292 (March 2005): 46–53; Hugh Ross, "Staving Off an Ice Age," *Today's New Reason to Believe*, April 1, 2005, http://www.reasons.org/staving-ice-age.

18. Rudolph Kuper and Stefan Kröpelin, "Climate-Controlled Holocene Occupation in the Sahara: Motor of Africa's Evolution," *Science* 313 (August 11, 2006): 803–7.

19. Wikipedia, s.v. "Gobi Desert," last modified January 9, 2011, http://en.wikipedia.org/wiki/Gobi_Desert.

20. Fernando T. Maestre et al., "Shrub Encroachment Can Reverse Desertification in Semi Arid Mediterranean Grasslands," *Ecology Letters* 12 (September 2009): 930–41.

21. C. Kevin Boyce and Jung-Eun Lee, "An Exceptional Role for Flowering Plant Physiology in the Expansion of Tropical Rainforests and Biodiversity," *Proceedings of the Royal Society B, Biological Sciences*, published online before print, June 16, 2010, doi: 10.1098/rspb.2010.0485.

22. Ibid.

23. Food and Agricultural Organization of the United Nations, *Livestock's Long Shadow: Environmental Issues and Options*, Rome 2006, http://www.fao.org/

docrep/010/a0701e/a0701e00.htm; Food and Agricultural Organization of the United Nations, *Livestock Impacts on the Environment*, Agricultural and Consumer Protection Department, November 2006, http://www.fao.org/ag/magazine/0612sp1.htm.
24. Trish J. Lavery et al., "Iron Defecation by Sperm Whales Stimulates Carbon Export in the Southern Ocean," *Proceedings of the Royal Society B*, published online before print, June 16, 2010, doi:10.1098/rspb.2010.0863.
25. Ibid., 4.

Chapter 5 Answers to Creation-Day Controversies

1. Ross, *Why the Universe Is the Way It Is*, 147–91.
2. R. Laird Harris, Gleason L. Archer Jr., and Bruce K. Waltke, *Theological Wordbook of the Old Testament* (Chicago: Moody Press, 1980), 1:199. Hereafter abbreviated as *TWOT*.
3. William Gesenius, *Gesenius' Hebrew and Chaldee Lexicon to the Old Testament Scriptures*, trans. Samuel Prideaux Tregelles (Grand Rapids: Baker, 1979): 254.
4. Ibid., 646.
5. Ibid., 689–90.
6. L. Paul Knauth and Martin J. Kennedy, "The Late Precambrian Greening of the Earth," *Nature* 460 (August 6, 2009): 728–32.
7. John H. Walton, *The Lost World of Genesis One* (Downers Grove, IL: InterVarsity, 2009). This book includes cover endorsements from scientists Francis S. Collins and Davis A. Young and from theologians Bruce K. Waltke and Tremper Longman III.
8. Lee Irons with Meredith G. Kline, "The Framework View," in *The Genesis Debate: Three Views on the Days of Creation*, ed. David G. Hagopian (Mission Viejo, CA: Crux Press, 2001), 217–56.
9. Belgic Confession, Article 2, in *Ecumenical Creeds and Reformed Confessions* (Grand Rapids: CRC Publications, 1988), 79.
10. Ross, *More Than a Theory*, 61–66.

Chapter 6 Answers to More Genesis Controversies

1. Fazale Rana with Hugh Ross, *Who Was Adam?* (Colorado Springs: NavPress, 2005), 123–37.
2. Ibid.
3. Ronald L. Numbers, *The Creationists: The Evolution of Scientific Creationism* (New York: Knopf, 1992).
4. Henry M. Morris III, *After Eden*, ed. Henry M. Morris and John D. Morris (Green Forest, AR: Master Books, 2003), 10, 107–14; Henry M. Morris, "The Coming Big Bang," *Back To Genesis*, no. 101 (May 1997), c; Douglas W. Phillips, "An Urgent Appeal to Pastors," *Back To Genesis*, no. 119 (November 1998), c; Henry M. Morris, "The Finished Works of God," *Back To Genesis*, no. 136 (April 2000), b.
5. *TWOT*, 2:672–73.
6. Ross, *Why the Universe Is the Way It Is*, 165–81.

Chapter 7 Unique Attributes of Humans

1. Hawking, *A Brief History of Time*, 175.

2. Esther Herrmann et al., "Humans Have Evolved Specialized Skills of Social Cognition: The Cultural Intelligence Hypothesis," *Science* 317 (September 7, 2007): 1360–66.

3. Ibid., 1360.

4. Keith Jensen, Josep Call, and Michael Tomasello, "Chimpanzees Are Vengeful but Not Spiteful," *Proceedings of the National Academy of Sciences, USA* 104 (August 7, 2007): 13046–50.

5. *TWOT*, 1:400.

6. Ibid., 2:721.

7. Humphrey Taylor, "The Religious and Other Beliefs of Americans 2003," The Harris Poll #11, February 26, 2003, http://www.harrisinteractive.com/harris_poll/index.asp?PID=359; David Masci, "The Paradoxical Relationship of Religion and Science," Pew Research Center Publications, November 6, 2009, http://pewresearch.org/pubs/1399/religion-and-science.

8. An uncut, unedited DVD of this debate is available from Reasons To Believe, *The Great Debate: Hugh Ross and Victor Stenger*, vol. 1 (Glendora, CA: RTB Live!, 2009), www.reasons.org/catalog/rtb-live-volume-1-formerly-rough-cuts-great-debate-hugh-ross-and-victor-stenger.

9. Merrill F. Unger, *Unger's Bible Dictionary*, 3rd ed. (Chicago: Moody Press, 1966), 1172.

10. Timothy Keller, *Counterfeit Gods* (New York: Dutton, 2009).

11. Francis Crick, *What Mad Pursuit* (New York: Basic Books, 1988), 138.

12. Richard Dawkins, *The Blind Watchmaker* (New York: W. W. Norton, 1987), 1.

Chapter 8 Origin of Soulish and Spiritual Qualities

1. Paul Davies, *The Fifth Miracle: The Search for the Origin and Meaning of Life* (New York: Simon & Schuster, 1999), 18.

2. Leslie Orgel, "The RNA World and the Origin of Life," first plenary lecture, *13th International Conference on the Origin of Life*, ISSOL '02, Oaxaca, Mexico, June 30–July 5, 2002.

3. Noam Lahav, *Biogenesis* (New York: Oxford University Press, 1999), 139.

4. Quoted by Jon Cohen in "Getting All Turned Around Over the Origins of Life on Earth," *Science* 267 (March 3, 1995): 1265. Bonner made this comment at *Physical Origin of Homochirality in Life*, a conference held in Santa Monica, California, February 1995.

5. William A. Bonner, "The Origin and Amplification of Biomolecular Chirality," *Origins of Life and Evolution of Biospheres* 21 (March 1991): 59–111.

6. Fazale Rana and Hugh Ross, *Origins of Life* (Colorado Springs: NavPress, 2004), 125–28.

7. See Rana and Ross, *Origins of Life*, 63–225.

8. The soulishness of *nepesh* animals is not to be confused with the New Testament's use of the term *soul*. In Greek, the language of the New Testament, the word for soul is *psychē*. *Psychē* refers to the spirit and/or sentience of a being. In Greek literature *psychē* almost always is used to refer to creatures that are both spiritual and sentient and rarely for animals that are merely sentient. With only one exception, namely Revelation 16:3, *psychē* in the New Testament refers exclusively to human beings.

9. Charles Darwin, *The Descent of Man*, in *From So Simple a Beginning: The Four Great Books by Charles Darwin*, edited by Edward O. Wilson (New York: W. W. Norton, 2006), 798.

10. Ibid.

11. Johan J. Bolhuis and Clive D. L. Wynne, "Can Evolution Explain How Minds Work?" *Nature* 458 (April 16, 2009): 832.

12. Ibid.

13. Ibid.

14. Ibid.

15. Ibid., 833.

16. Ibid.

17. C. R. Raby and N. S. Clayton, "Prospective Cognition in Animals," *Behavioural Processes* 80 (March 2009): 314–24.

18. Derek C. Penn, Keith J. Holyoak, and Daniel J. Povinelli, "Darwin's Mistake: Explaining the Discontinuity Between Human and Nonhuman Minds," *Behavioral and Brain Sciences* 31 (April 2008): 109–30, discussion on pages 130–78.

19. Ibid., 109.

20. Ibid.

Chapter 9 To Serve and Please

1. "Snowball Is a Rockin' to the Backstreet Boys," http://www.youtube.com/watch?v=utkb1nOJnD4 (accessed July 13, 2009).

2. Aniruddh D. Patel et al., "Experimental Evidence for Synchronization to a Musical Beat in a Nonhuman Animal," *Current Biology* 19 (May 26, 2009): 827–30.

3. Adena Schachner et al., "Spontaneous Motor Entrainment to Music in Multiple Vocal Mimicking Species," *Current Biology* 19 (May 26, 2009): 831–36.

4. Virginia Morell, "That Bird Can Boogie," *ScienceNOW*, April 30, 2009, http://sciencenow.sciencemag.org/cgi/content/full/2009/430/1?rss=1.

5. Alexandra Horowitz, "Disambiguating the 'Guilty Look': Salient Prompts to a Familiar Dog Behaviour," *Behavioural Processes* 81 (July 2009): 447–52.

6. Mark Petter et al., "Can Dogs (*Canis familiaris*) Detect Human Deception?" *Behavioural Processes* 82 (October 2009): 109–18.

7. Jonah Lehrer, "Small, Furry . . . and Smart," *Nature* 461 (October 15, 2009): 862–64.

8. Steven A. Kushner et al., "Modulation of Presynaptic Plasticity and Learning by the H-ras/Extracellular Signal-Regulated Kinase/Synapsin I Signaling Pathway," *Journal of Neuroscience* 25 (October 19, 2005): 9721–34; Ya-Ping Tang et al., "Genetic Enhancement of Learning and Memory in Mice," *Nature* 401 (September 2, 1999): 63–69; Rusiko Bourtchouladze et al., "A Mouse Model of Rubinstein-Taybi Syndrome: Defective Long-Term Memory Is Ameliorated by Inhibitors of Phosphodiesterase 4," *Proceedings of the National Academy of Sciences USA* 100 (September 2, 2003): 10518–22; Juan M. Alcarón et al., "Chromatin Acetylation, Memory, and LTP Are Impaired in CBP+/- Mice," *Neuron* 42 (June 24, 2004): 947–59; Dan Ehninger et al., "Reversing Neurodevelopmental Disorders in Adults," *Neuron* 60 (December 26, 2008): 950–60.

9. Hugh Ross, "Optimal Memory Designs and Benefits of Forgetting," *Today's New Reason to Believe*, November 9, 2009, http://www.reasons.org/OptimalMemoryDesignandBenefitsofForgetting.

Chapter 10 Top Ten *Nepesh*

1. C. R. Harington, "Pleistocene Remains of the Lion-like Cat (*Panthera atrox*) from the Yukon Territory and Northern Alaska," *Canadian Journal of Earth Sciences* 6 (October 1969): 1277–88.

2. Some good examples can be found in Genesis 49:9; Psalm 17:12; Proverbs 28:1; Isaiah 5:29; Ezekiel 19:1–9; 32:2; Micah 5:8; 1 Peter 5:8.

3. For more on how God designed carnivores to specifically benefit herbivores and minimize death and suffering for herbivores, see my book *More Than a Theory*, 197–200.

4. Melinda A. Zeder and Brian Hesse, "The Initial Domestication of Goats (*Capra hircus*) in the Zagros Mountains 10,000 Years Ago," *Science* 287 (March 24, 2000): 2254–57; Hugh Ross, *The Genesis Question* (Colorado Springs: NavPress, 2001), 186–87.

5. William F. Ruddiman, Stephen J. Vavrus, and John E. Kutzbach, "A Test of the Overdue-Glaciation Hypothesis," *Quaternary Science Reviews* 24 (January 2005): 1–10.

6. William F. Ruddiman, "How Did Humans First Alter Global Climate?" *Scientific American* 292 (March 2005): 46–53.

7. Ruddiman, Vavrus, and Kutzbach, "Overdue-Glaciation Hypothesis," 2.

8. Rana and Ross, *Who Was Adam?*, 55–95; Ross, *More Than a Theory*, 184–90.

Chapter 11 Lessons from the Animals

1. Charlie K. Cornwallis et al., "Promiscuity and the Evolutionary Transition to Complex Societies," *Nature* 466 (August 19, 2010): 969–72.

Chapter 12 Answers to Dinosaur Questions

1. In 1819 William Buckland, a vicar, paleontologist, and Oxford geology professor, unearthed bones in Stonesfield, England, that he identified as belonging to a huge carnivorous reptilian species that later was given the name Megalosaurus. Buckland published his findings and identification in the *Transactions of the Geological Society* in 1824.

2. Pfeiffer and Harrison, *Wycliffe Bible Commentary*, 488; Orr, *International Standard Bible Encyclopedia*, 1:427.

3. *TWOT*, 1:246.

4. Adam Britton, "Crocodilian Captive Care F.A.Q.," *Crocodilian.com*, http://www.crocodilian.com/crocfaq/faq-2.html (accessed August 3, 2009).

Chapter 13 Answers to the Problem of Suffering

1. Ross, *Why the Universe Is the Way It Is*, 147–91.

2. Victor J. Stenger, *God: The Failed Hypothesis* (Amherst, NY: Prometheus, 2007), 216.

3. This is not an implication that God created evil. Rather, God takes advantage of evil expressed by free-will beings he created to bring about an eventual higher good.

4. Stenger, *God: The Failed Hypothesis*, 221.

5. Ibid., 222.

Index

Hugh Ross (PhD, University of Toronto) is founder and president of Reasons To Believe (www.reasons.org). He is the author of many books, including *The Creator and the Cosmos*, *More Than a Theory*, and *Why the Universe Is the Way It Is*. An astronomer, Ross has addressed students and faculty on over three hundred campuses in the United States and abroad on a wide variety of science-faith topics. From science conferences to churches to government labs, Ross presents powerful evidence for a purpose-filled universe. He lives in the Los Angeles area.

About Reasons To Believe

Uniquely positioned within the science-faith discussion since 1986, Reasons To Believe (RTB) openly communicates that science and faith are, and always will be, allies, not enemies. Distinguished for bridging the gap between science and faith respectfully and with integrity, RTB welcomes dialogue with both skeptics and believers. Addressing topics such as the origin of the universe, the origin of life, and the history and destiny of humanity, RTB's website offers a vast array of helpful resources. Through their books, "Today's New Reason to Believe" blog, podcasts, and speaking events, RTB scholars present powerful reasons from science to believe in the God of the Bible as Creator.

For more information contact us via:
www.reasons.org
731 E. Arrow Highway
Glendora, CA 91740
(800) 482-7836
Or email us at customerservice@reasons.org

REASONS TO BELIEVE
Bridging the gap between science and faith.